PRAYERS
from GOD

Woody Dorrell

EDWARD WOODVILLE DORRELL, JR.

WestBow
PRESS
A DIVISION OF THOMAS NELSON

WestBow Press books may be ordered through booksellers or by contacting:

WestBow Press
A Division of Thomas Nelson
1663 Liberty Drive
Bloomington, IN 47403
www.westbowpress.com
1 (866) 928-1240

Australian Casey Stoner of Ducati Marlboro at 2007
Polini Malaysia Motorcycle Grand Prix
©Ahmad Faizel Yahya ! Dreamstime.com

ISBN: 978-1-4908-1957-0 (sc)
ISBN: 978-1-4908-1958-7 (e)

Library of Congress Control Number: 2013922626

Printed in the United States of America.

WestBow Press rev. date: 09/18/2014

The technique used, praying God's Word back to him, means starting with God's
Word and then modifying it as need be by modifying it slightly to fit in the flow
of words or by turning it into a request, thanks, or praise or to express the content
of the words in a different way. So, if the Scripture is not noted as one of the
above, a reference may be supplied, but the Scripture is not necessarily identical
to what is found in a particular version of the Bible. Most of the Scriptures
used started out as NIV, KJV, or Amplified and were then modified.

ACKNOWLEDGEMENTS

First and foremost I'd like to give all the praise and all the credit that comes my way to my Lord and Savior, Jesus Christ, and to the work of the Holy Spirit in my life and in the production of these prayers. How can I possibly deserve any credit for praying God's Word back to Him? He's the original author and is responsible for inspiring me to repeat it back to Him.

Secondly, I'd like to give credit to my daughter-in-love, Kathleen Robin Daust Dorrell, who typed the major part of this manuscript while handling six young'uns eleven and under with another one on the way. And I'd like to credit my wife, Lois Melita Gilmore Dorrell, who has put up with me through this process which has lasted for almost twenty years, encouraged me, acted as my sounding board, and performed a superior job of proofreading.

Then, too, I'd like to thank the congregation and leadership of First Baptist Church, Tullahoma (TN), for providing an environment that spawned these prayers and allowed them to be prayed out loud in their presence and for their encouragement and support along the way.

INTRODUCTION

About twenty years or so ago, I picked up a book entitled *Prayer: Life's Limitless Reach* by Jack Taylor in the church library. One statement Taylor made really got my attention: "I recommend continuous reading on the subject of prayer, biographies of great men of prayer, and repeated reading of certain prayer classics..."[1] Well, I definitely wanted to make a big improvement in my prayer life. You see, I wasn't an Ivah Bates whom Blackaby refers to as a knee in the body of Christ because she was such a great prayer warrior.[2] I was and probably still am a nerve. Now nerves are important, mind you, because they warn the body about what's wrong. But nerves typically get blamed for the pain even though they are ultimately saving the body if it pays attention to the pain. And I was tired of taking all the flak. I'd much rather pray, watch what I prayed for happen, then just sit back and smile, knowing I had a big part in bringing it about. Taylor also provided his list of the top twenty books about prayer ever written. So I decided I'd do it. And to God be the glory, I've been reading books on prayer ever since.

Now one of the comments in one of those books that really got to me concerned public prayer: "...leaving everything to spontaneity can lead to more vain repetitions than anything else! When you give your prayers no prior thought at all, you tend to say the same things over and over. You fall back on your store of previous thoughts and language. Phrases roll right off the tongue, but they're the same ones

---

[1] Taylor, Jack, *Prayer: Life's Limitless Reach Prayer: Life's Limitless Reach*, p.159.

[2] Blackaby, Henry T. & King, Claude V., *Experiencing God: Knowing and Doing the Will of God*, p. 162.

you used last week… You're acting much like a machine. The tape has been loaded, the 'play' button pressed, the volume adjusted, and now we can sit back and listen. In private prayer that is one thing, but in public prayer it surely falls short of being edifying to fellow believers over the long haul. They've heard it all before. The ones with good memories know what you're about to say before you say it! I'm arguing for giving conscious thought to prayer, and writing is one of the best ways to do that."[3] Other writers also indicated that most public prayers could be followed by phrases like 'portions of this prayer have been mechanically reproduced.' because they're using the same phrases we've used before.

I was called on to pray at church fairly often and felt intimidated when I was. And I felt that I usually did a less than adequate job. So, in order to do a much better job at praying in public at church, I took it that I needed to write prayers ahead of time—or at least prepare ahead of time. However, Matt 6:5 (Amp) says, "…when you pray, you must not be like the hypocrites, for they love to pray standing in the synagogues and the corners of the street, that they may be seen by people." There was a trade-off. Was I going to do a good job of edifying the church and glorifying God through my public prayers and cause some folk to think I'm trying to appear more spiritual than they or was I going to continue to say ho-hum prayers that neither glorify God nor edify the church?

So I decided if I was going to be serious about prayer it included being serious about prayers I prayed out loud in church. Just one problem—I didn't know what or how to pray. So I prayed about it. I asked God to tell me what to pray. I started with a clean slate and waited for the Lord to show me what to pray. The wait was sometimes months from one phrase to the next. Then I picked up a book that had a chapter on how to pray God's Word back to God. And I began using some of those techniques. My current technique is to read a Bible commentary that goes verse by verse and let the Lord focus my attention on what he wants me to pray. For example: from 2 Thes. 3:1b (Amp) I pray "May Your Word spread quickly, run its course, be glorified and triumphant." When you read the entire verse, you notice

_____

[3]   Briggs, Edward C., *A Pilgrim's Guide to Prayer*, pp 52-53.

the first part says we are to pray those words. Once the Lord focuses my attention on a verse and lets me know that this is something I can pray back to Him, I use *The Bible from 26 Translations*[4] to help me find the best translation or combination of translations to use. Another example is the end of Psalms 85:10 (Amp) "…righteousness and peace have kissed each other." If the words God has me focusing on don't pray directly back to Him, then I look for how to turn them into a request, thanks, or praise or to express the content of the words in a different way. This verse turned into "Help us find peace by making war on the sins in our lives." Sometimes it isn't a verse or a part of a verse that God causes me to focus on, but a concept. For example, the concept found in Luke 11:5-8 justifies praying for lost people I know. Another example is that reading selections of God's Word (Luke 19:10 & Gen. 3:8-10) caused me to be focused on the idea that God pursues each of us vigorously turns into "Hound of Heaven, we praise You because when it came time to pursue us You didn't leave the big dog on the porch." I attempt to use the ACTS (adoration-confession-thanksgiving-supplication) method of praying, remembering that the most important part of any prayer is the adoration, but certainly don't follow it strictly.

So over a period of almost twenty years I have allowed the Lord to lead me to prepare prayers ahead of time to be used in church. I don't like to say I write these prayers because I strongly believe the Holy Spirit leads me to pray what He wants prayed. One reason I believe this is true is that while I usually only have one prayer memorized when I am called on to pray, more often than not it seems to fit the occasion very well. Also, I have started each prayer by asking God to tell me what I need to pray. So while I've put these words on paper, memorized them, and prayed them aloud in church, I don't want to take any credit for what is written or for what effects these prayers create. Rather, I pray that all the credit and all the glory goes to my Lord and Savior, Jesus Christ, and to the work of the Holy Spirit, and, of course, ultimately to Jehovah Himself. I really consider Him the instigator and author of these prayers. And I purposely say, "To God be the glory." anytime

---

[4]   Vaughan, Curtis (ed.), *Bible from 26 Translations*.

anyone tries to give me any credit for one of these prayers. The intent of each prayer, even those that confess the sins of the church, is to glorify God and edify the church.[5] Of course, if there is any inaccuracy or anything that's not quite right, whether through carelessness or ignorance or if any of my personal prejudices sneak through, I accept all the blame.

There are two reasons why I call these 'Prayers from God.' First, much of most of these prayers is merely praying God's Word back to Him. Each prayer began with a clean slate and me asking God what I should pray. Each prayer is the result of prayer and Bible study and meditation and my desire to pray God's Word back to Him and to pray what God wants prayed. If I pray God's Word directly back to Him, which is often the case, then those words come from God word for word from the Bible. If I take God's Word and modify it so that it becomes a request, thanks, or a praise, then most of the words and ideas still come directly from God's Word. When I was a teenager I was confused by people who claimed to hear the "still, small voice" (See 1 Kings 19:12 Amp) of God. I thought they heard audible voices, but I never heard any. I have only encountered one person who told me that he heard audible voices not attributable to some human source and I believed him. It was a sixth-grade boy who said the voices were telling him to commit suicide. That obviously was Satan talking. So I am very skeptical whenever I hear anyone say that they hear God talking to them audibly. I certainly don't make that claim about these prayers; I still have never heard an audible voice that I could attribute to God. Currently this is how I understand God usually communicates to me: I have thoughts. These thoughts come from one of three sources: Satan, myself, or God. It's my job to figure out which thought comes from which source. I attribute to God those thoughts that agree with God's Word or are in accord with His nature and His will. I attribute those thoughts that are evil to come from Satan. The rest I attribute to myself. So, secondly, each one of these prayers is the product of only

---

[5]   See I Cor. 14:15-17 and John 11:41-42 to see that prayers prayed aloud in church should edify the audience.

thoughts that I have identified that came from God according to the method and criteria I just described.

Each of these prayers has been prayed out loud at First Baptist Church, Tullahoma, Tennessee, a Southern Baptist Church where I am a Deacon and youth Sunday School teacher. Almost all of these prayers were prayed as part of one of the following events: Monday Night Prayer Meeting, Wednesday Night Prayer Meeting, 8:30 Sunday Morning Worship Service, 11 O'clock Sunday Morning Worship Service, Sunday Evening Worship Service, a Pre-Service Deacon-Pastor Prayer Time, or some other church event. Offertory prayers were prayed mid service before the preaching or at the end of the service right before the offering, announcements, and dismissal.

Prayers from God

I call this the Motorcycle Prayer. It was prayed during a Monday Night Prayer Meeting. This prayer was an attempt to pray "Ye have not because ye ask not." James 4:2 (KJV) back to the Lord. Sometimes God helps us to see what we need to pray through our life experiences.

Lord God Almighty,

I finally got around to checking out the new guy in the office's motorcycle the other day. It was really snazzy. But what really intrigued me was the speedometer—it went all the way to 180mph. There were seven other bikes parked there. The Moto Guzz had a 140mph limit; the Harleys all had 120; and the Honda 750 and the Kamasaki had 80mph limits. When I got back to the office, I asked Eric about it. He said, "And you better believe me, it'll do every bit of it." In the back of my mind I said to myself Eric has ridden this thing at more than 180mph around here somewhere. So I pressed for more info. It was obvious that that bike was Eric's pride and joy. He couldn't stop telling me more and more details about it. He said his bike is a Ducati—that there are about two of those sold in Tennessee per year. A Ducati is the ultimate in motorcycles—kind of like a Ferrari car, and it's really a racing bike. In fact, he told me he paid about $20K for it but if he'd gotten all the racing options and add-ons it would have been close to $250,000. I kept asking how he resisted the temptation to break the speed limit around here when he had a bike that would go 180mph. He finally confided in me that every day that he rides it to work, on the way home he gets it up to 140mph on Fredonia Road over in Manchester.

O Lord, we confess that in You we have the Ducati of gods—the one that is the snazziest and comes with all the options and all the add-ons and all that power and all that speed, the one we could win every race with; but, Lord, we're not soaring on wings like eagles, we're not enjoying You the way Eric enjoys his Ducati. We're just putting along at what we consider a safe speed when we need to throw caution to the wind and let it all out—turn everything over to You, become completely dependent on You, follow Your every leading and let You take us wherever You want, and just enjoy the ride.

O Lord, we confess that with all that power and cattle on a thousand hills that You want us to ask for big things because You want to do great things for us and through us, yet we're too scared to ask for big things that would really glorify You. O Lord, help us to ask for the big things You want us to have.

O Lord, we confess that we're not just bubbling over ready to just tell all kinds of information about You like Eric is about his bike. O Lord, help us to make You our pride and joy.

Lord, Eric tells me that once he gets on, gets up some speed, squeezes in his knees, and tucks down that he almost feels like he's one with his Ducati. O Lord, help us to get close to You, to have such a grip on You that we're really one with You.

O Lord, may we not be able to resist the temptation to try out all Your power and all Your promises. And may You get all the glory.

Amen

Note: Eric didn't ride his bike to work when there was a threat of rain.

∞

This prayer was prayed at Monday Night Prayer Meeting prior to a visit I was supposed to have with Charles.

O Lord Who Likes to Be Pestered,

We praise You because You are a god who (Repeat this with each indented phrase below or not.)
    Loves sinners,
    Agonizes over the lost,
    Sent Jesus to die for the lost,
    Uses Your children to reach the lost.

Lord, over in Luke 11 You taught Your disciples how to pray. Lord, I consider that model prayer kindergarten praying since all the petitions are for the pray-er and because even a kindergartener can memorize that prayer and repeat it word for word without actually meaning it. Lord, help us to pray in the spirit of that prayer, actually meaning it. Another reason I call it kindergarten praying is that it asks for forgiveness of sins without accompanying it with any confession and repentance, and while there are some sins, like the sins of omission, that we don't always recognize, every growing Christian should confess every sin as soon as he recognizes it and ask for forgiveness and repent of it; and, for too many people, the Model Prayer is a cop out. This prayer, or one very similar to it, is the only prayer they pray asking for forgiveness; and the confession of individual sins doesn't happen, the asking for forgiveness of individual sins doesn't happen, and the repentance doesn't happen. Hence there is no Christian growth and the Christian stays in kindergarten. And the Christian goes his whole life and never gets promoted. Help us to keep our account with You very short.

But Lord there is one big difference at the end of this Model Prayer and the one in Matthew. There is no 'amen.' This seems to indicate that You weren't through teaching the disciples how to pray yet. And indeed, you next move on to what I call college-level praying: praying for others.

You talk about a man who has two friends, one who has bread and one who does not. Lord, by Your divine revelation, You have caused me to understand that You're not referring to the kind of bread one can buy in a grocery store, but You are talking about the Bread of Life that you have baked especially for sinners.

Guess what, Lord. I have two friends. And one of them is You; and You have a whole bakery full of that special bread. And I have another friend by the name of Charles who desperately needs a loaf of that bread. But Your Word indicates I won't get the bread for him by just asking once. Indeed, as we read on we are introduced to the concept of importunity, for which I substitute the word 'pestering.' Because of my pestering You over and over again, You'll finally give me the Bread of Life to take to him.

Lord, I beg of You, I plead with You. I have a friend who is on the journey of life. I have an encounter with him scheduled this week. And I have nothing to set before him. O Lord, give me a loaf of Your bread to take to him. O Lord, it's close to midnight in his life; and he is hungry.

Lord, in my humanness, I keep coming up with things I might convey to him that might influence him to come to faith. But, Lord, may I say nothing that comes from me. Lord, I have nothing. I don't have the power of the Holy Spirit; I don't have Holy Boldness; I don't have the burning words. O Lord, give me the power and the wisdom to enable me to do what otherwise I cannot do. Lord, give me the power to carry that loaf of bread to him; give me the wisdom to see which direction to go; give me the words that are needed, give me the leadership to convince and sway a man who has been saying no to You for over sixty years. O Lord, You have an abundance of bread; give some for this poor sinner named Charles. O Lord I'm standing between You and Charles; use me as a willing channel to carry Your bread to him.

O Lord, I'm asking You this because I think it's time. I've been pestering You about Charles for at least ten years. And You've now moved me on to the graduate-level praying for him. This is where You wanted to get me all along. You have moved me from just praying for him to be saved to praying for him again and again and again to the point where I have so much love for him I can hardly sit still. And Lord, You know as I beg You again and again and again to save Charles, I often cry and cry and cry and I have to stop praying so I can blow my nose. And then I pray for him again and again and again and I cry and cry and cry and have to stop praying so I can blow my nose. And there are times when I experience great heaviness and extreme agony and a great yearning that Charles submit to Your Holy Spirit that just gets stronger and stronger so much so that I am in pure agony. I have to stop praying; and when I do I find I'm out of breath and I check my forehead to see if I'm perhaps sweating blood.

Lord, I doubt if Charles knows I've been praying for him. But I'm sure he knows that his wife and son and others of his family have been praying for him. O Lord, would You honor their prayers along with mine? Would You prepare his heart and bring salvation to Charles this very week?

Please. Please. Please. Please. Please. Please with sugar on it.

And may You get all the glory and all the credit; and may I get none. And please, in the spirit of that Model Prayer, forgive me of every sin— especially pride and saying things that were better left unsaid so that unforgiven sin won't be a hindrance as I communicate with him. And Lord, if there is anyone I need to forgive or apologize to let me know right now so I can do that so those issues won't be a hindrance either.

May there be rejoicing in Heaven very, very soon.

Amen

Note: The idea of different levels of praying and that the interpretation of these verses primarily has to do with asking for salvation for a friend all came from John Rice's book *Prayer: Asking and Receiving* pages 79-85. Of interest is the fact that I have checked over two hundred fifty commentaries on and interpretations of these verses, both on line and in hardcopy, and I've not found a one that agrees with John Rice.

Note: Charles' wife called saying Charles changed his mind about that appointment. I'm still praying for Charles.

This prayer was the offertory prayer delivered near the end of at an 8:30 Sunday Morning Worship Service.

Precious Jesus,

You are our Shepherd. We are Your sheep. (See John 10:11)
May we not wander away,
But listen intently for and closely to Your voice;
And obey Your every command.

You are our Potter. We are Your clay. (See Isa. 64:8)
May we not resist Your shaping and become unmalleable,
But accept Your reproof with joy;
And conform to Your every squeeze.

You are our Vine. We are Your branches. (See John 15:5)
May we not become separated or shrivel up,
But cling to You and be pruned by You
And bear much fruit.

You are our Light. We are Your followers. (See John 1:7-9)
May we not walk in darkness,
But follow Your every guidance
And grow in love.

You are the Light of the World. We are Your reflectors. (See John 8:12)
May we not become dull or scratched,
But may our countenance and actions show Your glory
Just as Moses' did when he came down from the Mount Sinai. (See Ex. 34:29-30)

We've come to a time in this service set aside for rendering. When You were asked whether it was right to pay taxes to that despot Caesar, You asked whose image and whose inscription are on the coin. Then You said, "Render...unto Caesar the things that are Caesar's, and unto God the things that are God's." (See Matt. 22:21 KJV) Lord, the only things I know that have Your image on them are human beings; and sure enough, some of the human beings right here in this room also have Your name, Jesus Christ, inscribed in their hearts.

Lord, You are our Master. We are Your slaves. (See John 13:13-14)
May we not hold anything back,
But render unto You everything—
Body, mind, soul, heart, and will.

You are the Bread of Life. We are Your servers. (See John 6:35)
May none here go home hungry today.
And may we serve a loaf of that bread to a lost friend this week.

Amen

Inspired by Psalm 100:3. This was prayed at a Monday Night Prayer Meeting.

Heavenly Potter and Shepherd,

You are our Potter; we are Your clay.
You provided the stuff from which we were made.

You provided the spark and breath of life that started us up and keeps us going.

You continually try to mold us into what we need to be.

It is You who made us and not we ourselves. (See Ps. 100:3)

You are our Shepherd; we are Your sheep.

You have redeemed us and brought us into Your fold.

We are Your people, the sheep of Your pasture. (See Ps. 100:3)

You guide us, protect us, and watch over us.

We praise You because You are a god who never throws out His clay or abandons His sheep.

We have neither created ourselves nor made ourselves into what we are. We are what we are by the Grace of God. What we are is not cause to have pride in ourselves but is cause to praise You.

And we owe You big time.

We owe You (Repeat this with each indented phrase below or not.)

Total obedience and submission,

The sacrifice of praise,

Love with all our heart, soul, and might,

A walk with You in which we confess and repent of every sin in short order,

A life in which others see Jesus,

A deliberate effort to spread Your Gospel far and wide,

Enough love for the people that we encounter that we tell them about Jesus, and

Concern for the poor and needy and hurting.

But, Lord, too often our sins control us. They keep us from doing what we ought. We are blind to our pride, our arrogance, and our cognitive dissonance[1], while others see these in us right off. When it comes

---

[1]   See Appendix on Cognitive Dissonance.

time to confess, we deny we have sinned or say we can't remember, reinforcing our arrogance.

And, Lord, we rely on everything but You. We rely on the grocery store or the fast food place for food. We rely on our PC, laptop, I-pad, or cell phone for information to keep us straight and for social networking. We rely on our GPS for directions. We rely on the TV to determine our understanding of the world. We rely on Social Security, our 401(k), and our pension plan to provide for our future. Yet You are the one who ultimately provides our food, sets us straight, gives us the right directions; You are the one who should help us understand the world. You are the One to whom we need to be talking; and You are the One who is really providing for our future.

O Lord, some of us don't really know You because we never spend time with You. We say we pray, but we don't ever set aside even one hour a week to do it. Help us to commit to having a regular quiet time with You and follow through.

O Lord, may we follow hard after You. May our thirst and hunger for You be satisfied only to be replaced with an even deeper thirst and hunger for You. And may we be putty in Your hands and sheep that follow Your every command.

Amen

Monday Night Prayer Meeting was initiated by several church members to pray for the church and for the search for a new pastor. The nice thing about Monday Night Prayer Meeting is that one has the latitude to pray whatever the Lord has put on his heart.

O Lord Who God-breathed the Words of All Scripture,

Help each of us to constantly recognize that we're helpless to help ourself.

Let us be begging on the inside for Your control of our life.

Help us to think only of You and Your glory.

Let us be so consumed with Christ's glory that we lose ourselves in Your work.

Help us to be ultra-sensitive to sin in our life.

Let it be the sore point of our existence.

Let our sins burden us way beyond the point of tears.

Help us to deny our own desires.

Help us to not only deny, but put aside our own needs to think only of Your needs.

Help each of us to humble ourself before You and others, Lord.

Help us to hunger and thirst after Your righteousness.

May your Word be the joy of our life.

Help each of us to constantly pursue sanctification in our life.

Help us to be merciful to the hurting.

Help us to be merciful to the ones that are ill physically.

Help us to be merciful to the ones that are ill spiritually.

Lord, watch over our mind, our attitude, our inner being.

Lord, cleanse us from all sin.

Lord, let us be peacemakers by being confrontational with Your Good News when and where Your Spirit leads.

Lord, let us be persecuted for Your sake.

Lord, there is an old prayer that goes something like: Help us to resist the temptation to be so heavenly-minded that we are of no earthly good and help us to resist the temptation to be so earthly-minded that we are of no heavenly good. Lord forgive us for even considering that we might need to pray that first part, but, Lord, please accept the second part as our honest need.

We praise You once again because Your word became flesh and dwelt among us...full of grace and truth. (See John 1:14)

Please, Lord, because we mean it so much.

In Jesus' name,

Amen

∞

This was used as an offertory prayer in an 11 O'clock Sunday Morning Worship Service.

Lord God Almighty,

You scare us to death sometimes.
Your thunder booms directly overhead and we quiver in our boots.
Your fierce storms approach and we run for cover.
But when we consider that these events are completely insignificant when compared to solar storms or the big bang we think occurred when You said, "Let there be light," we're so in awe of You that we're scared to draw near.

But in Your infinite wisdom You gave us Jesus,
so that we might not be terrified, but drawn near with tender love.

Thank you for Jesus, our gentle shepherd, our victorious Savior, our very example of love.
O Lord, constantly remind us of Jesus.
We praise You for Jesus because through Him You can take all the evil, even the mistakes and sins of us, Your penitent children, and by Your

grace transform them so that they boomerang against Satan, enhance our character, and result in Your glory.

We praise You for the bad things that happen in our lives, as well as the good, and the in-between. And we praise you for those who offend us, because it is only through them we ever have opportunity to be forgiving like You, our Father in heaven.

Lord, it is our intense desire to worship You this morning.
Give us power by Thy Spirit to worship you now
    that we may (Repeat this with each indented phrase below or not.)
    completely forget the world,
    be brought into fullness of life,
    be refreshed, comforted, blessed, and challenged by Your Word, as
        it is preached this morning.

Lord, we don't have vast sums to give You this morning,
but a portion of what You have given us we return,
content to know that nothing is truly ours until we have dedicated it to You.

Lord, we are pardoned though the blood of Jesus.
Help us to confess our unconfessed sins
so we might feel a new sense of it and
so that we may worship You in Spirit and Truth. (See John 4:24)

Lord, we lift up those of our number who know You not.

Bless us with the knowledge that we are Yours and You are ours—forever.

In Jesus' precious name,
Amen

∞

The new pastor we had just called was not on the scene yet. Less than a year earlier, eighty of our membership left to form a new church because of differing opinions. This prayer took seven minutes. That would be way too long for most worship services, but this was prayed during Wednesday Night Prayer Meeting. At the time, our Wednesday Night Prayer Meetings were more like Bible studies. I led the session that night, did a Bible study on prayer, then ended with this prayer. I prefaced my prayer with the following:

In just a moment, I'm going to lead us in prayer. That doesn't mean I'm going to stand up here and pray out loud for your listening enjoyment. That doesn't mean I'm going to stand up here and pray as your representative. I hope it means we're going to pray together and I just happen to be the one saying the words out loud. Please pray with me.

Precious Jesus,

You came to us while we were still mired in sin, awakened us to the problem of sin in our lives, showed us the solution, forgave us, and made us God's children. Then, in effect, You took our weak hand in Your strong, nail-scarred hand and said[2], "Come now, I am going with you all the way and will bring you safe home to heaven. If you ever get into trouble or difficulty, just tell me about it. I will give you, without reproach, everything you need, and more besides, day by day, as long as you shall live."[3] O Lord, You are our daily refuge, our daily comfort, the source of rich and inexhaustible joy in our daily lives. Yet, even though we light up Your switchboard when the big problems of life hit, the rest of the time we grieve You because either we do not pray or do not pray as much as we should—in effect, severing the lines of communication between us and You and dooming our spiritual lives to be wimpy. O Lord, we have not because we ask not. (See James 4:2) We say we don't have time to pray, and we are left spiritually weak and emaciated without enough strength to fight against sin effectively or

---

[2]   Hallesby, Ole, *Prayer*, p.38.
[3]   Ibid.

to serve You properly. O Lord, we confess that the greatest sin we've committed since our conversion, the way in which we have grieved You the most, is our neglect of prayer. And that neglect, Lord, is the cause of many other sins, both sins of omission and sins of commission. O Lord, the countless opportunities for prayer we've not taken advantage of, the many answers to prayer we might have had, and, o Lord, the souls that might have been saved if only we had been praying for them. Lord, help us commit ourselves to praying down Your kingdom upon our lives and the lives of others. O Lord, help us to pray constantly.

Lord, "You ask so earnestly for the unity of Your people."[4] And we've failed You so miserably. "...encourage our unity... [by honoring] Your precious promise regarding united prayer"[5]—the one, Jesus, where You say that if two of us on earth agree about anything that we may ask and it shall be done for us by Your Father who is in heaven. (See Matt. 18:19) "Show us how to [so] join together in love and desire... that Your presence is evident by our faith in... [Your] answer."[6] We pray that all of us here tonight may pray as one. "Remove all selfishness and self-interest,"[7] all hindrances to our unity at least for these few moments while we pray. "Cast out the spirit of the world and the flesh through which Your precious promise loses its power."[8] Let our gratitude for Your love and for Your dying on the cross for our sins bind us together as one. "Grant especially"... [that we, Your people, may know without a shadow of doubt] that it is by the power of united prayer that.. [we] can bind and loose in Heaven (See Matt. 18:18), cast out Satan, save souls, ...[move] mountains, and hasten the coming of Your kingdom. And grant... ... [that as we may pray we are praying] with the power through which Your name and Word are [honored and] glorified."[9]

---

4   Murray, Andrew, *With Christ in the School of Prayer*, (Springdale, PA, 1981), p.116.
5   Ibid. p. 117.
6   Ibid.
7   Ibid.
8   Ibid.
9   Ibid.

Lord, claiming Your promise regarding united prayer, knowing that our request has already been granted even before we mouth the words, we Your people at FBC pray asking that we may be known as a people of prayer, that we may be known as a people of great faith, that we may be known as a people of Your Word, that we may be known as a people of great love and compassion, and that we may be known as a people whose prayers bring blessing and cause souls to be saved worldwide. And all this not because of someone's great misconception, but because of our strong, strong belief in the power of prayer and because of our humble submission time and again to your will. Lord, we ask for these things not out of denominational pride, or because we want to be thought better of because we belong to some great church, but only, Lord, only because we want Your name to be glorified and because we want your kingdom to grow by leaps and bounds in our lives and in our church and in our community and throughout the whole world. O Lord, many churches these days are buying into the value system of the world—fame, success, materialism, and celebrity status. They are trying to emulate the famous preachers and the megachurches who say, "We have such a large following because we give the people what they want." O Lord, some of these churches praise man more than they do You. Lord, let us not fall prey to this syndrome any more than we have. Instead of emulating other churches, let us find ourselves emulating Jesus. Instead of getting caught up in giving people what they want, let us get caught up in giving people what You want them to have. Better yet, Lord, let us get caught up in a passionate single-mindedness to do Your will. O Lord, break us time and time again, work our fingers to the bone, claim our sons and daughters for Your own, do whatever it takes, but grow Your kingdom through us.

Lord, we have gone so long without a full-time shepherd to lead us. We thank you for the opportunities to grow and to step up to new challenges we've had in this interim period. And we praise You for the work and leadership of Tom and Kenny during this time. Lord, be with Tom. Continue to bless him and his ministry wherever You lead him.

We now sense it's time to move on behind our tremendous Savior and a dedicated, full-time shepherd who will lead us to grow Your kingdom in this church. Lord, a man has been chosen to fill this position. We were careful not to pray for a great preacher, but only to pray for a preacher with a great God. O Lord, we sense You've been too good to us. Our first inkling is that You're sending us a great preacher who has a great God. O Lord, he came; we fell in love with him; then he called us his people; and we cried. O Lord, we praise You up one side and down the other for our new shepherd. Please, Lord, please, protect him and his family from harm and bring them safely to us. Help us to love him and to embrace him and his family into our fellowship here at FBC. Help us to accept him for who he is and to accept his mistakes and his humanness. And, Lord, when he gets here, let us smother him with love and help us to thrill his soul with our willingness to work as a church united and as individuals to be Your people, do your will and magnify Your name.

Also when he gets here, remind us that Jesus is the head of the church, that His lordship should be evident in the church as a whole and in each part of the church and in each of us individually. Lord, too often we look around and find ourselves in control. Please, Lord, help us to keep You in control of Your church and of our lives. Lord, You've given us each a job to do in the church. Help us to do it well and under Your constant direction so we can function as a coordinated body of Christ.

Lord, we have a great concern for this church. The last time we got a new shepherd it resulted in division rather than unity. Lord, forgive us for saying things that were better left unsaid, for thinking less of others than we should have, for hurting Your witness and Your work in this church and in this community. Lord, help us to forgive those who offended us and to apologize to those we might have offended. Then, let us be able to put it all behind us so that we can pray with a clear conscience so that our prayers might be answered. Lord, we pray, claiming Your precious promise regarding united prayer, that when our new shepherd comes it results in great unity. May all of us look for and find the good things about our new shepherd and our fellow church members and have only love for him and them. But, Lord, let our real focus be drawn to Jesus. May we be elevated to a higher level of love for You than we've ever had before. May we be elevated to a higher level of commitment to prayer and studying Your word so that we find our relationship with you constantly growing closer and stronger.

Lord, we cringe when we are reminded of the church at Laodicea— how they were neither hot nor cold and You were going to spit them out of Your mouth. Lord, we're guilty. We look at the number of baptisms we had the past several years and it's obvious we're not hot but we're not completely ice cold either. Lord, use Your Holy Spirit to light a fire under us and put a fire in us for the lost. Give us a compassion for the lost like to that of Jesus. Also, help us to be on fire for eliminating the sin in our life. Purge each of us individually from all sin so that when the Bridegroom comes He'll find a bride ready and anxious and pure.

Lord, we pray that our worship services may concentrate on praising You and honoring Your word. May they prove to be times when Your Holy Spirit gets our full attention. O Lord, let us find ourselves regularly committing ourselves to a deeper walk with You as a result of our worship services. Let us so focus on You and Your word and Your message for us that we become completely oblivious to the personalities conducting our worship services. Let us praise only You in our worship services.

Lord, some of us already have cold feet. We are questioning whether we're going to be able to live up to our new pastor's expectations. We recognize that he showed us a vision we've never even dared to dream before. Lord, now his dream is our dream, too. We know that we cannot even take one step toward the realization of that dream in our own power. But, Lord, we desperately want it because we know You want that for us and even more. Lord, as a love gift to You and to our new pastor, we pray, claiming your precious promise regarding united prayer, that You will require of us that we do whatever we must do to become that one local congregation in all of history—past, present, and future, that comes closest to being all that You want it to be.

Lord, be with the saints at Colonial Baptist Church. May they come to terms with and have peace about their pastor's leaving. May they feel Your grace and grow to love You more. Lord, be with the saints at the New Baptist Church of Tullahoma. May they feel Your grace and grow to love You more.

Lord, we lift up to You those whose names are on Table Talk and those we've just mentioned who need our prayer and our attention. We pray that You will heal each of them in accord with Your will and to Your glory. And we pray that You will use us as Your tools of mercy, love and attention to each of these and to others as Your Spirit leads.

Thy kingdom come, Thy will be done on earth as it is in Heaven. (See Matt. 6:10) Lord, let us both stand in the gap and pray it down and be ready and willing to be the means by which it is carried out.

To You be the glory forever. (See Heb. 13:21)

Amen

Note: Several ladies from the church cook Wednesday Night Supper and a large number of our fellowship all eat together before the other events of the evening. Table Talk is the name of a list of announcements and prayer requests placed on each table.

We have stewardship emphasis every November. This prayer was used in a November Sunday Morning Worship Service. See 1 Peter 4:10.

Lord God,

We come to you this morning recognizing You as king, sovereign of the universe, the one who has the deeds to all there is to own. We thank you for the privilege to be on earth to enjoy its beauty and grandeur, especially at this time of year, and to enjoy the fruits of the fields. Thank you, Lord, for all the great treasures You allow us to care take for our brief time here on earth.

Lord, help us to be better stewards—for in many ways we've failed. We've abused our environment; we've destroyed part of Your creation. Some of us have used the prosperity you've given us for our own comfort instead of for the furtherment of Your kingdom here on earth. Lord, some of us have been so busy doing our own thing that we've neglected our relationship with You—to the point that we're spiritually bankrupt. Lord, some of us have wasted time frivolously to the neglect of Your Word. Lord, we ask You to use this service this morning to cause us to recommit to being good stewards. We pray that Your Son will become real to us as we meditate on Your Word. We pray that we'll once again find ourselves regularly involved in praying with You to the extent that our thoughts become aligned with Your thoughts.

Lord, I recently encountered the statement that a parent is never happier than his saddest child. I immediately thought of a lady in our church whose son is suffering from a life-threatening condition and I knew the truth of the statement. Then I thought of others in our congregation whose children are sick, going through divorce, or having great problems. Then I thought of a family in our church whose son grew up in our church. He's now out on his own, but he has never become a Christian—despite many prayers. Then I thought of You, Lord, and said to myself, "Lord, this is You a billion times over—how many of Your children have not accepted Jesus despite Your great love and Your great sacrifice!" And I said to myself, "Lord, my great lack of stewardship is in the area of your gospel." Lord, we've been keeping it to ourselves instead of giving it away. Lord, forgive us. Help us, Lord, to feel Your grief, Your concern, Your love for the lost. Lord, accept our earnest request that any here this morning that are lost will come to know You.

Lord, meet the needs of those among us who are hurting—but also touch each one of us with your power to witness and a deep, deep concern for the lost.

In Jesus' name,
Amen

∞

This is the very first prayer that I prayed after committing to seeking to pray God's Word back to Him, writing prayers out ahead of time, memorizing the prayer, and then praying it out loud in church. This was used as an offertory prayer prayed just before the special music and the sermon in an 11 O'clock Sunday Morning Worship Service. In reality, it might have been better used as a morning prayer prayed at the beginning of the service.

Glorious God,

We struggle with our mental picture of You. We think of You as
- Creator of the universe—yet it is beyond human knowledge to understand how even one atom can be made from nothingness.
- Great Physician and the God who heals—yet our word "physician" describes a human who can heal absolutely nothing without Your complete cooperation.
- Father—yet our human fathers pale in significance in their love and care and protection for their children compared to You for Your children.

- Love—yet we can't even begin to fathom the depths and magnitude of Your love.
- Spirit—yet we can't help but ascribe to You hands and feet and voice and other human parts.

Lord, we confess that to some extent our mental picture of You is so inadequate is because we've not been diligent in our pursuit of knowing You.
- We've not spent enough time in Your Word.
- We've not been intimate in prayer with You as often as we should.

Lord, in Your infinite wisdom, you knew our limitations in understanding You and You provided Jesus—so that we might come to know you through Him.

Thank you, thank you, thank you for Jesus, our Christ-child, our brother, our shepherd, our Savior, our hero, our friend, our vine, our interpreter, our way to know You.

Lord, thank you for creating us, for giving us life, for giving us freedom, for giving us a conscience, for giving us the Law, for giving us grace, for giving us Jesus—sinless Jesus who took all our sins upon Himself, sinless Jesus who paid our penalty of death that we might overcome the power of sin and death in our lives, that we might have the abundant life, that we might be Your children, that we might please You and do Your will.

Lord, we ask that You help us worship you this morning by using Your Holy Spirit
- to help us completely forget the world
- to help us completely concentrate on Your Word as it is parted
- to help us be completely submissive to Your will as it becomes obvious.

Lord, convict each non-Christian here of his utter need for Jesus.

Lord, cause each Christian here to confess his sins daily so that he might feel forgiven and washed anew, so that he might conform to Your will in purpose, thought and action.

In Jesus' name,
Amen

∞

This was prayed at an 11 O'clock Worship Service. Our interim pastor preached. He had been our much-loved pastor many years earlier. His favorite TV show was "Gun Smoke."

Jehovah, God who keeps His covenant, God who honors his promises,

We praise you for being the same yesterday, today and tomorrow. We thank you, Lord, that we can rely on you not to change, that we can rely on You to keep your every commitment.

You promised
- that whatever we ask in Jesus name you will do (See John 14:13 and John 14:14) and
- that whatever we ask in prayer, believing, we shall receive. (See Matt. 21:22)

We claim those promises as we ask, in Jesus precious name, believing as much as you give us power to believe, that this morning your preached word would advance Your kingdom in our lives.

We know all too well that when a preacher shoots over our heads all it proves is that he doesn't know how to shoot. Therefore Lord, we ask You to use Your Holy Spirit to help Your servant take careful aim and shoot your message smack dab in the middle of each of our hearts. And use Your Holy Spirit to work in each of us so that our hearts are so receptive and malleable that that direct hit

- causes tears of remorse to well up in our eyes for the sin we've allowed to creep back into our lives since last we confessed to You
- brings a commitment to do Your will with a strength and determination like we've never had before
- brings such a submissiveness that we find ourselves muttering, "Yes, Lord. Yes, Lord. Anything you say, Lord."
- brings such love that we almost want people to have problems so we can meet their needs
- brings such a desire to practice Your presence in our lives that tomorrow at this time we can sing "All day long I've been with Jesus"[10] and it be true.

O Lord, make Jesus Christ, our crucified, risen and reigning savior, real and glorious to us moment by moment.

And, Lord, we especially ask that you discharge Your Word with armor-piercing bullets to those of our number who don't know Jesus as personal savior.
- Pierce their lack of understanding with Your truth
- Pierce their denial with conviction
- Pierce their reluctance with Your assurance
- Pierce their resistance with Your love

so that they might commit their lives this very morning to Your control.

Lord, thank you for Your promises and forgive us for having claimed so few of them.

Help us to see and do what brings glory to You.

In Jesus' precious name,
Amen

∞

---

[10] "All Day Long," Baptist Hymnal, 1991, #463.

Dismissal Prayer at the end of an 8:30 Sunday Morning Worship Service.

Precious Jesus,

We regret having to leave this fellowship of kindred minds.
We regret having to pause from focusing on You and Your Word.

But we know you leave us here on this earth not so much for our pleasure as to be your witnesses.

Therefore, help us to spread Your Word as we go.
So flood our souls with your spirit and love that our lives reflect You.
Let us witness of You verbally.
Let us preach You with our example.
Let our love for You cause others to be brought to Your fold.

Protect us from the power of sin.
Keep us from worldly thoughts.
Guide us in our pursuit the narrow way.

Dismiss us with Your love.

In Jesus' name,
Amen

∽

This revival prayer, in what I deemed miraculous fashion, got used in both Sunday morning worship services of a formal revival effort.

Lord God,

It is a humbling thing to be died for. At this time of revival we need to be reminded that Thy Son, Jesus Christ, did die for each one of us here. We are made humble by the knowledge that, while we were still mired in sin, Jesus, knowing we would never comprehend the enormousness of his love, took our sins upon himself, went to the cross and died for us.

Lord, forbid that personal pride should keep any of us here this morning from kneeling at the foot of the cross.

Also, at this time of revival we must acknowledge that the fire of our soul burns too low. That demon personal pride
- has kept us from yielding completely to Your will
- has caused us to keep entire areas of our lives out of Your hands
- has caused some of us to be satisfied with where we are in our relationship with You
- has blinded some of us to certain sins in our lives
- has deprived most of us of the blessings of daily meditating on your Word and of daily visiting Your prayer closet

O Lord, ride herd on us
- get our attention with Your Word this morning
- use Your Holy Spirit to convince and convict us of our sins
- then help us to confess our sins and to rededicate our lives completely to You—and then fill us with Your Holy Spirit

Then fan the flames so we have a strong, strong desire to be in close communion with you, 'til we burn with a white heat, on fire for Your church and for Your kingdom in our lives. And give us an unquenchable thirst and an unsatisfiable hunger for Your righteousness and Your Word and a consuming passion for lost souls.

Lord, we confess that in our own power we are unable to properly worship You this morning. So we ask that You use Your Holy Spirit to cause us to so dwell on the Christ as he hung on the cross and died for us that
- we can't help but offer You the sacrifice of praise
- when we place our tithes and offerings in the offering plate our attitude makes You smile

- as we sing hallelujahs and hosannas to Your name it is truly music to Your ears

But, Lord, let our supreme act of worship this morning be the humbling of ourselves as we set aside our personal pride and desires and completely submit our entire lives to Your full control.

Then let our attitude be that of gratitude because Jesus did die for us.

In the name and nature of our Living Savior,

Amen

Prayed before a children's musical in a Sunday Night worship Service.

Heavenly Father,

We thank You for the children here this evening.

We thank You for the gift of children
We thank you for the gift of their laughter and enthusiasm
We thank You for the gift of their music

Lord, use their music to warm our hearts with love for You.
Use their music to lead them to a greater faith in You.
Use their music to lead them to invest their lives in Jesus so that they might always have a song in their hearts for You.

Lord, help each of us to encourage these children to continue to praise You all the days of their lives.

To You be the glory.
Amen

This prayer was used as an offertory prayer in a Sunday morning worship service. To God be the glory.

Glorious God,

The whole world is full of your glory. (See Isa. 6:3)
The telescope reveals your infinite glory.
The microscope shows us your utmost glory.
The naked eye sees your surpassing glory in the beauty of the world around us.
But Your Word seems to suggest that all this is but a small part of your total glory.
O Lord, we praise You because You are great and greatly to be praised. (See Ps. 48:1)

We understand that man is the crowning glory of Your creation, but Your Word teaches that man's glory is fleeting—like the flowers of the field and the blades of grass. (See Ps. 103:15-16) Remind us that only Your glory is worth living for. Help us so dedicate our lives to You that we find our glory in seeking Your glory.

Lord, teach us to pray "to Your glory, in full surrender to Your will, in full assurance of faith, in the name [and nature and character] of Jesus [Christ], and with a perseverance that, if need be, refuses to be denied."[11]

Lord, help us to see and do what glorifies you.

Use these tithes and offerings for Your glory. May this service be used only for Your glory.

Supply all our needs according to your riches in glory in Jesus Christ. (See Phil. 4:19)

To You, Lord, be the glory both now and forever. (See Heb. 13:21)

Amen.

∞

---

[11] Murray, Andrew, *With Christ in the School of Prayer*, (Springdale, PA, 1981), p. 12.

This was an offertory in an 11 O'clock Sunday Morning Worship Service. In some small way this prayer resulted from one of our Ministerial Staff referring to Sunday as the Sabbath in a previous service. The official stance of most Southern Baptists is "The first day of week is the Lord's Day. It is a Christian institution for regular observance. It commemorates the resurrection of Christ from the dead and should be employed in exercises of worship and spiritual devotion..."[12]

Father in Heaven,

We choose not to bring You burnt offerings or blood sacrifices this morning because Jesus fulfilled the Law. He was the ultimate sacrifice that paid the price of sin once and for all. Instead we bring You the sacrifice of praise. (See Heb. 13:15)

We praise You because You are worthy, o Lord, to receive glory and honor and power for You created all things and by Your will they exist and were created. (See Rev. 4:11)

We praise You because You have clothed us with garments of salvation and arrayed us with robes of righteousness. (See Isa. 61:10)

We praise You because You alone do marvelous deeds. (See Ps. 86:10)

We praise You because Your love endures forever. (See Ps. 138:8)

We choose not to observe this day as the Sabbath because Jesus fulfilled the Law and hence the Sabbath. Instead we place all our burdens and our entire lives and our faith in Jesus and obtain our rest in Him. Lord, in the tradition of Christians since New Testament times, we celebrate this day as the Lord's Day and commemorate the resurrection of Your son, Jesus Christ. Lord, forbid that anyone here should continue to seek meaning in life by acquiring things or by seeking fame or fortune or

---

[12]   The Baptist Faith and Message, A Statement Adopted by the Southern Baptist Convention, (Nashville,1963), p.14.

by trying to live a good life or by doing good deeds. Rather help them find their rest by submitting to Jesus.

Lord, we choose not to bring tithes and offerings out of habit or duty or coercion or out of concern for what others might think, but rather, with Your help, we bring them out of love for You and our thankfulness for Jesus and because we truly want to invest our money in Your church and Your kingdom.

We choose not to confess our sins this morning and not feel remorse. Instead we agree with You that our sins are horrible, despicable, and deplorable and their consequences are grievous. Lord, we plead with You to help us never do them again.

Lord, we choose not to just go through the motions of worship this morning. Instead we ask You to use Your Holy Spirit to help us be so in tune with your message that it convicts us of our need to submit ourselves to You as empty vessels. Then fill us with Your Spirit so that all we want to do is be Your person and do Your will and magnify Your name.

Lord, to You be the glory forever. (See Heb. 13:21)

Amen

∞

This was used as an offertory prayer at an 8:30 Sunday Morning Worship Service prayed before the sermon and special music. It emphasizes participation.

God Almighty, Full of Grace,

Just as Moses and the Israelites praised You, we praise You for our strength and for our song and for our salvation. (See Ex. 15:2)

We also praise You because You are gracious and compassionate, slow to anger and rich in love. (See Ps. 145:8)

And we praise You because You change the times and seasons and set up kings and depose them. (See Dan. 2:21)

Lord, help us to be more than just spectators here this evening.

Let us sing the songs and mean the words.

Let us pray and not just bow our heads and close our eyes.

Let us give our money and not just pass the plate.

Let us be caught up in the message of the words of the special music and be moved emotionally.

Let us show our love and adoration of You by being obedient to Your Word as it is read and preached.

Let us not fall asleep during the sermon nor let our minds wander, but hang on every word.

Let us not sit idly by as the appeal is made but let us commit our lives as Your Spirit leads.

And, Lord, as we leave this place let us be able to say truthfully that we have worshipped You in spirit and truth. (See John 4:24)

Lord, we feel the need to pray for others.

Be merciful to the hurting.

For the lost we pray that Your Word spread rapidly, run its course, and be glorified and triumphant. (See 2 Thes. 3:1)

Be with Christians worldwide. Let Your spirit of holiness rule their lives. Keep them from the world, sanctify them, and help them to be one in love.

May our lives be controlled by only one purpose—to please You.

To you be the glory both now and forever. (See Heb. 13:21)

Amen

Prayed at a Sunday Evening Worship Service. See Luke 10:2 for the inspiration for this prayer.

Lord of the Harvest,

We thank you for the laborers who planted and watered so that we were brought into a saving knowledge of Jesus Christ. We praise You for the work of the Holy Spirit that convicted us of our sin and convinced us of our need for Jesus. Lord, as we look at the world we see that the fields are indeed ripe. Please, Lord, send many laborers unto the harvest. Lord, help us to have a concern for the spiritual condition of our fellow man like that of Jesus. Help us be peacemakers by being confrontational with Your Good News when and where Your Spirit leads. Help us to fill our barns with seeds planted in lost souls. O Lord, help us to pray down Your saving grace upon the lost.

Lord, we ask that the seeds in your message tonight find only good soil to fall upon in our hearts. May the seeds sprout, put down deep roots and grow trees with an abundance of good fruit in our lives.

May these tithes and offerings be used to grow Your kingdom in our hearts and the hearts of others. May Your Word spread quickly, run its course, and be glorified and triumphant. (See 2 Thes. 3:1)

To You, Lord, be the glory forever. (See Heb. 13:21)

Amen

Used as an offertory prayer in an 11 O'clock Sunday Morning Worship Service. This prayer began as an effort to pray 1 Peter1:16, Leviticus 20:26, and Leviticus 11:44 back to God.

O Holy One,

There is an old prayer that says "Help me to resist the temptation to be so heavenly minded as to be no earthly good and help me to resist the temptation to be so earthly minded as to be no heavenly good." We confess that we fall into the latter category—we've let the secular world and the press of everyday affairs so dominate our time and our lives that we completely forget You for long periods of time. Forgive us, Lord. Use Your Holy Spirit and this service to refocus our eyes upon Jesus and to help us recommit our lives to being Your people and doing Your will.

Help us in our pursuit of the narrow way. Help us to be holy as You are holy. Let holiness rule every aspect of our lives. Help us to be holy by being obedient. But let us obey You rather than rules. Help us to not be so concerned with the letter of the law that we lose its spirit.

Use Your Holy Spirit to quicken us through the conviction of sin and to bring us to Christ by grace and to sanctify us.

Let our efforts to be holy not result in self-righteousness, but let them result in the selflessness of true holiness.

Let us not exercise our freedom to the point of sin. Help us to separate ourselves from sin and cleave to You.

May we think as You think and will as You will.

Give us grace to match our trials.

Help those of us who are on our feet maintain a compassion for those who aren't. Give us a word of encouragement for those living in a world of hurt.

Keep us from the evil one.

Renew our spirits with the realization that we're Your possessions.

May these tithes and offerings represent but a small token of our love for You.

Let us get caught in a passionate single-mindedness to do Your will.

To You be the glory both now and forever. (See Heb. 13:21)

Amen

∞

This was prayed at the first 11 O'clock Sunday Morning worship Service that our new pastor was on the scene. When I prayed this aloud the list of 'You are' statements was shorter and slightly different. I had used a list I found published somewhere, but when I decided I would publish these prayers and tried to find the source, I failed. So I came up with a new list.

The Lord, My Shepherd,

You are the good shepherd who leads us by the quiet waters. (See Ps. 23:1)
You are the Comforter who wipes away our tears. (See John 14:16 KJV)
You are the Author and Finisher of our Faith. (See Heb. 12:2)
You are our Gate, our Door, our Way to the Father. (See John 10:7)
You are our Passover Lamb who sacrificed himself so we can live. (See 1 Cor. 5:7)
You are the Rock we can run to when things get rough. (See 1 Cor. 10:4)
You are our Counselor whose advice is never wrong. (See John 14:16)
You are the Father who waits anxiously with open arms for the prodigal. (See Luke 15:11-32)
You are our Great High Priest who intercedes with the Father on our behalf. (See Heb. 4:14)

You are our Prince of Peace, Lord of Lords and King of Kings. (See Isa. 9:6 and 1 Tim. 6:15)

O Lord, we praise You because You are our everything.
We praise You because You loved us while we were yet sinners.
We praise You because You placed a desire in us to seek You.

O Lord, our soul pants for You like the deer pants for water. (See Ps. 42:1) Please, Lord, use this service to give us an understanding of You that causes us to want You even more, causes us to pore over Your Word, and causes us too strive to constantly be in touch with You. Lord, use this service to grow Your kingdom in our lives. So focus our eyes on Jesus that we can't take them off for days to come.

O Lord, take our money and use it for Your bills.
Take our time and use it for Your work.
Take our lives and use them as Your witnesses.

Good Shepherd, bless us with the knowledge and the assurance that no one can snatch us out of Your hand (See John 10:29) and that You are ours and we are Yours—forever.

O Lord, we ninety-nine sheep pray desperately for the return of the one lost sheep. We pray for those of our fellowship who haven't been in fellowship with us in a long time; and we pray for those who have never been brought into the fold. O Lord, please open Your arms wide and use us to head them in Your direction.

O Lord, may Your earthly shepherd here feed Your sheep this morning. And may Your sheep hear Your voice and follow You.

Amen

Prayed at the beginning of Sunday School.

O Lord Who God-breathed the Words of Scripture,

Help us to study Your words now. Use Your Holy Spirit to help us to understand what You want Your words to communicate to us right now. Let that message sink into our thoughts and hearts, let us keep it in our memory, obey it constantly in our life, and let it shape and mold our daily life and every act. May Your written word be honored and may it be used for doctrine, for reproof, for correction, and instruction in righteousness. (See 2 Tim. 3:16-17) Supply all our needs according to the riches of Your glory. (See Phil. 4:19)

Amen

❦

Prayed as an offertory prayer at a Sunday Evening Worship service. I sometimes find myself mentally criticizing others because they praise God for things He has done or thank Him for who He is. Technically we should thank Him for what He has done and praise Him for who He is. But I find myself committing the same faux pas. I do know that the adoration part of a public prayer is by far the most important part and that I always feel better if I invest part of my prayer in praising God.

Jehovah, God who keeps His covenant,

We praise You because all that You are You have always been,
and all that You are and have always been, You will always be.
We praise You because nothing You have said about Yourself will ever be changed.
We praise You because nothing the inspired prophets and apostles have written about You will ever be rescinded.
We praise You because You are the one and only constant in life.
We praise You because we can rest in You without fear or doubt and face tomorrows without anxiety.

O Lord, we deplore the lack of stability in all earthly things. And yet, the very ability to change is a golden treasure, a gift from You of such fabulous worth as to call for constant thanksgiving.

O Lord, we so thank You for the magnificent change that happened in our lives that resulted in us becoming Your redeemed children, destined to spend eternity with You.

O Lord, we thank You that You have asked us to take Your yoke upon us, learn of You, (See Matt. 11:29) and strive toward the abundant life which only comes through change after change as we grow as Christians.

O Lord, use this service to help each of us recognize what needs to be changed in our lives right now. Then help us to change from resisting Your Holy Spirit to praising Your name all day long.

Lord, we know that You feel the same today toward the sick, the broken, and the sinful as is recorded in Your Word when You sent Your only begotten Son into the world to die for all mankind. Please, Lord, have mercy on these by helping us change our attitude so that we have the same compassion toward these as Jesus did.

May these tithes and offerings be used to change the hearts of those resisting Your Spirit.

And may all the changes we make and all the changes we resist be for Your glory.

Amen.

Prayed as an offertory prayer at an 11 O'clock Sunday Morning Worship Service. If the Holy Spirit doesn't communicate to us during the service, from God's perspective the service is a failure.

Lord Who Is Always Near,

If we ascend up to Heaven, You are there.
If we make our bed in hell, behold, You are there.
If we take wings of a morning and dwell in the uttermost parts of the sea, even there shall Your hand lead us, and Your right hand shall hold us. (See Ps. 139:8-10)

Lord, Jacob said, "Surely the Lord is in this place, and I knew it not." (Gen.28:16 KJV)
Let us also experience You and know that it's You.
Use Your Holy Spirit to reveal the Father and the Son to us this morning.
Make Yourself so real to us that You become the wonder of our lives.
As we get into Your Word this morning may Your Word get into us.
O Lord, may we experience Your Living Word this morning. Make Jesus so real to us that we so submit our lives that we consider everything a loss compared to the surpassing greatness of knowing Christ Jesus as lord and savior. (See Phil. 3:8)

O Lord, we know that Your Word says, "Blessed are the pure in heart for they shall see God." (Matt. 5:8 KJV) Please, cleanse us of sin and wrong motive, purify our hearts.

O Lord, we desire to be putty in Your hands. Please, Lord, help us to set aside every personal desire and to want only what You want.

May our tithes and offerings acknowledge not only Your presence here and everywhere but also our love for You.

Lord, we pray for all those who do no know You or do not sense Your presence. Use Your Holy Word, Your Holy Spirit, circumstances, and us as need be to enlighten them. And involve us in praying down Your kingdom on their lives.

Lord, when this service ends may we be able to say that we tasted of You and found that You are good. (See Ps. 34:8)

Amen.

⬿

Monday Night Prayer Meeting is usually five-to-ten minutes of sharing concerns and then the rest of the time is spent praying. People pray one at a time as they feel led. Usually the crowd is small so there is plenty of time for whoever wants to pray whatever the Lord leads them to pray.

O Perfect One,

Which of us has not at least once said to ourselves that if we were in charge we would have created a world in which there was not pain or suffering or hunger or sorrow. O Lord, forgive our arrogance. Must we be reminded that the reason you do not change or cannot change is because any change in perfection results in imperfection. And not only are You perfect, Lord, but all of Your plans are perfect, too.

O Lord, instill in each of us the desire to be perfect by being perfectly submissive to Your plan and Your will. O Lord, in Your good time, finish and fulfill the good work You began in us.

Lord, help us to set our sights on being Your perfect church. Let not anyone of us be able to say, "Jesus, sometimes I feel like You and I are the only idealists in this church," O Lord, let us be a church full of saints with enough faith in You to believe we can be Your perfect church. Raise up in Your people at FBC a stubborn tenacity to do Your will, to obey Your Word, and to cast off everything that would oppose Your Spirit (See Matt.12:28) and then move us into the realm that is willing to pay the price and lay hold of Your kingdom. O Lord, we're tired of mediocrity, tired of the status quo, tired of being defeated by an already defeated enemy.

Give us the power to be Your perfect church. And, Lord, if we must fall short of perfection, let us at least end up being the prayingest, lovingest, soul-winningest church of all time.

Amen.

∞

This prayer was prayed during a Sunday evening Revival service. I found out a few services later that the evangelist really appreciated this prayer.

Lord God,

Somewhere in Your Word it says, "To obey is better than sacrifice." (1 Sam. 15:22 KJV) Lord, those words are really bothering me. You see, I was planning to sacrifice a couple hours down here today, put some money in these offering plates, sing some hymns, listen to a couple of sermons, and tell myself that I've done my part—I've worshiped You. Then the rest of the week can go on as normal. But I guess Your Holy Spirit has been working on me—making me feel guilty, making me think that I'm wasting my time down here unless I actually try to be obedient to whatever it is that You are trying to tell me today.

Lord, can You help me out just a bit? First off, could You help me listen? You wouldn't believe how far my mind can wander during a sermon. Then again, You probably would.

Secondly, could You make Your message as clear as a bell? You know how dense I am and how big words and theological concepts sometimes go right over my head. And a lot of times after the sermon is over I don't have a clue as to what the preacher was trying to say, much less what You might have been trying to tell me.

And, Lord, you know my favorite excuse for not obeying You is that I wasn't absolutely sure what You wanted me to do. Help me acknowledge that what You're asking me to do really is Your will for my life. Let me be 100% sure.

And then, Lord, would You help me to feel so much love for You that I really want to do whatever it is that You're asking me to do or help me to feel so sorry, so remorseful for my past disobedience that I really want to change and start obeying You now or help me to come to the logical, rational conclusion that what You're asking me to do is the very best thing for my life? Either way, considering how resistant I am to change, Lord, would You also give me a little push to help me make that commitment?

Then, Lord, after I make that commitment—considering how little will power I have, would You help me to rely on You moment by moment for strength to follow through?

And, Lord, while You're at it, if there is anybody else here who needs to be obedient to Your message for them this evening, would You do these same things for them, too?

Amen

∞

This Sunday Night offertory prayer is almost 100% God's Word prayed back to Him.

Be praised, adored, and thanked, O Lord, the God of Israel, forever and ever. Yours, O Lord, is the greatness and the power and the glory and the victory and the majesty: for all that is in the heavens and the earth is Yours. Yours is the kingdom, O Lord, and Yours it is to be exalted as Head over all.

Both riches and honor come from You, and You reign over all. In Your hands are power and might. In Your hand it is to make great and to give strength to all.

Now, therefore, our God, we thank You and praise Your glorious name and all those attributes which that name denotes.

But who. . .[are we here tonight that we] should retain strength and be able to offer [these tithes and offerings] thus so willingly? For all things come from You, and of Your own [hand] we have given [to] You. (1 Chron. 29:10-14 Amp)

To You be the glory forever and ever. (See Heb. 13:21)

Amen.

This prayer was prayed during a Monday Night Prayer Meeting. Confession is good for the soul, but it usually better accepted in a prayer that is not part of a Sunday Morning Worship Service.

Lord God Almighty,

Holy and awesome is Your name.
There is no one holy like You, no not one.
O Lord, You are so pure, so perfect, so awesome.
O Lord, we humble ourselves before You. We tremble before You.
O Lord, we praise you because You supply all our needs according to the riches of Your glory in Christ Jesus. (See Phil. 4:19)
We praise You because You give us life—not just physical life but eternal life and abundant life.

O Lord, we want to say we love You. But we hesitate, not because we know You know our heart at this very moment, but because we know that You have known all day and all week and we know that somehow

41

You measure love in terms of obedience. O Lord, in truth, we do love You more than anything for periods of time, but then we look around and we find ourselves loving pleasure more than You or loving things more than You. And when we discover it, sometimes we don't even say, "Oops." Please, Lord, help us to maintain Your rightful position in our lives—we're doing a miserable job all by ourselves. O Lord, we confess that sometimes we feel we don't deserve to be in Your family. At best we feel like black sheep. We've let sin get the upper hand. It keeps us from being the person You want us to be. Instead of being Your witness and doing Your work, we found ourselves meeting our own needs and not telling anyone about You today. O Lord, we took our focus off of You today. O Lord, we keep trying to do things on our own. Please, help us to continually recognize that we're helpless to help ourselves. O Lord, we're begging on the inside for Your control in our life.

O Lord, involve us so much in the study of Your Word that Your Holy Spirit gets the upper hand in our life. Help us to be ultra-sensitive to sin in our lives. Let it be the sore point of our existence. Let our sins burden us beyond the point of tears. Help us to deny our own desires. Help us not only deny but to put aside our own desires and needs and think only of your needs. Help us to humble ourselves before You and others. Help us to hunger and thirst after righteousness. May Your Word be the joy of our life. O Lord, move us from being just nominal Christians to being Christians that radiate Jesus. O Lord, help us to put on the full armor of God and to take every thought captive to the obedience of Jesus. (Combining thoughts from Eph. 6:11 and 2 Cor. 10:5)

O Lord, teach us to pray. Involve us so much in prayer that Your will and Your work get done in and through our life and the lives of others. Teach us to pray Your words and Your thoughts and Your will. Teach us to persevere until our prayer matches Yours and You use us to accomplish Your will. Teach us to pray "to Your glory, in full surrender to Your will, in full assurance of faith, in the name [and nature and character] of Jesus [Christ], and with a perseverance that, if need be, refuses to be denied."[13] Clothe us with power to pray down God's kingdom on those around us. Teach us to be Your fellow workers in the intercession by which the kingdom is to be revealed on earth.

Lord, our hearts rejoice with those of our church family who rejoice and weep with those who weep. Lord, please comfort those who are grieving. Help them to feel Your love. Lord, please be with those who are experiencing illness. Lord, in our own humanness we would ask that You would snap your fingers and miraculously heal each of these. But we know that's not the way in which You will be most glorified. Please, Lord, instead, deal with each situation in the manner in which You will be most glorified. And use us to be Your tools of attention and mercy as Your Spirit leads.

Lord, we ask You to bless the church that meets in this building. Lord, we pray that we may continually strive to be united in love as we draw and are drawn closer to You and Your purpose. Please, Lord, cleanse us so that we may be a suitable bride for the Bridegroom. And, Lord, we pray again, as a love gift to You and our new pastor and so that Your name may be glorified on earth as it's never been before, that You will require of us to do whatever it takes to become that one local congregation in all of history—past, present, and future, that comes closest to being all You want it to be.

O Lord, because we want it so much.

Amen.

∞

Prayed at a Monday Night Prayer Meeting. After adoration, confession is probably the most important element of prayer. Recognize that many people are uncomfortable with anyone confessing the sins of the church—saying you shouldn't ever say anything negative about the

---

[13]   Murray, Andrew, *With Christ in the School of Prayer*, (Springdale, PA, 1981), p. 12.

church. God is more interested in honesty and repentance. Recognize that it's not you making them uncomfortable, but the Holy Spirit.

God Who Empowered Moses to Part the Water, God Who Empowered Samson and Gideon and Paul, empower this church to do Your bidding. Lord, as individuals, we ask very humbly, may we walk with You. May we commune with You so we know what Your bidding is. Then may we come to want only what You want and do only what You want us to do.

Lord, we come confessing our sins—not just admitting them but agreeing with You that they're deplorable, wanting never to repeat even one of them again. O Lord, we didn't intend to do these ahead of time, but we did them anyway.

Lord, we've not been as quick to forgive as we should. May we willingly and anxiously forgive those who offend us because we know it is only through them that we ever have opportunity to be forgiving like You, our Father in Heaven.

We've not put You first in everything. Lord, let us not allow ambition, pleasure, loved ones, friendships, desire for money, or our own plans interfere with our surrender and service to You.

Lord, we've been doing a miserable job of reaching the lost for You. May we have as much concern for them as You do. May we witness consistently with our mouth for our Lord Jesus Christ.

Lord, we've not been as loving as we should be. May we love our fellow church members with a love that revels in the good things that happens to them and weeps in their misfortunes.

Lord, we've been tightfisted with our money. May we strive to be as generous in all our dealing with You and our fellow man as You have been with us.

Lord, we've not multiplied the talents that You've given us as we should. May we be good stewards and dependable and have a good reputation among our fellow men.

Lord, we have dishonored Your Holy Temple, our bodies. We've overeaten or put things in our bodies we shouldn't have or not gotten enough exercise. O Lord, may we use our bodies only in ways that glorify You.

Lord, we've been guilty of not giving You the glory and the credit for everything good about us. We've been close mouthed or accepting when people praise us rather than making sure You get the credit and the glory. May we talk about what You have done rather than what we have done.

Lord, at times we've failed to do Your will. May we not let our feelings of inadequacy keep us from attempting the things You want us to do.

Lord we've been lazy. May we give an honest day's work. May we not waste any of the valuable time You've given us.

Lord, at times we've had a poor attitude. May we not complain or find fault or have a critical attitude toward any person or thing. May we not become impatient with others.
Lord, we've allowed Satan to get a toehold in our lives. May we avoid unwholesome TV and movies and radio and magazines and novels and put only good stuff in our minds. May we not engage in empty and unprofitable conversation.

Lord, at times we forget to thank You. May we thank you for all things, both good and bad.

Lord, we get our priorities all messed up. May we not be taken up with the cares of this world, but rather make You and Your Word our major focus.

Lord, we confess that we find some people hard to love. May we harbor no prejudices against those who are different. May we see what You see in all those we come into contact with.

Lord, our prayer life is not what it should be. May we be consistent in our daily private prayer life. May we be able to say that all day long I've been with Jesus.

Lord, we've been complaining about our government leaders. May we be submissive to the leadership You place over us. May we render unto Caesar what is Caesar's and unto You what is Yours.

Lord, we've missed opportunities to help others. May we minister to others as Your Spirit leads.

Lord, we have a big problem with personal pride. May we humble ourselves before You and others.

Lord, we have let the world dictate our lives. May we be more concerned with what will be pleasing to You than in what others might think.

Lord, we've lied to You and to ourselves. May we be honest and true in admitting our sins.

Lord, if we've sinned against any one, let us confess it to You and make things right with them.

Lord, we pray all these things that we may be cleansed of the wrongdoing in our lives and so that we can pray with a clear conscience, because we don't just want to be a holy people, but we want our prayers to be able to have great effect. We want to be able to pray down Your kingdom on those around us. O Lord, use us as individuals and as a church to stand in the gap and intercede for those who are lost and going to hell. May we plead for them with the same love that Jesus had for us as he allowed himself to be crucified. O Lord, change us as a church from what we are to the prayingest, soul-winningest, lovingingest church that ever existed on planet earth. O Lord, use Your Holy Spirit to convict us of our lethargy, our unwillingness to change, our pride, or whatever it is that's keeping us from being able to take that next step in Your direction. O Lord, we ask these things not for us but because we sense You want us to ask for them. O Lord, light a fire under us and put a fire in us.

In the name and nature and character of Jesus Christ,

Amen

∞

This was prayed at Monday Night Prayer Meeting. The new prayer ministry mentioned is a prayer room to be populated with church members praying one hour at a time. It has become the most precious hour of the week for me.

Adonai, Lord and Master,

Help us to deny our own desires. Help us to not only deny but to put aside our own desires and needs and think only of Your needs. Help us to humble ourselves before You and others.

Involve us so much in the study of Your Word that Your Holy Spirit gets the upper hand in our lives. Help us to hunger and thirst after Your righteousness and Your Word. May Your Word be the joy of our life. O Lord, move us from being just nominal Christians to being Christians that radiate the love of Jesus, Christians that do mightier works than Jesus did. O Lord, move us from struggling with the fundamentals of the faith to taking giant steps toward spiritual maturity. O Lord, help us to put on Christ, to put on the full armor of God, and to take every thought captive to the obedience of Jesus. (Combining thoughts from Rom. 13:14 & Eph. 6:11 & 2 Cor. 10:5)

O Lord, use Your new Prayer Ministry as a means of growing Your Kingdom in our lives and the lives of others. Help each of us to so honor our commitment that You are honored. Turn that hour into Your hour. Lord, instead of a chore turn that hour into a great blessing. Teach us to pray Your words and Your thoughts and Your will. Teach us to persevere until our prayer matches Yours and You use us to accomplish Your will. Teach us to pray "to Your glory, in full surrender to Your will, in full assurance of faith, in the name [and nature and character] of Jesus [Christ], and with a perseverance that, if need be, refuses to be denied."[14] Clothe us with the power to pray down Your kingdom on those around us. Teach us to be Your fellow workers in the intercession by which the kingdom is to be revealed on earth. May our praying cause more praying not just in our lives but the lives of others. Teach us to "labor for an inward stillness… [where] we no longer entertain our own… thoughts and vain opinions… and [where] we wait…that we may know… [Your] will."[15] And when Your will becomes obvious, give us the boldness to do it. Let us say, "Yes, Lord, yes. Anything You say." Then help us follow through. O Lord, involve us so much in prayer that Your will and Your work gets done in and through our life and in the lives of others.

Lord, we pray for the local congregation that meets in this building. Let us not reason and argue among ourselves, but merely let us obey Your Word and Your command. Let us fear our own ideas and opinions. May we be obedient to all those You have set over us. May we not grumble but only obey. May we have only love for all our brothers and sisters in Christ. Lord, we pray that we may continually strive to be united in love for You and in purpose. Please, Lord, cleanse us so that we may be a suitable bride for the Bridegroom. And may we have great love for and be totally submissive to the Bridegroom. May the recognition of Your presence be a constant in our lives. May those who attend our services sense that this is a place where You are at work. O Lord, we ask that there be a great outpouring of Your Holy Spirit on this church. Break

---

[14]   Murray, Andrew, *With Christ in the School of Prayer*, (Springdale, PA, 1981), p. 12.

[15]   Longfellow, Henry Wadsworth, *The Poems of Henry Wadsworth Longfellow*, pp 423-424.

us again and again and again. Make us desperate for Your control. Then fill each of us to overflowing with Your Holy Spirit. And, Lord, we pray once again, as a love gift to You and so that Your name may be glorified on earth as it's never been done before, that You will require of us to do whatever it takes to become that one local congregation in all of history, past, present and future, that comes closest to being all that You wanted it to be. O Lord, test us and try us, allow us to be persecuted for Your sake, O Lord, may we ask for everything You intend for us to have. Lord, give us the boldness to ask for more enthusiasm for Your work than we have for our favorite team, more dedication to Your cause than we have for our job, more love for You than we have for anything. O Lord, ask us to make a great sacrifice for You.

Lord, I pray for the families of this church. Whatever binds them together as a family unit, make that stronger. Be with the children in those families. Help them to find you. May we bring them up and nurture them into a saving relationship with you. Lord, I pray for some husbands that aren't Christians.

O Lord, because we want it so much and because You're worth it.

Amen.

Prayed as an offertory prayer at an 8:30 Sunday Morning Worship Service. The Deacon Fellowship has a Worship Support Committee which is responsible for organizing Deacon support during our worship services. The committee has organized things such that each Deacon ends up praying during a Sunday Morning Worship Service about four or five times a year.

Lord of Salvation,

We praise You because You have the goodness to want only the very best for us.

We praise You because you have the wisdom to plan the very best for us. We praise You because you have the power to achieve the very best for us.

O Lord, we praise You because You have put Your plan in place and sacrificed Your Son to do it.

O Lord, let us not accept second best. Let us submit to Your plan for our lives.

Lord, use this service to get buy-in. Use Your Holy Spirit to convict of sin and to convince of the need for Jesus. Use Your preached word to expose the plan and lay bare Your great love for us. Use our prayers to bring Your kingdom down upon us. O Lord, may Your magnificent plan come to fruition right before our eyes this evening. May the angels in Heaven find reason to rejoice.

Lord, some of us have bought into Your plan, but we're spiritually bankrupt because we haven't made enough prayerful deposits. We haven't given You the first fruits of our lives. Use Your Holy Spirit and this service to move us to the point of giving prayer and Bible study and Your will the priority you want them to have in our lives.

May these tithes and offerings be used to advance Your plan in this world.

May we so humble our hearts before You this morning and so honor Your Word and so praise your name that You feel worshipped.

Lord, teach us to so live that You and Your love constantly grow nearer, dearer and clearer.

Amen

Prayed as an offertory prayer for a Sunday Morning Worship Service. People love to hear God praised with words that come from God's Word. If you want to receive compliments on your prayer include lots of praise that comes from God's Word. But, of course, it's a sin to pray for the purpose of getting man's praise.

Lord of Lords, King of kings,

You only have immortality, dwelling in the light which no man can approach, whom no man has seen nor can see. (See 1 Tim. 6:16) Great and marvelous are Your works, Lord God Almighty. Just and true are Your ways, Thou King of Saints. Who shall not fear You, O Lord, and glorify Your name? For You are holy. (See Rev. 15:3-4) Indeed, You are infinite, eternal, and unchangeable in Your holiness. In fact, You are also infinite, eternal, and unchangeable in Your wisdom, and in Your power, and in Your justice, and in Your goodness and truth, and in Your entire being.[16] O Lord, we worship You in the splendor of Your majesty.

Lord, in these moments of meditation ahead may we "labor for an inward stillness, [in which] we no longer entertain our own... thoughts and vain opinions... [and in which] we wait... that we may know... [Your]will."[17] Prepare us for Your message, Lord.

Then reveal Your mind to us through the special music, through Your preached word, and through Your holy written Word. Speak to us in a mighty way. May Your words sink deep into our hearts. May they shape and mold our actions and our daily life. O Lord, may Your Word not return void during this service, but may it explode within our hearts.

---

[16]   Westminster Shorter Catechism, General Assembly of the Church of Scotland, p. 1 (Answer to Question 4, What Is God?).

[17]   Longfellow, Henry Wadsworth, *The Poems of Henry Wadsworth Longfellow*, pp 423-424.

Lord, may Your Holy Spirit also work in a mighty way during this service. May there come such a move of Your Spirit, such a brooding and hovering, such a release of power, that Your Word falls on only receptive hearts, that there is deep conviction of sin, that there is the desperate realization that we're helpless to help ourselves, that there is the universal understanding here that only Jesus can solve our problems.

O Lord, may we end up offering You not just a portion of our money this morning, but also every ounce of our being. O Lord, may we throw caution to the wind, jump off the deep end, and fling ourselves into Your open arms.

Lord, burst our bubble of personal pride this morning with Your sharp, two-edged sword so that we might find our glory by seeking Your glory.

Then may we give You all the glory, both now and forever. (See Heb. 13:21)

Amen

∞

Prayed at Monday Night Prayer Meeting. While this prayer may seem conversational, keep in mind that the very nature of most public prayers make them monologues rather than dialogues. However, it is very desirous to have conversational prayers in private that are, in effect, dialogues.

Precious Jesus,

As we pray tonight, will You be our go-between—just as You've promised? Will You say to the Father, "Father, the folk at FBC are here to speak to You. They're not coming on their own merits or righteousness. Rather they are here based on mine. They are here in My name. I'm sure that You remember that I paid the price so that they might have access to You. They have a few things to ask You." Then, Jesus, let us be able to picture in our minds the Father saying, "Of course, I remember, Son. You made each of them one of ours. Because they came through You, they are always welcome here. Let them make their requests known to Me. Let them ask whatever they may."

O Jesus, may we pray with a boldness that only comes from knowing that You're interceding for us—that You and the Holy Spirit are assisting us as we pray. O Lord and Savior, impress upon us what we should be praying. Let us not pray for anything that we can do in our own power. Let us pray for only what You can do. Lord, we ask that You do what only You can do. Lord, we ask not only that You go between us and the Father, but would You go between us and Satan and separate us from him.

Lord God Almighty, there is great tragedy going on all around us. People all around us, people everywhere, people by the billions are lost and going to Hell not because of their sins but because we Your church are abrogating our responsibility. We're not interceding for them. Lord, we confess to being unconcerned, lazy, apathetic, complacent. O Lord, we confess to being the weak link. May we be obedient to the point that when it's Your will and it's Your time it gets done because we prayed for it. O Lord, Satan is having a field day with us. Please, Lord, put Your compassion for the lost in us. O Lord, move each of us from saying that we desire to be like You, that we try to imitate You to being able to say that for us to live is Christ. Lord, we're here this evening to ask You to bring down Your kingdom on this world. Start right here with us, start right here in this church, start right here in this community. Use the spark that is smoldering here at FBC to light a fire in this church. O Lord, light a fire under us and put a fire in us. O Lord, then fan the flames till there is an all-consuming passion to know You and Your Word and do Your will.

Lord, as we pray would You change us from saying the right words about the lost to having Your heart for them. Lord, we ask You to extend mercy and bring salvation to the people of Tullahoma and nearby. Because Jesus interceded and mediated for them, Father, we are asking based on what He did. He needs a human being on earth to ask for Him because He is in Heaven now. So as He taught, we are asking for Your Kingdom to come and Your will be done in the lives of the lost of Tullahoma. We're asking for laborers to be sent here. We're asking to be the ones who stand in the gap and pray it down. We're asking these things based entirely on the redemptive work Jesus has already done.

Lord, may we have the honor of spreading Your Good News. We're asking this for Christ and through Christ. Set us free from being so much hearers of the Word only and not doers. (See James 1:22) May we be Your co-laborers. May we have the honor of regularly conveying Your awesomeness to others. Lord, we beg You to use us to spread Your Good News. Wear us out knocking on doors, distributing tracts, being Your witness, doing whatever it takes. Lord, may we be the ones who enforce Your victory down here on earth. May we be Your voice, Your hands, Your feet. May we do what You would do if You were here in the flesh.

Lord, grow our faith. Help us to accept Your Word for what it says. Let us not waste time trying to rationalize it away. Let us believe so much in Your Word that we claim its promises.

To You be the glory both now and forever. (See Heb. 13:21)

Amen

Prayed at a Monday Night Prayer Meeting. While the words may seem to be important, our attitude is often what God is most interested in. That is why attempting to pray what the Holy Spirit seems to be telling us God wants is so appropriate.

Jehovah,

The Hebrews of old chose not to speak Your name to make sure there was no way they could break the third commandment. We wonder how they could have a right relationship with You and never call You by name. We chose to honor Your name not by avoiding its use but by treating it with great respect and using it to address You in a respectful manner. O Lord, we enjoy addressing You by all the various names You've provided for us in Your Word. We love to think on the attributes that they bring to mind. O Lord, we love to address You by the names that describe You. O Lord, we chose to honor Your name by using it often—as we pray to You. O Lord, we chose to honor Your name by living lives that acknowledge You and by praising Your name often. Lord, we chose to honor Your name this evening by praying for what we believe that Jesus would pray for if He were here in person.

Lord, one of Your servants wrote that "prayer is striking the winning blow...that service is just gathering the results."[18] Lord, we're here to strike the winning blow. Lord, we strike the winning blow, as we pray that
- the praying habit would catch on like wildfire around here
- all the activities of this church get undergirded with prayer
- that prayers become so prolific in this congregation that Your will gets accomplished regularly
- that Your kingdom pours continuously out of heaven as a result of the constant intercessory prayers made by this congregation
- that every member of this church be praying regularly for at least one lost soul

---

[18] Gordon, S.D., *Quiet Talks on Prayer*, p.19.

- that every member's private prayer life blossoms
- that You become the sole author of our prayers
- that our praying would beget more praying
- that we pray for things that only You can do
- that we pray for everything that You intend for us to have

Lord, we strike the winning blow, as we pray that
- You will send many laborers to the harvest
- You will burden us with Your agony, Your concern, Your love for the lost
- You will use our prayers to cause souls to be saved worldwide
- Your focus becomes our focus
- witnessing and spreading Your Word becomes our way of life
- we might have the privilege of daily representing Your awesomeness to someone
- we might cultivate, water, plant seeds, hoe and harvest, and give You all the credit and glory
- this church might continuously point people to Jesus
- Your Word spread quickly, run its course, and be glorified and triumphant (See 2 Thes. 3:1)

Lord, we strike the winning blow as we pray that
- the proclamation of Your inerrant Word remain the centerpiece of our worship services
- we do nothing in our worship services that does not glorify You and Your name
- every worship service result in changed lives, committed and recommitted to Your service
- all the unchurched of this community would get a personal invitation to attend our worship services
- circumstances will arise that will cause people who need to be in our worship services to be here
- we will reach everyone in Tullahoma with the Good News of Jesus Christ in a fashion that they really do understand it and believe it

- this church remains one in the bond of love
- we spend so much time in Your word that Your Word gets into us
- that the inactive members of this church become convicted that they need to come back to church

Lord, we strike the winning blow, as we pray
- the devil be defeated in our lives
- Thy will be done in and through us

Lord, as a love gift to You, we pray asking that You would require of us to do whatever it takes to become that one church in all history that comes closest to being all that You want it to be.

Amen

❦

Prayed as an offertory prayer at an 8:30 Sunday Morning Worship Service. One of the main purposes of praise and adoration is to cause us to recognize how humble we should be.

O Lord, Almighty and Omnipotent God Who Knows No Barrier and Who Cannot Fail,

No one is like You. No, not one. We have had to invent words that we can use for no other reason than to describe You, and still You are magnificent beyond description. Your magnificence not only exceeds our vocabulary, it exceeds our very comprehension. And Your glory outshines the sun. O Lord, we are nothing compared to You.

Only You are worthy to be praised all day long. We praise You because Your kingdom is an eternal kingdom and Your dominion endures from generation to generation. (See Dan. 4:3) We praise You because You have delivered us out of darkness into marvelous light. (See 1 Pet. 2:9) We praise You because You rule over all things. We praise You because in Your hand are the depths of the earth, and the mountain peaks belong to You. (See Ps. 95:4) O Lord, we could go on and on, but for our shallowness and our exhaustibility.

Lord, we have come to the time in this service when we are ready to give You a gift, a portion of the money You've allowed us to come by. And we recognize that it's also attitude evaluation time, because we recall that You're not so much interested in our gift as You are our attitude. Lord, we confess that our attitude is less than perfect. Lord, maybe the first thing we should ask, even before we give you our gift, is for You to give us a gift, the gift of a right attitude.

But Christ taught that the gift above all gifts that You want to give in answer to prayer is the Holy Spirit. He fills the heart with Your love and gives knowledge of You. We long for a lot more of that than what we've got. He breathes the mind and life of Christ into us, so we can live as Jesus did, in and for Your love. We long for a lot more of that than what we've got. He supplies power from Heaven for our walk and work. We long for a lot more of that than what we've got. O Lord, we confess that the reason we don't have more than what we've got is that we've been quenching Your Holy Spirit. (See 1 Thes. 5:19) It's like we've relegated Him to one of two rooms of our soul. O Lord, use the special music this morning, the preached word, Your Holy written word, and Your Holy Spirit to talk us into flinging open those interior doors of our souls and taking the hinges off. O Lord, may we give Your Holy Spirit full sway in every area of our lives, may we obey His every urging so that the next time we're ready to give our gifts to You our attitude is much improved.

O Lord, may any here who have never received this gift above all gifts be receptive to Your will today.

Amen

Prayed at a Monday Night Prayer Service. Reminding God of why He should answer our prayers causes us to revisit our status with God.

Lord,

It has been said that "prayer is striking the winning blow...that service is just gathering the results. Lord, we're here to strike the winning blow."[19]

But first, Lord, we want to give You good reason to answer our prayers. Answer our prayers, Lord, because we choose to honor Your name. May we honor Your name by treating our government leaders and anyone who has a place of authority in our lives with great respect even when we wholeheartedly disagree with them. We choose to honor Your name by living decent, respectful lives that give Your detractors no reason to think less of You. We choose to honor Your name by respecting all people and working to uplift those who are downtrodden or experiencing injustice.

Lord, answer our prayers because we chose to acknowledge Your character. Lord, we can extol Your character all day long. We praise You because of Your love and Your immutability and Your eternalness and Your omniscience and omnipotence and omnipresence and Your integrity and Your sovereignty and Your authority and, Lord, we can go on and on.

Lord, answer our prayers because we acknowledge Your glory. Lord, no one is like You, no not one. You are magnificent beyond description. Your glory outshines the sun. We are nothing compared to You.

Lord, answer our prayers because of our relationship with Jesus. Because of His redeeming blood, we are not just Your creation, but we are Your children. Lord, answer our prayer because we are Your servants down here doing Your work. Lord, answer our prayers because what we are asking is what You want done. It's what Jesus would ask if He were here in person.

---

[19]   Gordon, S.D., *Quiet Talks on Prayer*, p.19.

Lord, answer our prayers because Jesus and Your Holy Spirit are interceding on our behalf, begging You to give us what we need.

Lord, we come tonight asking—
asking out of the minds You gave us,
asking what we understand the Spirit wants us to ask,
asking in Jesus name, claiming to represent Him, claiming to be asking what we think He would be asking if He were here in person,
asking abiding in Christ, being in constant fellowship with Him, obediently accepting His will for our lives,
asking in faith, without any doubt You'll do what we ask because what we ask is consistent with Your will,
asking in humility, recognizing our need for You, knowing who You are,
asking in sincerity, meaning our request with every ounce of our being.

Lord, we strike the winning blow, as we pray that
prayer would become the mindset of this church,
no activity takes place in this church without it being prayed for,
prayer permeates this church—that prayers become so prolific in this church that Your will gets accomplished,
that Your kingdom pours continuously out of heaven as a result of the constant intercessory prayers made in this church,
that our prayer closets never gather any dust,
that You become the sole author of our prayers.

Lord, we strike the winning blow, as we pray that
Your Good News will get preached to every people group on earth,
every local congregation in the entire world will honor Your Word,
the universal church will be united in love for You and each other and obedience to You,
Your Good News will find its way to every true seeker in the world,
through spiritual disciplines—prayer, Bible study, meditation, fasting, etc. we become best friends with You.

May Your Word spread quickly, run its course, and be glorified and triumphant. (See 2 Thes. 3:1)

Amen

∞

Janice experienced severe depression. It was so bad she couldn't even come to church anymore. Janice suffered for like a year and got no relief from the doctors. One Monday night Al was the first one to pray; and he prayed for only one thing—for Janice's depression to go away. Then everyone who prayed that evening prayed for Janice and that was the only thing they prayed for. Later that night Janice's depression lifted. Janice is the Bible leader for Morning Glories, a Tuesday morning women's Bible study that draws women not only from our congregation but from all of Tullahoma and the surrounding area. The following was prayed at a Monday Night Prayer Meeting.

Father of Faith,

It has been said that we become like the one with whom we spend the most time. Lord, we're here this evening to spend time with You. We cultivate Your companionship as our dearest friend and we desire to be like You. You see, we deplore certain aspects of our lives. We pledge again and again that we're going to change certain things in our lives. But still we've not changed. Lord, in intimate and firsthand interaction with Your Spirit remake us in Your likeness. Lord, we've put our faith in You to save our souls, now help us to put our faith in You to run our lives. Lord, bestow on us Your gift of faith so we can respond to the gentle overture of Your Holy Spirit, so we can put enough childlike trust in Christ, our Savior, Friend, and Master to give Him control. Work in our lives by Your Spirit and through your own gracious Word so that we may comply with Your will. In Your good time, finish and fulfill the good work You began in us. (See Phil. 1:6) Lord, we give our consent for You to do whatever You deem best for us.

Lord, in order to make us more like You, help us to spend more time with You. Help us to develop a closer relationship with You by spending time in our prayer closets. In the words of the psalmist: Help us to dwell in the secret place of the Most High so we shall abide under the shadow of the Almighty. (See Ps. 91:1) Help us to make prayer a way of life. Let us be in constant communication with You. May we always have our minds and hearts open to Your every communication to us.

Lord, in order to make us more like You, help us to spend more time in Your Word. Lord, as we look at Your Word this evening, may Your words sink into our thoughts and heart. May we meditate on them and "keep them in our memory, obey them constantly in our life, and let them shape and mold our daily life and every act."[20]

Lord, in order to make us more like You, help us to spend more time with Your people. O Lord, may we be a people who are continually about Your work, encouraging and edifying each other to greater obedience to Your Word. May there be great love for fellow believers in this church.

O Lord, make us more like You by helping us to have such a love for our fellow believers that we agonize when they agonize and rejoice when they rejoice. O Lord, make us more like You by giving us such a concern for our fellow man that his spiritual welfare is more important to us than our physical welfare.

O Lord, may we have 100% faith in You as the liberator, the one who unshackles the chains of alcohol and drugs and anger and pride. O Lord, may we have 100% faith in You as a healer. O Lord, as a church use us to liberate folk from the shackles that are binding them. Use us to heal those who need healing. Use us to minister as Your Spirit leads.

O Lord, increase our faith and increase our resemblance to You in proportion to the time we spend in hearing and meditating on Your

---

[20] Torrey, R. A., How to Pray, p. 55.

Word and the time we spend in communing with You and being with Your people.

Amen

∾

The following prayer was prayed at a Monday Night Prayer Meeting for an upcoming revival effort called "Days of Looking Up."

Blessed Redeemer,

We pray for our "Days of Looking Up." May we come prepared to be blessed. O Lord, may it be a time when we look up and what do we see but You looking down from Heaven. O Lord, may our gaze meet Your gaze so that we feel bathed in Your love. May the radiance of Your love so fall on us that we reflect Your love to all those around us.

And as evidence of Your love, may we feel Your rebuke and discipline. (See Heb. 12:6) May our sins so accuse us that we feel totally exposed. O Lord, may the ones we've swept under the rug haunt us. May the ones we've been so blatant about bring us to tears, may the ones we've been in denial about lambaste us, and may the ones we don't even know about rear their ugly heads. O Lord, may our confession be complete, may we be in complete agreement with You about our sins. May we be made pure in heart so that we cannot only see You, but we can also see the Father.

O Lord, so sharpen our focus on You that we get a true image of the Father. And, Lord, may our image of You and the Father be so real that our faith becomes unshakable.

And, Lord, as we hear and read Your Word may it just melt us. As a result of looking up so much may we not become a stiff-necked people, but rather just the opposite, a people so desperate to know and do Your will that we invest major amounts of time in poring over your Word and meditating on it, and major amounts of time in prayer just waiting to know Your will.

O Lord, may the "Days of Looking Up" result in a readjustment of our mindset. Use Your Holy Spirit to move us to a new high in which we are so committed to You, so submissive to Your will, so attuned to Your will, and so in touch with You that we could truly say that Christ lives through us and that we have the mind of Christ.

O Lord, when the "Days of Looking Up" end may we be able to have days of looking back when we can say that was when You gave us such a passion for prayer, such a passion for praise, and such a passion for Your Word. May we be able to say that that was when we ended up rededicating ourselves to greater involvement in Your work, to greater submission to Your will, to greater contribution of our time, talent, and treasure. O Lord, may we be able to look back and say that was when we caught on fire for being Your witness. And, Lord, may many be able to look back and say that was when they gave their life to You.

O Lord, because we want it so much,

Amen

∞

Prayed as an offertory prayer at a Sunday Night Worship Service. I serve as a Sunday night usher so that I am occasionally called on to pray the offertory prayer on Sunday night.

Bread of Heaven,

Hungry people are here to be fed tonight. We hunger and thirst after Your righteousness. And it's Your fault. You put this strong desire in us to fill the God-shaped void You created us with. So give us a heaping helping of Your Word tonight along with generous portions of Your love and understanding. O Lord, let us go home tonight as sheep who have been fed, confident that we have understood what You wanted to tell us tonight, ready to obey Your message. O Lord, may we never tire of hearing Your Word proclaimed.

O Lord, hungry people are here tonight to feast on Jesus. Lord, we want You for our appetizer. We want You for our main course. We want You for dessert. Fill our plate to overflowing. Run our cup over. Feed us till we want no more.[21]

O Lord, there are people in our everyday lives who are hungering for You but don't even know You. O Lord, may we have the privilege of representing Your awesomeness to them. Or may we somehow so reflect Your love that they see You. Lord, use us to lead them to Your table. O Lord, cause us to go into the highways and hedges to invite people to attend Your banquet. (See Luke 14:23)

May these tithes and offerings be used to fill chairs at Your banquet table.

To You be the glory both now and forever. (See Heb. 13:21)

Amen

∞

Prayed at Monday Night Prayer Meeting. God's needs really are more important than ours.

O Lord Who Ordered the Whole Universe,

Help this poor, wretched soul get his priorities right. And help us as a church put the most important things first. Lord, it's so hard to choose between two good things. Give us enough godly wisdom to, when faced with the choice between two things that are both seemingly Your will, make the right decision.

---

[21] Williams, William. "Guide Me, O Thou Great Jehovah.", 1745.

Lord, we know it is said we should carry everything to You in prayer, but we wonder if when we do so if we aren't spending too much energy thinking about our needs and not enough thinking about Your needs. Too often we want You to see things from our perspective instead of wanting to see things from Your perspective. Help us to see what we most need to pray for. Help us to give priority to praying for the things that are most weighing on Your mind.

Lord, we spend a lot of time around the church house praying for the physically ill—and rightfully so. But You didn't send Jesus to die on the cross for the physically ill. And we know that sometimes physical illness is a tool You use for Your purposes—as in the case of the man who was blind since birth, and that sometimes You are most glorified when the laws You set in place take their natural course. Lord, may our prayers reflect Your concern for the spiritually dying. Or better yet, Lord, intensify our concern for the lost until it matches Yours.

Lord, we're coming up to a time in our church when we will be concentrating on a new budget and on stewardship. And we'll be praying that we become better stewards of our time, talents, and money. But a few years back I came across the statement that a parent is never happier than his saddest child. At the time I immediately thought of a lady in our church whose son was suffering from a life-threatening condition and I knew the truth of the statement. Then I thought of others whose children were sick or were going through divorce or had great problems. Then I thought of a family in our church whose son grew up in our church, he's been out on his own for many years now, but he has never become a Christian—despite many prayers. Then I thought of You, Lord, and said to myself, "Lord, this is You a billion times over—how many of Your children have not accepted Jesus despite Your great love and Your great sacrifice!" And I said to myself, "Lord, my greatest lack of stewardship is in the area of spreading Your gospel." Lord, we've been keeping it to ourselves rather than giving it away. Lord should I be praying for my stewardship of Your Word before I pray for my stewardship in the areas of time, talents, and money?

Lord, some churches primarily preach a social gospel—visiting the sick, feeding the hungry, clothing the naked, running social programs to help the poor and the down and out and we know that when we've done any of these things we've, in effect, done it to Jesus. But we wonder if our most important task as a church is to minister to Jesus and to make the world a better place to go to Hell from.

Lord, the thought crossed my mind recently as to where I stood on Your growth chart for me. Am I even 10% of what Your goal is for me? Lord, I recognize that I am supposed to work out my own salvation to a certain extent, that my personal holiness is up to how much I put myself in Your hands and let You run my life. Lord, which would You have me put first—my personal Christian growth or efforts to witness to someone? Lord, I confess that I've used the excuse for not witnessing to someone that I wasn't a mature enough Christian.

Lord, Rick Warren in his book, *The Purpose-Driven Church*, said he tells his people: "Have you ever wondered why God leaves us here on earth, with all its pain, sorrow, and sin, after we accept Christ? Why doesn't He just zap us immediately to Heaven and spare us from all this? After all, we can have worship, fellowship, pray, sing, hear God's Word and even have fun in Heaven. In fact, there are only two things you can't do in heaven that you can do on earth: sin and witness to unbelievers."[22] Then he asks his church members which of these two they think Christ has left us here to do. O Lord, is the primary reason You've left us down here not to worship You but to witness for You?

Lord, I know there is a right mix somewhere, but somehow I get the strong, strong feeling that You want us to make praying for the lost a high, high priority in our lives and in Your church. Lord, You must weep when You look for someone to stand in the gap for these and find Your people busy praying for other things. Lord, may praying for the lost become the norm in this church. Lord, I especially pray for Steve

---

[22] Warren, Rick, *The Purpose-Driven Church*, p. 116.

and Stephen, Hunter, Kristin, Josh, Jason, Chris, Beth, John, Nathan, Eric, Kirk, Stephen, and Chris.

Lord, we pray that You would lift the veil of Satan's deceptions from each of these such that they can be so confronted with Your Good News that they can't resist.

Now, Lord, I've said the words; I've meant the words. O Lord, I want to feel Your agony for these. Work on changing me to have a heart like Yours for these and use me to do whatever part You have for me.

O Lord, may Your priorities be our priorities.

Amen

∞

Prayed as an offertory prayer at an 8:30 Sunday Morning Worship Service. Praise often focuses on some of God's attributes. Almost invariably, when assembling a prayer, the praise part is the first part that I deal with—even before I have a clue about what the rest of the prayer will include.

Lord Jehovah,

We've drug in this morning—wounded by our encounters with the world this week. Wipe away our tears of anguish, heal our wounded spirits, take away our fears, take our burdens upon Yourself and give us the joy of gladness so we can praise You with gladness of hearts.

We praise You because everything that You have ever been You still are. We praise You because we don't have to worry about when Your love for us is going to stop. O Lord, we praise You because the best way to cope with change in our lives is to rely on the one thing that doesn't change, namely You. Thank you for being our firm anchor in the storms of life. Lord, we praise You because even though Your Word says that You do not change Your mind that doesn't mean that You're not responsive and willing to react to our problems and our requests. Thank You for being consistent with Your character even when we don't understand or would have had You do differently. O Lord, we praise You because You do not change. O Lord, must we be reminded that You cannot change because any change in perfection would result in imperfection.

Lord, please accept our humble efforts at worshipping You this morning because they are sincere. Please accept these tithes and offerings this morning because they are given out of love.

O Lord, take advantage of us while we're feeling worshipful to have Your way with us. Move us from praising You with our lips to praising You with our lives. So focus our eyes on Jesus that Your will becomes the focus of our lives. Use the special music and the preached word and Your holy written Word to melt us until we become putty in Your hands. Then in intimate and firsthand interaction with Your Holy Spirit remake us in Your likeness.

O Lord, may the veil of Satan's deceptions be lifted here this morning and may personal pride and selfishness and rebellion and materialism be set aside and may all our doubts fall away and may Your will for our lives become crystal clear.

And, Lord, when this service is over may we be able to say that Your kingdom has won a great victory here and much new territory has been claimed.

And may Your word spread quickly, run its course, be glorified and triumphant. (See 2 Thes. 3:1) And to You be the glory both now and forever. (See Heb. 13:21)

Amen

Prayed during a Pre-Service Deacon-Pastor Prayer Time for an 8:30 Sunday Morning Worship Service.

O Holy One,

With Your permission and cooperation we're going to try to worship you this morning.

Plans have already been made as to what songs are to be sung, what sermon is to be preached, what Scripture is to be read, and the order of service. Please, Lord, use Your Holy Spirit to change anything that needs to be changed, fine tune anything that needs to be fine tuned. Please, Lord, let Your Holy Spirit take control.

Lord, plans have already been made as to who's coming and who's not. Plans have already been made as to where people are going to sit and how much people are going to participate—what they're not going to do. Lord, please use Your Holy Spirit to change anything that needs to be changed. Please, Lord, let You Holy Spirit take control.

Lord, plans have already been made in Heaven as to what needs to take place down here on earth for Your will to be accomplished in our lives this morning. Please, Lord, use Your Holy Spirit to change anything in our lives that needs to be changed. Please, Lord, let Your Holy Spirit take control.

Lord, plans have already been made by Satan as to what can be done to minimize the effectiveness of this time of worship and its long-term impact. Please, Lord, use Your power from on high to claim victory here this morning. May Satan's veil of deception be lifted, may his tactics be exposed, may his stranglehold on us be released.

O Lord, may there be an unplanned rejoicing by the angels in Heaven because of what takes place here this morning.

Amen

Prayed during a Pre-Service Deacon-Pastor Prayer Time for an 8:30 Sunday Morning Worship Service.

Lord Jehovah,

We are gathering in Your name this morning for the stated purpose of worshipping You. There have been times in the past when we have done this and nothing has happened. We just went through the motions and You didn't get worshipped and we were no better for the experience. Externally it looked as though we were worshipping You, but internally nothing really happened. Lord, use Your Holy Spirit to help us be very sincere this morning about worshipping You so when this service is over we will know that You have been worshipped because we know our lives have been changed by You.

Lord, some here this morning will be babes in Christ. Give them milk to grow on.
Some will have only trusted You to save their souls. Move them this morning to trust You to run their lives.
Some will be floundering in the fundamentals of the faith. Help them firm up their foundations and step out in faith.
Some will be plodding along the narrow path. Put a lilt in their step.
Some will be stagnated. Stir them up, Lord.
Some will be headed down the wrong path. Put a road block in their way.
Some will be curiosity seekers. Help them to really understand.
Some will be here for the wrong reasons. Get their attention and plant some seeds.
Some will be lost and seeking. Find them and show them what they're looking for.

And, Lord, may these internal changes cause external results.

Amen

Prayed at a Monday Night Prayer Meeting.

Lord Who Is Always Near,

Most of us drove all the way down here—and will drive all the way back home—just to pray with these folk of kindred mind for this church and for Your kingdom. We didn't come down here to parade our spirituality before each other or to be seen, but rather to glorify You and to undergird this church with prayer.

First off, we want to remove any show stoppers in this process of prayer. We remind You and ourselves that we are here as Your children who want to defend Your good name and as Your servants who want to do Your work. Lord, we also come confessing. We have not sought Your kingdom and Your righteousness first all the time. Help us, Lord. We confess to being impatient—we have wanted the things we've prayed for to happen quicker. Forgive our lack of faith. Lord, we ask for more faith. Lord, we have offended people and not even known it. Forgive us and help us to be more sensitive to other people's feelings. Lord, if there is any sin that keeps us from getting Your full attention for our prayers, burden us with.

Lord, we didn't come down here to waste Your time. We are here because we believe in You and we believe in prayer. We don't want to waste our time praying for something that You don't want. We're not here to change Your mind. So if You don't mind, we'll just ask for what we're sure You want to happen.

Lord, we know that there are a whole lot of things that You want to happen, but in Your infinite wisdom You gave mankind freedom of will so that we can very easily thwart Your intentional will by either not praying for it or by not obeying Your will for our lives. So that's why we're here tonight—to do some praying so there'll be more obeying.

Lord, if You don't mind we'll limit our praying to praying for those things that are closest and dearest to our hearts since that's what we know about and that's what we tend to think You might involve us getting done. Lord, we ask that the goings on at FBC change. First off, may neither church politics nor denominational politics nor state politics nor national politics be an issue here because we're so busy pushing Your agenda. May rumors die on the vine because we're so busy abiding in the vine and spreading Your truth. May spiritual growth be a constant in this church because of the amount of attention paid to Your biblical directives. May we become a church that is so caught up in giving You the glory that You get all the credit, too. Lord, may this church gain a reputation that glorifies Your name—a reputation, Lord, that causes people to acknowledge You. Lord, may there be things happen here that no one can explain any other way than to admit that You caused them to happen. Lord, may many lost people of this community feel the influence of this church and seek Your will. Lord, we're asking that we will be so obedient to Your Word that Your Word spreads quickly, is glorified, and triumphant. (See 2 Thes. 3:1) Lord, may every lost person in this community receive a personal invitation to accept Jesus Christ as Lord and Savior as a result of the praying that goes on in this church. Lord, we would ask that Your Holy Spirit so take control that this church becomes so united in purpose and in love that your earthly kingdom puts down deep roots here and starts spreading like wildfire.

Amen

∞

Prayed at a Monday Night Prayer Meeting.

Lord God,

I was feeling smug the other day until once again I ran up on the statement that you love God only as much as you love the person you

73

love the least. Lord, if that's true, I'm in big trouble. Please, Lord, help me to love the unlovable. Help me to love those that don't like me. Help me to love those whose sins I detest. O Lord, I really have a hard time separating the sin from the sinners at times. Lord, forgive me for enjoying the troubles of my enemies. Forgive me for wishing something bad would happen to Saddam Hussein.

Lord, as we pray for Your church tonight, we ask that we may be a people of great love. May we have wall-to-wall love for each other. May we rejoice when our brothers rejoice, may we weep when they weep. May our visitors recognize that this is a church full of people who love You and love each other. May we be anxious to forgive and slow to think less of our brother.

Lord, may we be a church who has eyes like Yours—able to look at all people through eyes of love, able to see great potential, able to see their great need for Jesus. Help us to genuinely care for what happens to all people. O Lord, burden us with the lost. Help us to feel Your anguish. Help us to forget our own desires and to think only of them. O Lord, as we think upon Your great love we can't help but ask You to use us to bring Your kingdom into the lives of the lost that we come into contact with. May we pray for them by name. Help us to love by sharing Your love.

May we no longer live to and for ourselves, but to and for Him who died and was raised again for our sake.

Amen

Prayed during a Pre-Service Deacon-Pastor Prayer Time for an 8:30 Sunday Morning Worship Service.

Lord God,

As we gather in Your name, may we know You're in our midst. May we sense that You have called this meeting—and we know that is true because the church is doing Your work here on earth. And may we sense that You specifically invited us. And that is also true because we know that You put this desire in us that caused us to be here today. Lord, may we recognize You as the Big Boss here this morning. As the preacher and worship leader lead us may we recognize that it is really You who have given them words to say and directed them as to what songs to sing. Lord, may the messages Your Holy Spirit impresses upon us this morning have the same impact upon us as if we had been given them as action items by our big boss at work.

Lord, we pray that each person here will exercise their free will to choose to obey You. We pray that each free will here will will Your will. May we as a church put our free will in full subjugation to Your authority. Help us to deny our own desires and to want only what You want. Bring us to perfect harmony, perfect unity.

Lord, we ask You to do everything You want to do this morning. Put a burden on us to pray for what we should be praying for.

Amen

Prayed at a Monday Night Prayer Meeting. Confession is good for the soul.

Lord Jehovah,

Somewhere in 1 Samuel it says: "He who is the Glory of Israel does not lie or change His mind, for He is not a human being, that He should change His mind." (1 Sam 15:29 NIV) O Lord, we praise You because You never need to change Your mind because You are always right. Must we be reminded that any change in perfection will result in imperfection.

Lord, Your Word also says, "Be ye therefore perfect, even as Your Father which is in heaven is perfect." (Matt 5:48 KJV) Please pardon the expression, but we're having a devil of a time trying to be perfect. We readily confess that
- we don't always resist temptation
- we sometimes doubt
- we sometimes lack trust
- we sometimes don't love You with all our heart
- we sometimes have bad thoughts
- we sometimes do bad things
- we sometimes aren't merciful to those who need mercy
- we sometimes aren't meek and long-suffering

In fact, Lord, we're so short of perfection we can't even get our 'fessing caught up good. We're lucky to remember most of our sins of commission, much less even recognize most of our sins of omission.

O Lord, we're just a bunch of wannabes—we want to be all that You want us to be. And we try. In fact, You probably think we're very trying at times. But, Lord, one of two things is going to have to happen for us to be perfect. We're either going to have to rely on Jesus' holiness for our holiness or else we are going to have to go to be with Jesus.

In the meanwhile, Lord, help us to continue to strive toward the perfection You request. Help us as a church to spur one another to grow. May we as a church be continually providing opportunities to grow closer to You.

Lord, there is a story I remember about two boys who were fooling around one Sunday afternoon when one said to the other, "Why don't we go down to the church house and check out the girls?" They did; and they both got saved that night. O Lord, imperfect as we are, will You also use us to accomplish Your perfect will, just as You used that young man and that church that night. O Lord, use us as individuals to invite people to Your banquet table. Use us as a church to spread Your feast and make it so inviting that people can't resist.

And to You be the glory both now and forever,

Amen

∽

Prayed at an 8:30 Sunday Morning Worship Service.

O Lord Who Created the Heavens and Stretched Them out above Us (See Isa. 42:5),
    Who Calls Us to Righteousness and Desires to Hold Us in His Hand and Keeps Us Forever,
    Who Spread forth the Earth and Everything on It,
    Who Gives Life and Breath to All Who Walk on It, and
    Who Gave Us Jesus
        to open the Eyes of the Blind,
        to release Prisoners from Bondage,
        to give Rest to the Weary, and
        to die for Us,

We praise You and glorify Your name. We will not give Your praise to another. We will not take Your glory for our own.

O Lord, open our eyes to the truths You have for us here this morning.
    Bring us out of the bondage of our sins.
    Bring us out of the bondage of materialism and self-pride and hedonism and of concerning ourselves too much with what other people think.

O Lord, help us to lay all of our burdens on You here this morning and to put our trust in You completely.

Lord, You have brought us to this time and to this place, this never-to-be-repeated set of circumstances, for a reason. Help us to understand exactly what You want us to do here this morning. Then give us the strength to seize the moment and do it.

Then, Lord, may we sing unto You a new song and go out of this place singing Your praises from one end of the earth to the other because we have accepted Your love and Your salvation and Your complete control of our life.

May Your Word spread quickly, run its course, be glorified and triumphant. (See 2 Thes. 3:1) And may these tithes and offerings be used to spread that Word near and far.

Amen

∞

Prayed at a Monday Night Prayer Meeting.

Sovereign Lord,

We humble ourselves before Your throne and confess our not praying as much as we should. Why are most of us so busy we don't have time to get serious about prayer? You must weep often when you seek someone to stand in the gap and find no one. Your heart must ache for us, Your people, to rise up and be what You've called us to be.

O Lord, cleanse us and break us of the curses we've allowed to rule over us and keep us from spending the time with You that we should. Cleanse us of the sins of apathy and complacency that keep us from realizing what we need to be praying for. Cleanse us from the sins of lack of faith and unbelief that keep us from asking for what we know we need. Cleanse us from the sin of not asking for what we know You want us to have.

Lord, Satan seems to know just the right time to tempt us. Help us to recognize the most important times we need to be praying.

Lord, we have more confessing to do. We're stuck, Lord. We're kind of like the dieter who has plateaued. We experienced Christian growth for a while, but it seems as though now we're just busy playing church—going to all the meetings, putting up a good front, enjoying the fellowship, and being a good boy or girl. But Lord, we're still kicking the dog the same number of times every night. Lord, too many of us are like the people I know at work who are just waiting around to retire. They figure that they've done their part already and so it's okay to coast the rest of the way. We figure that we're good enough the way we are, so we'll just rely on Jesus' blood and coast the rest of the way.

Lord, we've confessed our sin. Now we're asking You to solve our problem 'cause we know we sure can't solve it by ourselves. But, Lord, we know that sometimes the only way You can get some people's attention is after they've been laid low with some serious illness or catastrophe. But, Lord, we'd much rather You just hit us like a brick with Your message. Please, Lord, get our attention and don't let go until we've let You change us. O Lord, please, get us out of our rut.

O Lord, raise up in Your people at FBC a stubborn tenacity to do Your will, to obey Your Word, to cast off everything that would oppose Your Spirit, and move us to a realm that is willing to pay any price to lay hold of Your kingdom. "Fill us with Your Spirit. Baptize us in fire. Let there be an impartation of ...[Your] Spirit, grace and supplication. Let there be an anointing of ...Your people who are tired of the status quo, who are tired of mediocrity,"[23] who are tired of being defeated by a defeated enemy. O Lord, may every member of this church make a giant improvement in his or her walk with You. And may we not be remiss in thanking You and giving You all the glory.

Amen

Prayed at a Monday Night Prayer Meeting. Note that Monday Night Prayer Meeting provided an opportunity for each person to pray every Monday night, while other services, for the most part, only afforded opportunities when called upon.

Lord Jehovah,

We delight in the beauty of Your creation. We delight in the beauty of a rainbow that stretches across the sky, the new moon shining on a snow-covered world, a butterfly.

We delight in the inner workings of Your universe. As we study Your world, everywhere we see evidence of Your handiwork.

We delight in Your rich communication to us. Your Word is so full and so mind-expanding. As we study Your Word we are overwhelmed by how it all fits together and by how You continually give us more understanding as we study.

---

[23] Weblog post. *Acts4Prayer*. N.p., n.d. Web. 3 July 2013. http://www.acts4prayer.com/forgive.html

We delight in Your Son, Jesus. O Lord, we delight in the great love He demonstrated for us.

O Lord, we delight in You. For You created us and adopted us into Your family and blessed us so magnificently. O Lord, we delight in delighting in You. Please, Lord, help us to delight in You more and more.

Lord, we recognize that parents and teachers take pleasure in seeing their children and students value what they value, do the same types of things that they do. And, Lord, as we study Your Word we come to realize that You, too, delight in what reflects You and Your values. You delighted in Jesus as He reflected You perfectly in this world.(See Col. 1:19) Your great desire is that we, Your children, will also value what You value, think the same thoughts as You think, and do the same things You would do if You were in our shoes. O Lord, help us to be able to delight You with our lives. Help us to be holy even as You are holy. Help us to see and do what pleases You, both as individuals and as a church. Help us to reflect You in all that we do.

And to You be the glory, both now and forever. (See Heb. 13:21)

Amen

∞

Prayed as an offertory prayer for an 8:30 Sunday Morning Worship Service.

Lord of Love,

We are troubled in mind. We are sure that there is nothing in us that could attract the love of one as holy and righteous as You.[24] Yet You have declared Your unchanging love for us by providing Jesus Christ.

---

[24] Linne, Blair. "Perfection of Beauty." *The Attributes of God Lyrics*. N.p., n.d. Web. 3 July 2013. <http://www.lampmode.com/taoglyrics/>.

If nothing in us can win Your love, nothing in the entire universe can prevent You from loving us. Your love is uncaused and undeserved. You are Yourself the only reason for the love with which we are loved. Lord, use this service and Your Holy Spirit to urge us to accept that love that has found us. And use this service to help us realize that once we accept Your love, You accept us as one of Yours, we become part of Your family, that You bless us with Your Holy Spirit and with eternal life, that You discipline us as evidence of Your love, and that You hold us in Your hand and will never let go. Then that love can cast out fears, and our troubled hearts can be at peace, trusting not in what we are but in what You have declared Yourself to be.

But when we think on this love, Lord, we become troubled in mind again because we don't know which to do first, praise You or thank You.

O Lord, we praise You for love that gave us life and breath. We praise You for love that drew salvation's plan. We praise You for love that groaned upon a tree. We praise You for love that is unfailing. O Lord, we are compelled to praise You because we know You. But as we praise You we become troubled in mind, for there is not time enough in our entire lifetime to adequately praise You.

O Lord, we give You these tithes as offerings this morning out of thanks. And also out of thanks we rededicate our lives, Lord and Master, to be your slaves—to do Your will as You reveal it to us. But again we are troubled in mind. For no matter how much we do, we know it can't adequately thank You for your love.

O Lord, thank you so much for the troubles in our mind.

May we see and do what glorifies You.

Amen

∞

Prayed as an offertory prayer for an 8:30 Sunday Morning Worship Service.

Father in Heaven, Judge over All,

We have said the words, "I forgive." But inwardly we still want to hear them say that we were right and they were wrong. Help us to forgive and forget. Lord, may we leave all the issues of fairness to You. May we have enough faith to trust that You'll make things right in the long run. Let us give alms to the poor and needy as well as those who are trying to take advantage of us and not give it a second thought. May we turn the job of being judge and jury over to You. Yes, Lord, we have to make value judgments about what is right and wrong, but let the only person we judge be ourselves. Help us to hate the sin and love the sinner. O Lord, why do we have such a hard time separating the two? Help us to see others from Your perspective.

O Lord, we thank You for being totally unfair—when it came to our sins. Thank you for not letting us have what we deserved. Thank you for picking up the tab and then forgetting how big the bill was. Thank you for lifting us from the ash heap and making us joint-heirs with Jesus. Thank you for clothing us in garments of salvation and arraying us with robes of righteousness. (See Isa. 61:10)

O Lord, in all fairness, these tithes and offerings we bring this morning are a farce, because we owe everything to You.

O Lord, use the rest of this service to help others choose Your unfair love over Your fair judgment. And, Lord, help each of us spread that unfair love by being forgiving at every opportunity.

May Your word spread quickly, run its course, and be glorified and triumphant. (See 2 Thes. 3:1)

Amen

Prayed as an offertory prayer for an 8:30 Sunday Morning Worship Service.

O Lord Who Foils the Plans of Nations and Thwarts the Purposes of Peoples,

Your plans stand firm forever.
As do the plans of Your heart from generation to generation (See Ps. 33:11)
You do as You please with the powers of heaven and the peoples of the earth.
No one can hold back Your plan. (See Dan. 4:35)

We praise You because Your plan allows us to choose eternal life and abundant life. But Your plan also allows us to choose what You call 'the path of destruction,' (See Matt. 7:13-14) what Satan sometimes calls 'doing our own thing.'

O Lord, thank You for limiting Satan and his power. Left to his own, he might make Jobs of us all. Left to his own, he might make earth a personal hell for each of us.

O Lord, we confess that at times we aren't 100% sure that You're really in control down here, at times we question whether You are intimately involved in the details of our every day affairs.

But Lord, You pursued us. You hemmed us in. You planned the very coincidences that resulted in our accepting Jesus as Lord and Savior. And, as we look back on our lives, we can now see that most of the trials sent our way have been custom made for our eternal good.

O Lord, You've gone and done it again. Here we are at one of those never-to-be-repeated set of circumstances that You like to arrange. And You have arranged for us to be here. Yes, we chose to come. But Your Holy Spirit planted the idea in our minds and nurtured it. And, if Your servants here have been in accord with Your will, You have choreographed every song that is to be sung and every word that is to be said. O Lord, help us not to miss what You have to say to us this morning. Restrain Satan from diverting our attention. Use Your Holy Spirit to cause us to recognize Your personal message for us this morning and to take it very seriously.

Lord, we praise You for not violating our free will. But we praise You even more for interfering in our lives. And our prayer this morning is that Your concerted efforts to further establish Your Kingdom in our lives will be very successful. May we exercise our free will to choose Your will for our lives.

And, Lord, use these tithes and offerings to further Your plans here on earth.

In accord with Jesus' strong desires we pray.

Amen

∞

Prayed as an offertory prayer for an 8:30 Sunday Morning Worship Service. Based on Ex. 20:5, Ex 34:14, Deut. 4:24, Deut 5:9.

Jealous One,

We recall that You are sometimes called a jealous god, but we tend to forget or ignore the fact that one of Your names is Jealous. We know that it describes that aspect of Your character that wants us to have eyes only for You, that aspect that, in final analysis, shows Your love is not the selfish love that we associate with jealousy here on earth but is an unselfish love that desperately wants only the very best for us. O Lord, Your jealousy is not the kind that blinds, but rather the kind that opens eyes to truth. O Lord, only You could have all the positive aspects of jealousy and none of the negative.

O Lord, we thank You for Your jealous love—a love that won't leave us alone—In more ways than one.

O Lord, we confess that we, too, are jealous, but ours is not a sinless jealousy. We are jealous of those who are more thankful than we. We are jealous of all those who walk closer to You than we. We are jealous of those who got to walk with Jesus here on earth. We are jealous of the Peter, Paul, John, Stephen and the others whose faith worked miracles, stood true, and caused others to believe. And, Lord, we confess that we are jealous for this church, wanting it to be the best that it can be. And, Lord, by our actions we seem to show that we want You only for ourselves—as we so often ignore Your plea to spread Your Word.

O Lord, use this service to purify our love for You. Use this service to change our jealousness to zealousness for You and what You want us to have and do. Use this service to cause us to become so thankful that we just have to tell others about You. Use this service to grow our faith in You—to the point that we're willing to give our life for You.

Lord, we've come to a time in this service when we offer up to You our tithes and offerings. In reality we need to offer up all our possessions. O Lord, some of our possessions possess us more than we possess them. Lord, we want to own nothing but You.

Lord, we also want to offer up our loved ones to You. We fear there are times that we love them more than we love You. Please, Lord, they will be safe if we commit them to You. In fact, nothing is really safe until we commit it to You.

Let us bask in Your jealous love and help us to see and do what glorifies You.

Amen

The Power Team© came. Over five hundred people came forward as a result! This prayer was prayed as an offertory prayer at a Sunday Night Service.

O Lord,

Now that the smoke has cleared and the Power Team© has gone home, we praise you because things will never return to normal around here again. We stand in awe of what You have done.

We praise You for victory after victory after victory after victory.

Lord we praise You for allowing us to see the results of Your Holy Spirit working in a mighty way in our midst. Lord, we've heard and read about such things, but now we've seen it with our own eyes.

O Lord, never again will we be quite so narrow-minded and skeptical. Never again will we pray small prayers, never again will we think that You can't use creative ways to carry out Your sovereign plan. Never again will we doubt that You can't pour out Your blessings far above anything that we could even imagine. Never again will we question whether You still perform miracles here on earth.

O Lord, thank You for allowing us to think that we had some small part in what went on. But we know that what took place here was something that only You could do.

O Lord, we praise You because You allowed us to see what You can do with those who give their time and talents totally to you. O Lord, Your Word says, "For the eyes of the Lord move to and fro throughout the earth that He may strongly support those whose heart is completely His." (2 Cor. 16:9 NASB) Lord, as we celebrate Your great victory tonight by hearing these testimonies, move each of us ever so much closer to being one of those upon whom Your eyes come to rest.

And we ask this not for selfish reasons, Lord, but we ask for Your Kingdom and because there are still billions we need to reach.

O Lord, may Your word spread quickly, run its course, be glorified and triumphant. (See 2 Thes. 3:1) And to You be the glory both now and forever. (See Heb. 13:21)

Amen

∞

Prayed during a Monday Night Prayer Meeting

Lord Almighty,

We come confessing. We know that daily reading Your Word and meditating on it and that regularly spending significant amounts of time in our prayer closets and that continuous expressions of gratitude and praise and that constant submissiveness and servanthood are so vital to our Christian walk. Yet most of us spend more time watching TV every day that we spend engaged in these practices. Therefore we remain far less than You want us to be and experience far less that You want to give us.

Some of us blame Satan for our failure in the very processes that You have provided to build us up so we can resist him. O Lord, many of us have tried again and again to conquer some of these disciplines. Some of the highly disciplined, super spiritual among us have mastered some of these. But, Lord, most of us are tired of trying and failing. After repeated attempts to establish these habits in our lives, we have just slipped back to life as usual.

Lord, in desperation I come to You, asking not that You give us the strength and perseverance and diligence to add these disciplines to our lives and maintain their practice 'til we go to be with You, but rather that You make us so desperate for You, so in love with You that we just can't get enough of You and these disciplines just become the constant, natural, spontaneous expressions of our love for You and our desire to know You better.

Lord, we also come confessing that we are too self-sufficient. We come to church pretending that everything is okay, that we're strong and sufficient. We accumulate material possessions to give us a sense of security. We feel confident as long as we have good health, a good job, money in the bank, and some measure of influence in the circles we travel.

But, Lord, in the back of our minds we know that all that we have comes from You. And without Your blessing we know that all that we have is of no value. And we know that our whole life is but a vapor. But, Lord, move us from just having head knowledge to having the proper perspective on how much we really need You. Move us to the point where we are actually relying totally on You and submitting to You as the Shepherd of our lives.

Help us to be so honest with ourselves that we recognize our need to be completely reliant on You. As we think about how we are nothing and how You are our everything and how Jesus died for our sins, may it make us so desperate for You or so love you that it drives us to our Bibles, drives us to our prayer closets, compels us to praise You all day long, and causes us to submit to Your every request.

O Lord, whom have we in Heaven but You?
And earth has nothing we desire but You.
Our flesh and our hearts may fail,
But You are the strength of our hearts and our portion forever. (See Ps. 73:25-26)

Amen

Parts of this prayer are heavily influenced by Joseph M. Stowell's "Who Needs God" in Jan/Feb 1997 issue of *Moody*.

Prayed during a Monday Night Prayer Meeting. Whether appropriate or not, these prayers are, in some degree, influenced by what others are praying. Praying for our preacher, the church staff, government leaders, and the sick are common subjects of other people's payers on Monday night. So these prayers usually short change those items in favor of other things that are on God's mind. That doesn't mean these and other issues aren't prayed for at other times.

Lord Jehovah,

We often admire people who are elevated to high positions. But usually, Lord, it's the position that we respect and not the individual. We often say that the best way to ruin a man is to elect him to office or promote him to boss. O Lord, we know all too well the saying, "Power corrupts, and absolute power corrupts absolutely." Not even David, a man after Your own heart, could handle the amount of power he had wisely all the time. O Lord, only You are worthy, only You are wise enough, only You have enough love to handle large amounts of power. Only You deserve absolute power. O Lord, we thank You that You are the only one who is omnipotent. We praise You for Your omnipotence.

Lord, I come confessing. My parents were well intentioned but they were not perfect. They indirectly taught me some false values. Lord, I find myself still listening to those voices from my childhood that taught me false values. Lord, I have performance anxiety. I'm scared of failure. I often get nervous when I speak in front of a group. Lord, I too often find myself trying to please others instead of trying to please the one who never yells at me, the one who loves me regardless of my performance, the one who lets me suffer the perfect consequences of my actions. Lord, I find myself worrying about my health, worrying about job security, worrying about my loved ones' safety when they're flying or out on the road and overdue. And yet I know that my worrying is an obvious lack of trust in You and Your provision. Lord, I know that I'm not the only one in this church who has hang-ups because of still being chained to some of the voices from childhood that taught false values. Lord, help us all who fit into this category to recognize that we are slave to those voices and that they are gods that we are paying tribute to. Lord, help each of us to turn those voices over to You and ask You to quiet them forever. O Lord, for all of us, let us be so close to You and so involved in Your work that the only inner voice we hear is the gentle voice of Your Holy Spirit.

Help us as a church to be more willing to confess our sins to You and to each other. And, Lord, may we as a church be non-condemning and totally supportive of each other.

Lord, there was a man who so insisted upon unconditional surrender that there is now a place called the Courthouse at Appomattox, VA, that is known as a place of surrender. Lord, You gave us a Savior who so insisted on unconditional surrender that this place, FBC, according to Your great plan should be known as a place of surrender. O Lord, for Your kingdom's sake and for Your glory, we pray that there may be so much surrendering, so much absolute surrendering in this place that this place gains a worldwide reputation as a place of surrender.

Lord, we Your people stand in great need of completely surrendering to You. Lord, some of us have already turned it all over to You. But we find the old life keeps creeping back in and taking over. O Lord, help us to keep surrendering again and again. Help us to stay in a continual state of surrender to Your will. Let us be desperate for Your control of our lives.

Lord, others of us who are Your people have trusted You for our salvation, but we've not trusted You with our lives or maybe we've trusted You with only some small part of our lives. O Lord, we're ripe for plucking. You see, we try over and over again to change certain habits that Your Holy Spirit brings to our attention regularly, but we keep failing big time. O Lord, flaunt our powerlessness to change ourselves in our faces. Bring us to the stark realization that You're the only one who has the power to change us. Lord, a bunch of us are keeping our cards close to the vest and are willing to surrender only part of our lives at a time to You. O Lord, keep insisting on absolute total surrender and grow our faith through trials and tribulation.

O Lord, we long for Your perfect teaching, Your perfect discipline, and Your perfect direction in our lives. We yearn for Your perfect care. We are desperate for Your perfect companionship. And we'd give anything for Your perfect peace in our lives. O Lord, may there be so much surrender going on here that our thankfulness causes us to spread the Good News.

O Lord, may we grow to such a state of surrender here that
- We've got wall-to-wall love in every room
- Unity reigns, Jesus reigns, and Your kingdom reigns in our lives
- "Yes, Lord, yes" echoes in the halls constantly
- Every financial need is met when it arises with money left over
- Your message so saturates this community that it causes a whole heap of more surrendering

O Lord, may there be a great movement, a great surrender here, like the one in Appomattox, one where troops by the thousand and ten thousands quit fighting and unconditionally surrendered.

O Lord, may You be our commander-in-chief; may You be the chairman of our joint chiefs-of-staff. O Lord, may You be the executive officer of our lives.

O Lord, be with our earthly shepherd here. Keep him close to Your breast, keep him a kingdom man, keep Jesus ever before him, and keep him coming back to his prayer closet for more. Bless him through Your victories.

Amen

Prayed at Monday Night Prayer Meeting.

Jehovah Jireh, God Who Provides,

We praise You and thank You for Your great provision, the sacrifice above all sacrifices, the sacrifice that ended the sacrificial system, the sacrifice that compels us to give You the sacrifice of praise, the sacrifice that compels us to give You the sacrifice of thanksgiving.

Lord, if we thought it could happen, we'd take up a big offering and purchase a piece of Your Kingdom and bring it right here to Tullahoma and give everybody a piece.

Lord, if only we could figure out how to do it, we'd send up the space shuttle to get a piece of Heaven and land it out at the airport and spread it all around.

Lord, if it were within our power, we'd be so good and righteous that You'd have to reward us with enough perfect peace we'd be able to share it with our neighbors.

Lord, if we didn't already know it wouldn't work, we'd stage a spectacular miracle in the skies over Tullahoma to make people believe in You.

Lord, if we were absolutely sure it would do the trick, we'd die so others would come to know Jesus.

But, Lord, we know that apart from You we can do nothing—to bring about Your kingdom here on earth. And Your Word tells us to stand in the gap and intercede for those who are facing judgment. O Lord, help us to stay connected to You so we can pray down Your Kingdom on others. O Lord, may You not pour Your wrath on the people of Tullahoma because an intercessor is not found. Lord, we're here to do the job. Give us on-the-job training on how to do it right. O Lord, we're not here to change Your mind about the people of Tullahoma, we're here to share Your mind about them. Reproduce your heart for them in us. May we agonize over them as You do. May we love them as You do. May we pray for them as Jesus would do if He were here in person.

O Lord, may we continue to pray for the people of Tullahoma until we submit to Your will. Wean us from what we want to what You want and then use us to get it done.

Thy Kingdom come, Thy will be done, in Tullahoma as in heaven.

O Lord, we praise You and thank You for Your great provision and sacrifice.

Amen

∞

Prayed as an offertory prayer at an 11 O'clock Sunday Morning Worship Service.

O Lord Who Inspired the Words of Scripture,

We praise You because Your Word is living and powerful and sharper than any two-edged sword, piercing even to the division of the soul and spirit, and of the joints and marrow, and is the discerner of the thoughts and intents of the soul. (See Heb 4:12)

O Lord, may Your Word operate on and in our lives this morning, penetrating to the depths of our souls, exposing and sifting and analyzing and judging the very thoughts and purposes of our hearts. (See Heb 4:12) May Your Word comfort the disturbed and disturb the comfortable here this morning.

And may Your servant here divide Your Word rightly this morning— according to Your direction, and may we be convicted of Your truth. May his preaching not be with persuasive words of human wisdom, but in demonstration of the Spirit and of power, that the faith of us listening not be in the wisdom of men, but in your power. (See 1 Cor. 2:4-5)

Lord, help us to not walk in the counsel of the wicked, or stand in the path where sinners walk, or sit in the seat of mockers, but to delight in Your word and upon Your word to meditate both day and night. (See Ps. 1:1-2)

O Lord, may Your Word not return void here this morning.
But may it accomplish what You please.
And may it prosper in the thing for which You sent it. (See Isa. 55:11)

And may these offerings be used to spread Your Word far and near.

Amen

∽

Prayed at a Monday Night Prayer Meeting.

O Lord Who Scoffs at the Wisdom of Men,

We praise You because your very nature is that of truth and wisdom.
We thank You because Your Word points us toward true wisdom.
We thank You because Solomon, to whom You gave wisdom the equal of which has not been seen before or since, wrote "The fear of the Lord is the beginning of wisdom, and the knowledge of the Holy One is insight." (Prob. 9:10 ESV)
We thank You for the mind that You created us with and the environment that You placed us in or the parents that You blessed us with or the spark that You put in us or whatever it was that led us to recognize that, indeed, You are God and are worthy of our awe and reverential worship.

Too, Lord, we wish to thank You for our salvation. You see, not only did Jesus die on the cross for our sins, Your Holy Spirit worked in our lives until we made that decision—so much so that we hesitate to take credit for our decision, but prefer to give credit where credit is due: to You, Lord, for Your great plan and Your great work in our lives to bring us to repentance and salvation.

Lord, we thank You because You made us new creatures in Christ. We thank You because You gave us a new song. Lord, we thank You that You have given us the helmet of salvation to help protect us from Satan and sin; but, Lord, we recognize that our minds must be continually renewed.

O Lord, just like water is percolated through coffee grounds again and again until it takes on a deep brown color and is called coffee, help us to percolate our minds through Your Word again and again in a manner such that our minds take on the qualities that will enable it to be called a mind like Christ's.

O Lord, as we meditate on Your Word may Your Word assimilate itself in our minds. May we learn to think like Scripture. May the words of Christ richly dwell in us. Help us to set our minds on things that are above, not on things that are on earth. (See Col. 3:2)

Help us to refute arguments and every lofty opinion that sets itself against the true knowledge of Christ and take every thought captive to the obedience of Christ. (See 2 Cor. 10:5)

Grant us wisdom, give us discernment, help us to recognize the difference between better and best. We pray for more insight, the kind Solomon referred to, the kind that comes from knowing You. May we be a people of one mind—Your mind.

Lord, conventional wisdom says that a mind is a terrible thing to waste. I lift to You all those who have wasted their minds on conventional wisdom. Help us to do the wise thing and be so obedient to Your Word that it causes some of these to put their faith in You.

O, the depth of Your riches and Your wisdom and Your knowledge. O God, how unsearchable are Your judgments and how inscrutable are Your ways. For who has known your mind or who has been Your counselor? For from You and through You and to You are all things. (See Rom. 11:33-34,36)

To You be glory forever. (See Heb. 13:21)

Amen

∞

Prayed at an 11 O'clock Sunday Morning Worship Service as an offertory prayer.

Father-Creator,

As we stand here enjoying the moment,
may we remember whose day this is.

As we stand here just enjoying life,
may we remember who gives us every breath.

As we sit our body down in just a moment,
may we remember whose temple it is.

As we sit in comfort on our padded pews,
may we remember whose house this is and whose world it sits on.

As we see and interact with the people here,
may we remember whose children most of them are.

As we sing,
may we remember whose virtues we're extolling.

As we pray silently,
may we remember who is listening to our every word.

As we bring these tithes and offerings,
may we remember who really owns everything we have.

As we read Scripture,
may we remember who God-breathed every word.

As we stare at this preacher up here,
may we remember who placed his call on him.

As we listen to the sermon,
may we remember who gave this preacher a message just for us.

As we think about our problems,
may we remember who died on the cross just for us.

As we remember You, Lord,
please remember us with the assurance of Your love and tender care
and all-sufficient grace.

And as we feel the gentle tugging of your Holy Spirit this morning,
may we respond with all we have.

And as we dwell on the grace and love You have given us,
may we feel the urgent need to share it free of change no strings
attached.

Amen

One of the nice things about Monday Night Prayer Meeting is that one can pray for a long time, whereas prayers for worship services usually need to be limited. I always tried to keep offertory prayers to one page; but, of course, tried to let the Holy Spirit lead.

Omnipotent Father,

We could come to You tonight with our shopping list of physical and spiritual needs for ourselves and our church and fellow church members, but we know You already know what our needs are and are going to take care of them—even though we haven't even recognized some of them yet. We know that we are more precious to You than the lilies of the fields and the birds.

We could come with some grand and glorious scheme to glorify You and Your name and try to convince You to do it. But You've already thought up all the ideas and made up Your mind about which ones are worth pursuing.

Lord, we could have enough faith, or say the right words, or use the right formula so that we could pray for anything we want and get it. At least that's what some people believe. But, Lord, we praise You for the spiritual wisdom to understand that that's not how prayer works.

Lord, we could try to hold You to Your promises we find in Scripture. But that might mean we don't have confidence in Your promises. Sometimes we might find just the right Scripture to guarantee what we want, then take it before You and try to hold You to Your word. We could treat Your Word like a catalog and skip over the promises that aren't too appealing and just ask You to fulfill those that we kinda like.

Lord, we could try to talk You into releasing part of that huge treasure of blessings You have for us there in Heaven. Lord, let us not waste our spiritual energy trying to convince You to do what You're already doing. Lord, we're not here to ask You for any of the mundane things like material or physical blessings we so often think about as part of our world. Lord, set us free from earthly thoughts and desires.

But, Lord, we come asking that Your power be released into this world to do immeasurably more than we can even imagine. (See Eph. 3:20) We're asking for the same power that raised Jesus from the dead, the same power that set Jesus on the throne to reign forever. May our prayers set Your will into motion. Bring Your perfect will into this circumstance, this church, this community by Your power in Your way.

Do Your will on earth the same way You've already done it in Heaven.

Lord, we ask You to concentrate Your power to bring down Your Kingdom upon us, on our personal lives, on our church, on this community. May this church continually be about the activity of exposing its people and the people of this community to Your power to change lives. Power and might are in Your hands, and no one can withstand You. (2 Chron. 20:6) O Lord, the power is in Your hands and it stands at the ready.

Praise be to You, O Lord, who with his hands has fulfilled what You have promised with Your mouth. When we consider Your power, the ultimate power, the only real power, and when we see Your power focused on our problems—we can only watch expectantly for how You will do Your work in Your way in Your time. What do we have to fear, Lord? Your "power is so rich and so mobile that all we have to do is name the persons or things we desire to have Your power applied to and You, the Lord of Power, will direct the necessary power to the desired place at once."[25]

But, Lord, in order to consistently tap Your power in Heaven, we know we must stay in Your will. Lord, use Your power to help keep us in Your will, to keep us asking for things that You want to happen. May

---

[25]   Hallesby, Ole, *Prayer*, p.65.

we have complete faith that what we ask for is going to happen because we know it's Your will.

Lord, we'd be willing to be miserable and suffering to be in Your perfect will. We're willing to die to ourselves to be in Your perfect will. O Lord, try us, put us to the test, grow our faith through hardship, but purify our love to the point that our every thought coincides with Yours so we can bring down Your power upon this lost world.

O Lord, You have created us to be an expression of Your will. May we give ourselves completely to You so that our minds may be able to prove it good, acceptable, and perfect. (See Rom. 12:2) O Lord, may we be able to say with the Psalmist that Your promises have been thoroughly tested and Your servant loves them. (See Ps. 119:140) May we be able to say with the Psalmist, "I delight to do Your will, O God. Your laws are written on my heart." (See Ps. 40:8 my version) O Lord, Your will is a perfect fit for our lives. O Lord, You created each of us physically unique, and Your plan for our lives is not a generic one either. Your will for our lives was created and planned just for us. You didn't get Your will for us off the rack, but You custom made it specifically for us. May our body, spirit, and soul live in perfect harmony—completely submitted to Your will. May our bodies never again do what we don't want to do, what You don't want us to do. O Lord, may we live and move and have being in You. (See Acts 17:28)

Lord, fill us with the knowledge of Your will through spiritual wisdom and understanding. O, the depths of the riches of Your wisdom and knowledge. How unsearchable are Your judgments, and Your paths are beyond tracing out. (See Rom. 11:33)

Lord, we're not here to tell You how to accomplish Your plan. Please do it Your own way. We know that You are always working out Your perfect will in response to our prayers. When we surrender our situation to You, we know You are moving it toward the best, most beneficial, long-term resolution. Your ways are higher than our ways.

Lord, about some things we are 100% sure what Your will is. Lord, I personally know of a pile of youth who have invited Jesus into their lives but have not followed through by being baptized. I specifically pray for Josh, Kristin, Steven, Hunter, Chris, Jason. I pray for the Rachel, Adam and Jim. Lord I pray for salvation for Patrick and Kristin and Beth. Lord, I pray for the husbands and fathers of some of our church members to be saved—specifically Steve and John.

Lord, for those things for which we don't know 100% for sure what Your will is we pray that Your will be done. Lord, help us to know Your will so we can pray Your will.

O Lord, thank you for Jesus—not the messenger but the Message. May we know Your Word—Your perfect message. May we understand Your perfect will by knowing Your perfect Word—Jesus. O Jesus, express Yourself through us. May Your life flow through us just like the vine's life flows through the branches.

O Lord, as we pray, be in us. Speak through our mouths. Put Your thoughts in our minds. Put Your words in our mouths. Put Your desires in our hearts. We desire to be pliable in Your hands and molded by You.

O Lord, we give You willing minds that they may become tablets upon which You inscribe Your desires. O Lord, we delight in You. Create our desires. O Lord, I want to be 170 pounds of willingness through which You can channel. O Lord, use our willingness, our openness to Your every desire as a pipeline to communicate between Your heart and the world.

We pray to get into that portion of the world that would shut You out. May we be Your tool to reach the lost.

Jesus, work in our lives more to cause us to want Your will more. May we feed regularly upon Your Word—to the point where it nourishes and strengthens our spiritual immune system, produces spiritual growth, increases our spiritual strength, and enhances spiritual awareness. May we pray without ceasing, live by faith, and be continually filled with Your Spirit.

O Lord, search us, know our thoughts, know our ways. Show us any wrong directions in our paths. Put our feet back on Your path. May we settle for nothing less than all You have for us.

Let us hear You speak. Teach us to recognize Your voice. Create spiritual hunger in us. Cause us to crave Your presence.

We lay our hearts and minds before You. Write Your will on them.

Amen

Note: This prayer is composed from notes taken from *Power Praying* by Jennifer Kennedy Dean.

∞

Prayed as an offertory prayer at an 8:30 Sunday Morning Worship Service.

Loving Father,

When we came to our senses and, in effect, said, "Father I have sinned against Heaven and against You. I am no longer worthy to be called Your child. Make me like Your hired men," You, in effect, while we were still far off, came running full speed, filled with compassion, threw Your arms around us and kissed us, and then You said to Your servants, "Quick, bring the best robe and put it on us, put a ring on our finger and sandals on our feet. Bring the fatted calf and kill it. Let' s have a feast and celebrate. For this child of mine was dead, but is alive again." (See Luke 15:21-24)

O Father, You have clothed us with garments of salvation and arrayed us with robes of righteousness. (See Isa. 61:10)

Blessed are we whose transgressions are forgiven, whose sins are covered. (See Ps. 32.1) Blessed are we who have Your love and know it and realize Your love endures forever. O Father, You have overwhelmed us with Your love.

O Father, Your great love for us spawns a desire in us to respond in kind. Indeed, at times we have so much love for You that our bodies ache to do Your will. O Father, just tell us what field You want plowed, what barn You want cleaned out, and we will run to do it. Just tell us what enemy You want to fight and we'll be on the front line fighting like three wild cats. At times we feel like our heart is just going to burst with love for You. O Father, may our love for You never wane. Help us to have so much love for You that we can't control it.

O Father, tears come to our eyes because we see Your great concern for those other wayward ones out there still trying to do their own thing. O Lord, we pray with every ounce of our being that they too would come to their senses. May they seek you while You still may be found. (See Isa. 55:6)

May this service be used to express our love for You, to heighten our concern for Your concerns, and to help us come to our senses. May these tithes and offerings be given in love.

And, O Father, may we <u>never</u> leave Your presence again.

Amen

While this prayer was used as an offertory prayer in a Sunday Morning Worship Service it is probably better suited as a morning prayer.

Eternal Law Giver,

There are those we know who scoff at Your law. And they don't like You either.

But, Lord, we've come here to praise You and tell You we love You because

- Out of Your great love and infinite wisdom, You have not only created the universe and put us in it, but You have given us the rules that enable us to find peace and live in harmony with You and Your creation.
- You have given us the precepts for guiding our path
- You have given us an instruction manual for living our lives that, if we could but follow perfectly, would enable us to be the best person we could possibly be here on earth.
- Your law acts like a school teacher pointing out our every sin

And, but for the limits You put on us, we would have unlimited praise and unlimited love for You, Lord, because Your law brought us to our knees repenting of our sins, begging Jesus to come and take control.

O Lord, we praise You because Your law does not restrict us, but Your law has set us free, not just free from the guilt of sin, but free to live within Your perfect law.

O Lord, may everything done in this service in some way honor You and Your perfect plan of using the law to bring us to Jesus.

O Lord, continue to search us. Continue to show us the wrong directions in our lives. Use this service to put our feet back on Your path. Guide us into all Truth. (See John 16:13) May sin come into contact with Your grace here this morning. O Lord, we delight in Your commandments. (See Ps. 119:47)

O Lord, we pray for those we know who are trying to obey Your law in their own power. And we pray for those we know who scoff at Your law. Our prayer this morning is that Your law will continue to serve its usefulness by bringing these to the recognition of their sins. And may we as Your people be so true to our calling that they turn to Jesus in their great need.

May Your Word serve as a lamp unto our feet, a light unto our path. (See Ps. 119:105)

Amen

Prayed at a Monday Night Prayer Meeting.

O Lord Who Spoke Creation into Being,

We praise You for Your creative word.
We praise You for Your spoken word, Your written Word, and Your living Word.
We praise You because Your actions always match Your words.
O Lord, Your words are never idle.

O Lord, we praise You because You said You loved us and proved it by sending Jesus.
O Lord, we praise You because You are always true to Your word.

O Lord, we confess that all too often our actions have not matched our words. Help us to live lives that match our words. Help us to live lives that match what we sing on Sunday morning. Help us to live lives that match the words we affirm in our hearts as the message is preached on Sundays. Help us to live lives that match Your Word.

Lord, hit us up side of the head with Your Word. Hit us over the head with Your Truth. Inoculate those of us that are immune to sermons with your Holy Spirit. Light a fire under those of us that haven't done anything in forty years except raise an occasional eyebrow. Put a fire in us for Your Word that sets not only this whole church on fire but sets this entire town on fire for Jesus.

Lord, help us to resist temptation. May we be so in the mind set of resisting temptation that Satan flees. Lord, may we not be in a mode where we are waiting to see what Your will is before we decide whether or not we're going to do it. May we be ready to do Your will no matter what it is.

Lord, we ask You to do what only You can do. Lord, I know some boys who are allowing shyness and peer pressure to prevent them from doing Your will. Help them to rely on You to give them the strength to do what they can't do by themselves.

In accord with Jesus' strong desires we pray.

Amen

∞

Prayed at a Sunday Morning Worship Service.

Lord God Almighty,

Elijah was a human just like we are, and he prayed <u>earnestly</u> for it not to rain, and no rain fell for three-and-a-half years. (See James 5:17)

Then, Lord, for Your glory and so that it might be known without a doubt that You are the one and only true god, Elijah prayed again on Mt. Carmel, praying in absolute faith because he knew he was praying for what You wanted to happen. And before 450 prophets of Baal and 400 prophets of Asherah and before a large crowd of Israelites and after the altar and sacrifice were drenched three times, You answered his prayer by bringing fire to consume the sacrifice and the altar.

O Lord, we also feel like Elijah. We too are living in a time when we're part of a dwindling number of true believers. Increasingly we find ourselves in situations where we feel like we're the only true believer. We too find ourselves being the lone voice willing to proclaim Your Word. O Lord, we too are living in a time when Your people are limping between two opinions. (See 1 Kings 18:21)

O Lord, we say that You are our God and that we love You. In fact, we've been singing the words right here this morning. But some of our actions say otherwise. Materialism and worldliness and our own desires and opinions dominate our thoughts and actions.

O Lord, there is not a person here who has not compromised themselves to fall into line with what our culture defines as acceptable. Lord, we've come here this morning feeling comfortable—because we know we're safe. A worship service won't threaten our comfort zones—or at least we won't let it. We've already made up our mind about what we won't do. Lord, we're becoming spiritual weaklings because we've drawn the line on what we will or won't do for You. Lord, some here would rather die and go to hell than accept You as Lord and Savior. Lord, some here have invited You into their hearts, but they are letting shyness or peer pressure keep them from making a public profession or following through with baptism. Lord, some here have accepted You as Savior, but they are letting self stand in the way of submitting to You as Lord also. Lord, some of us have drawn the lines in certain areas of our lives and keep You out of those areas altogether. Lord, some of us just need to rely on You to help us to resist the sin that keeps creeping back into our lives.

Lord, we pray earnestly this morning, because we know it is Your will, that because of what happens here this morning You will be glorified and that many may once again affirm that You are the one and only god. Lord, we pray that You will do what only You can do here this morning. Break down our comfort zones, give us strength to do what we haven't been able to do by ourselves, bring the fire of the Holy Spirit that we may be consumed with doing Your will. O Lord, put Satan to flight. And may You win a great victory here this morning.

Amen

∞

Used as an offertory in a Sunday Morning Worship Service.

O Lord Who Makes All Things New,

We thank You for another new day. We thank You for the new life we see all about us: babies in the nursery, babies in Christ stirring baptismal waters, the growth we see in our own Christian lives. But mostly we thank You because You made us new creatures in Christ. And we praise You because our salvation didn't depend on how smart we were, or how good we were, or how rich we were, or on whom we knew, but only on our submitting to You. And we can't even take full credit for that because we know Your Holy Spirit played the major role.

Lord, we've come to Your filling station this morning running on fumes. Once again we let sin win all too many battles this week. Once again we allowed the world to get our focus and keep it for long periods of time. Once again we found ourselves doing our own thing, trying to satisfy some of our own selfish desires. Once again at times we found ourselves trying to be self-sufficient. Once again at times we disappointed You with the amount of time we spent in prayer and Bible study. Once again we went all week without telling a single soul about Jesus.

O Lord, we can't afford to just ask You to recharge our battery and put $2 worth in our tank again. We can't afford to limp along from Sunday to Sunday like we've been doing, Lord, 'cause today is the first day of the rest of our life, and we really want the rest of our life to really count for Your kingdom. And we know that won't happen if we just continue as we are.

But, Lord, we know precisely what we need to do—we need to just once again or maybe for the very first time just totally submit to You again. But we don't seem to have the will power or the spiritual discipline or whatever it takes to do it and follow through. So, Lord, we ask You to use Your Holy Word, Your preached word, Your Holy Spirit, and whatever else it takes to convict us of the fact that we are the greatest sinner who ever lived because we have broken the greatest commandment ever given—to love You with all our heart, soul, and might. O Lord, may we not just feel guilty, but may we feel so devastated that we empty ourselves of everything but You, that we can say, "Fill 'er up, Lord, fill 'er up." Then Lord, fill us with us with enthusiasm and eagerness to do Your will. O Lord, just fill us with You!

Then, Lord, may we find ourselves so in love with You, so dedicated to finding and doing Your will that You use us to accomplish for Your kingdom things that we would never have done our own power.

O Lord, may Your strength and power be made perfect in our weakness (See 2 Cor. 12:9) here this morning.

O Lord, because we need it so much.
O Lord, because it's what you want to happen here this morning.

And, Lord, may each of us go away from here this morning having You in our hearts, Christ in our focus, and Your Holy Spirit on our case.

Amen

∞

Prayed during a Monday Night Prayer Meeting.

Lord,

We don't have to look far to see a bunch of folks on the road to Hell. In fact, we don't even have to leave Tullahoma to see a whole mission field.

Lord, may none of these end up going to Hell because we live such hypocritical lives that it turns them off to Jesus.

Lord, may none of these end up going to Hell because we don't pray for them, May none of these end up going to hell because we don't pray for them enough. May none of these end up going to hell because we don't pray for more workers for the harvest. May none of these end up going to Hell because we pray for stones and snakes when You want to give bread and fish. (See Matt. 7:9-10)

Lord, may none of these end up going to Hell because we are so busy playing church we forget all about them. May none of these end up going to Hell because we are so busy doing our own thing that we ignore them. May none of these end up going to Hell because we are so involved in the things of the world that we lose sight of them.

Lord, may none of these end up going to Hell because we are remiss in telling them about Jesus. May none of these end up going to Hell because all the signs on the wide and easy road they are traveling say "To Heaven," and we don't have the love to tell them the signs are wrong. Lord, may none of these end up going to Hell because we don't go into the highways and hedges and invite them to your banquet. (See Luke 14:23)

Lord, may none of these end up going to Hell because we don't feel your love and concern and agony for them. May none of these end up going to Hell because we don't care enough to ask them where they were going to spend eternity. May none of these end up going to Hell because we don't pay attention to Your voice and Your message in our own lives. May none of these end up going to Hell because we think we aren't prepared to witness to them.

Lord, may none of these end up going to Hell because we as a church don't make Your agenda our agenda. May none of these end up going to Hell because we as a church are so disunited that Your message can't be heard over the clamor. May none of these end up going to Hell because Your Word and Your truths aren't proclaimed boldly from our pulpits and through our lives.

O Lord, may none of these end up going to Hell because we leave some stone unturned. But, Lord, may the only reason any of these end up going to Hell be because they want to. And, Lord, if any of these aren't so set in their ways that You can't change them, use circumstances, Your Holy Spirit, and us as need be to bring them to their senses.

O Lord, we pray for each and every person in this community that does not know You as Lord and Savior. May each of these hear Your Good News in a manner in which they really do understand. We pray for more workers to glean the fields. We pray for more nets to cast upon the waters. We pray for a healthy dose of Your concern for the lost. We pray for the blessed joy of seeing others come to know Jesus as Lord and Savior. O Lord, infect us with desire to seek out and witness to the lost, and let it grow like a plague in this congregation.

Amen

Prayed during a Sunday Night Worship Service and then again, slightly modified, in an opening assembly in Youth Sunday School.

"Almighty Heavenly Father, [God] of Limitless Power and Glory and Unimaginable Awesomeness,"[26]

What a mighty God You are. There is nothing You can't do. No sickness You can't heal. no miracle You can't perform. No problem You can't solve. No life You can't revitalize. No sin You can't forgive. O Lord, be our object of worship this evening as we bring You the sacrifices of praise and thanksgiving through song, as we show our obedience to You by presenting You with these tithes and offerings, as we acknowledge Your claim on our lives by praying to You and You only, as we honor You by proclaiming Your Word boldly from this pulpit, and as we please You by submitting our lives to Your will. May it all be for Your glory.

O Lord, You keep our "astronomers on the edge of their seats with new... [displays] of... [Your] power"[27] the rest of us usually don't even hear about. And our scientists who look through microscopes see details of Your creation the rest of us usually don't even think about. But, O Lord, we who see only a small part of Your creation and who understand Your power and Your plan only from our very limited perspectives have more to praise You for than we can do in our entire lifetime. O Lord, You are a "god of majesty and might who is [infinitely] worthy"[28] to be praised. But what really blows us away, Lord, is that while You are the all-powerful God of Creation, God of the entire universe, You are also our God, a god who is gracious and kind, a god who loves us more than anything, a god who, in effect, tucks us in at night, kisses us, and checks on us *constantly* while we sleep. You forgive and encourage. You are a god who gives faith and confidence to draw near, to actually enter Your presence and talk with You as a

---

[26]   Jeremiah, David, *Prayer, the Great Adventure*, p. 87.

[27]   Ibid. p. 87-88.

[28]   Ibid. p. 87.

small child would talk with his loving parent—all because of the plan You inaugurated whereby Jesus Christ died for our sins. O Lord, that one great act, that great demonstration of Your great love, that giving of Yourself on the cross, combined with the proof we have of Your power over the grave gives us reason to have need to lose ourselves in worshipping You. O Lord, if we knew Your address and could connect all the computers in the whole world to the internet and dedicate them to the task of sending You praise all day long for the next billion years, it would be but a drop in the bucket compared to how much we really need to praise You. O Lord, we cannot think more highly of You than You are. We can't imagine You being more holy than You are because You are already "at the pinnacle of righteousness and holiness and greatness."[29]

Lord, we know that what would please You the most, what would worship You the most here this evening, is if we were to make a quantum leap in our faith and commitment to You. And we know that You have already used Bro. J. to prepare a sermon for us through which You can communicate Your personal message for each of us, a message designed to do exactly that—to move us from where we've been spiritually stuck for longer than we care to mention down the road a 'fur' piece, a lot closer to where we need to be. And we know that he and others have already watered the seeds You want planted here this evening with their prayers, and quite possibly with their tears. But, Lord, we also know from past experience that that sermon is going to turn into nothing but another conversation piece unless somehow that personal message You have for us turns into the fervent prayer of our lives. O Lord, we pray for exactly that to happen here this evening. May Your Word be so powerful, may Your Holy Spirit be so effective, may Your truths become so important to us here this evening that we can resist Your urgings no longer. May our resistance just fall away. May our concern for what others might think just disappear. And may Your kingdom gain a great victory in each of our lives here this evening. O

---

[29] Ibid. p. 91.

Lord, because we need it so much. O Lord, because it's what You want to happen here this evening.

To You be the glory and dominion forever and ever. (See 1 Pet. 5:11)

Amen

Note: This prayer was written after reading chapter 5 of David Jeremiah's *Prayer, the Great Adventure*

∞

This prayer was prayed during a Monday Night Prayer Meeting. Victory Sunday was a Sunday for which efforts were made to try to achieve the highest Sunday School attendance of the year.

Sovereign Lord,

We praise You because You really are the absolute sovereign of the universe. We praise You because Your throne is not empty. You are seated and in control. You are an awesome and a mighty god. We praise You because You're not an absentee ruler who made the earth and then just left the engine running. We praise You because You are a hands-on god who is actively involved in energizing the world and keeping it working.

We praise You because You know everything inside and out. And, if something needs fixing, You can do it. Nothing is too difficult for You.

We praise You because when You make a promise—we better believe we can believe You're going to keep it.

Lord, we praise You because You don't have bad moods. You're the same yesterday, today and tomorrow.

Lord, we praise You for anointing Jesus king of Israel, king of the Jews, king of Heaven, King of the Ages, the king of the saints, and the Prince of the kings of the earth. O Lord of lords, King of kings, help us to anoint Him king of our lives. O Lord, He has put everything in subjection under His feet. O Lord, we want him not just to be sovereign of our lives, but sovereign of our relationships, sovereign of our workplace, sovereign of our everything. Lord, help us to be His loyal subjects.

Lord, we pray for this church. May it be so united that it causes the world to believe the message it's broadcasting. O Lord, may we all be so united with You, so in lock step with You, that we feel the heartbeat of Jesus and we too are seeking and saving that which is lost. (See Luke 19:10) Father, use us to glorify the Son. Lord, may we pray what Jesus would pray. Help us to take hold of the discipline that You supply with Your grace.

O Lord, we've become so like the world and invited the world into the church. Please, keep us from the Evil One. Sanctify us.

O Lord, there is no one so lost or so far from You that Your divine power can't reach their heart and transform them. Lord, I would like You to transform ten boys: Nathan and Eric, Josh, Jason, and Chris, Steven, Hunter, and Jackson, and Will and Frankie. Lord, move them from where they are to being baptized as demonstration of what has taken place in their lives. Lord, in my wildest dream I see all of these boys coming forward on Victory Sunday. I think I know what I want, but if that's not what You want, then I don't want it.

To You, Lord who is able to do superabundantly far over and above all that we dare ask or think according to the power that works within us, to You be the glory in the Church and in Christ Jesus throughout all generations for ever and ever. (See Eph. 3:20-21)

Amen

Prayed as an offertory prayer at a Sunday Morning Worship service.

O Lord Who Loved Us before We Were Born,

Totally awesome is Your creation. Absolutely compelling is the beauty of Your handiwork. Deeply profound and perfect was Your plan from the very beginning.

O Lord, Your gracious humbling of Yourself to come in the form of a baby, Your agonizing on the cross to pay for our sins, Your miraculous resurrection, and Your great love for even the most sinful and most rebellious continually amaze us.

O Lord, Your love and power overwhelm us. We can but respond with the applause of praise. We praise You because You are more concerned than we are about our paper cuts and chigger bites and hangnails and zits. We praise You because You temper us and discipline us. You allow trials to come our way to test us and try us and to grow our faith and perseverance and character. And You allow us to suffer the consequences of our actions. O Lord, we praise You because when the big problems of life hit and we don't know where else to turn You are there to walk with us through the valley of the shadow of death and comfort us. O Lord, we praise You because when Satan tempts us You grace us with the power to resist.

O Lord, Your great power and Your great love set You apart from all others. O Lord, we confess that we have sinned because at times we have thought more of ourselves or less of You than we should. We have deified man and tried to humanize You. O Lord, holy and awesome is Your name. (See Ps. 111:9) Lord, our entire lifetime isn't long enough to even write down a number large enough or to find units big enough to define Your power or Your love.

O Lord, we've come here this morning to give You a present, not just these tithes and offerings, not just the sacrifice of praise and thanksgiving, not just our worship, but also this moment in eternity. Use this time to set our hearts aright. Use it to reenergize our love for You. Use it to help us understand that from Your vantage point You can see all things perfectly and therefore know exactly what is best for us. Use this present moment to influence our future moments for Your kingdom.

O Lord, some of us have let You get Your foot in the door, but we've been holding the door tight ever since. May this be the moment when we just completely let go and let You come in and take complete control.

O Lord, Your will where You will when You will.

Amen

❧

Prayed at Monday Night Prayer Meeting.

O Lord Who Consumed the Very Stones upon Which Elijah Placed His Offering on Mt Carmel,

We praise You because You are the one and only god in all the universe and in all that's not in the universe. We praise You because even though we can't see you with our eyes, hear You with our ears, or feel You with our fingers, we can see the evidence of Your handiwork everywhere, and we know that You're still in the business of consuming stones in answer to prayer.

O Lord, we know that Elijah prayed earnestly and that it didn't rain for three-and-a-half years. O Lord, we come this evening praying earnestly—with all the oomph we can muster. O Lord, we didn't come here to be seen or heard by others. We didn't come to support the pastor or just to undergird the programs of this church with prayer. O Lord, we didn't come to waste Your time or our time. We've come because of Your great love for us and Your great sacrifice and because Your Holy

Spirit brought us here us to pray for Your will for this church and this circumstance. O Lord, we've come to set Your plan in motion in this place.

O Lord, it has been said that You can do more with one person 100% committed to You than You can with 100 people 90% committed to you. O Lord, we confess that we're some of those 90%-ers, if that good. O Lord, we desperately want to be 100%-ers. Yes, we're tired of trying to do Your will in our own power. Yes, we're tired of trying to witness when You haven't prepared the way. Yes, we're tired of being the hypocrites that others offer up as excuses for why they'll not follow You. O Lord, we're tired of being an embarrassment to You and Your kingdom. But, Lord, the real reason we want to be 100%-ers is not for any selfish reasons but solely because You want us to be and You need us to be for Your Kingdom's sake.

O Lord, we confess the sin of holding back certain areas of our life from Your control, to having a mental list of things we won't do for You, places where we draw the line. O Lord, help us to turn them over to You at this very moment. O Lord, please, if we don't, knock the props out from under our self-sufficiency, bring us to our knees one way or another.

O Lord, we know that You can use small vessels but You don't use dirty ones. Please help us to resist every temptation. May we treat temptation like a challenge—a challenge You'll help us win. And, Lord, for any battles we lose may our confession be immediate and our remorse bring us to complete dependence on You.

O Lord, may we be so in tune with You that our prayers pulsate with exactly the thoughts that Jesus would be praying if He were here in person. O Lord, may our hearts be so filled with love that we feel a compelling need to spread Your Word.

Lord, it sometimes seems like a Sunday School picnic around here. Everyone is having a good time, there's lots of good fellowship, and everyone is getting fed real well. O Lord, for some of us Sunday down at the church house has become an end in itself. We're doing our part by being there and doing our normal thing. We go home satisfied that we have fulfilled our obligation to You. Some of us are just glad to have our names in the Lamb's Book of Life and to get fed every Sunday. Lord, some of us spend so much energy preparing Sunday School lessons or in personal spiritual development that we've made it a substitute for outreach and personal soul winning.

O Lord, so fill us with Your Holy Spirit that we become obsessed with You. So fill us with Your Holy Spirit that we can't get the lost off our minds. Saturate us with the oil of Your Spirit and set us on fire for You. Then consume us, just as You consumed those rocks on Mt. Carmel. Consume us with Your work and Your fire. Use us for Your fuel.

O Lord, may we be so consumed that
- The whole world will note that here are some folk that have been with Jesus
- The whole world will have to admit that You are alive and well and have work full-time down at FBC
- We don't have to beg people to accept Jesus, but people will continually come begging to receive Jesus

O Lord, we earnestly pray that You will come and take absolute, complete control. And may Your victory here be even greater than the one You experienced at Mt. Carmel.

Amen

Prayed at Monday Night Prayer Meeting.

O Lord Who Gives the Power to Patiently Endure and Who Supplies Encouragement,

We come praying the prayer of Agur. O Lord, may we be neither rich nor poor. (See Prov. 30:8–9) May we not have the burden of being overly concerned with money. May we not waste time on entering sweepstakes or buying lottery tickets. May we not be obsessed with the stock market. May we have no desire to be wealthy here on earth. May we not become rich like the Laodiceans who claimed to have need of nothing.

O Lord, we confess great need—first and foremost, Lord, we need You. O Lord, You are our Vine—without You we can do nothing. (See John 15:5) O Lord, You are our heart's desire[30]—without You we are devastated.

O Lord, we need Your leadership. We fail miserably when we pursue our own leanings. We flounder when we don't pay attention to Your urgings. Please, Lord, use Your Word to guide our path. Use Your Holy Spirit to guide our every move. Use Your church to put opportunities to accomplish Your will in our path. With unfailing love, lead this people whom You have redeemed. Guide them in strength to where Your holiness dwells.

O Lord, we need Your gold. The same gold that You counseled the Laodiceans to purchase—gold that has been tried in the fire. May we buy Your gold so we can be truly rich. (See Rev. 3:18)

And, Lord, we need Your white raiment (See Rev. 3:18) to cover our shame. O Lord, may we truly desire to be holy, as You are holy. (See 1 Pet. 1:16) May we seek to clothe ourselves with garments that have the label inside that says "Made in Heaven."

---

[30] Nystrom, Martin J., "As the Deer", 1981 and Psalm 42:1.

And, O Lord, we need your eye salve (See Rev. 3:18) so we can see Your truths, so we can see how much we need You. O Lord, at times it's hard to put our trust in You because what we see with our human eyes is so clear. Help us give up the right to be right. Help us to walk by faith instead of sight. Help us to see things from Your perspective.

But, o Lord, we have great need to bring Your message to the lost. We have great need to intercede for them. O Lord, please send more workers to the harvest. Lord, we pay for Your Word to be spread quickly, run its course, be glorified and triumphant. (See 2 Thes. 3:1) Lord, we pray for this congregation to catch Your love for the lost. May it become a driving force behind our prayers. May it be the activity that unites us in purpose. May every lost soul in this community get the gospel explained to them in a way that they really understand. O Lord, may the natural consequences of sin bring many to their senses.

And may it be all for Your glory.

Amen

∞

For quite a while our church visitation program began right after Monday Might Prayer Meeting.

Lord Almighty, King of Glory,

We praise you because You are the one who does all things well, (See Mark 7:37) who never sleeps or slumbers, (See Ps. 121:3) who guides us with His gaze fixed constantly upon us.

"Forbid it, Lord, that our roots become firmly attached to this earth, that we should fall in love with things. Help us understand that this pilgrimage of life is but an introduction, a preface, a training school, for what is to come. Then shall we see all of life in its true perspective.

Then shall we not fall in love with the things of time, but come to love the things that endure."[31]

O Lord, You are from everlasting to everlasting, the Alpha and Omega. Only You deserve our wholehearted devotion. May we seek Your kingdom and your righteousness. May we spend time with You daily. May we keep up a running conversation with You all day long. O Lord, may our love for You know no end or any bound.

O Lord, Your Word endures forever. Heaven and earth will pass away but Your Words will remain forever. (See Matt. 24:35) O Lord, may we delight in Your Word both day and night. May we so love Your Word that we can't get enough of it. May we so love Your Word that we carry it everywhere with us in our heart. May we so love Your Word that we live it.

O Lord, about the only other things here on earth that are eternal besides You and Your Word are the people. O Lord, may we love the people with a love like Jesus did when He was here. May we love the unlovely. May we love the sick. May we love the destitute. May we love those who hate us. O Lord, may we love them with the same passion that Jesus did when he was here. O Lord, may we love them so much that we intercede for them day and night, night and day. May we love them so much that we proclaim Your Word to them until they get the message. May we love them so much that Your angels are kept busy sewing garments of salvation and robes of righteousness.

O Lord, as we go out visiting tonight may we spread love everywhere we go.

Amen

---

31 Marshall, Peter. "Liberation from Materialism." *The Voice: Biblical and Theological Resources for Growing Christians.* CRI/Voice, Institute, n.d. Web. 4 July 2013. <http://www.crivoice.org/prayers.html#TFamily>.

Prayed as an offertory prayer at an 8:30 Sunday Morning Worship Service. After renovating our sanctuary and returning to two morning services, it was decided the 8:30 service would be a traditional service and the 11:00 service would be a contemporary service. At that time my wife and I decided we would primarily go to the traditional service. So most Sunday Morning Worship Services mentioned will be traditional services held at 8:30.

Holy, holy, holy are You, Lord of Hosts,

Truly we are standing on holy ground here this morning. But, Lord, we know who else is here. Lately every time the church doors are open Satan just sashays right in. It's almost as if he's already made reservations down at his place for a whole passel of folk and the only thing that can throw a monkey wrench into his plans is if something happens here he hadn't planned for. So he's shown up to make sure everything here stays status quo.

He's working behind the scenes to provide opportunity and suggest motive for some of our youth down front to talk and pass notes during the sermon again. He's already got a list of kids he's counting on going out the front on their way to the bathroom during the rest of the service. He's looking for a way to turn up the heat in the choir loft. He's going to do everything necessary to draw our attention away from Your Word. And then, just to be on the safe side, he's planning on using his number one strategy—to try to get us to doubt Your Word. If us not claiming Your promises or applying Your Word to our lives is proof we really don't believe it, he's been very successful so far. O Lord, the Father of Lies will once again tell us we should procrastinate here this morning, once again putting off doing exactly what we know You want us to do here. O Lord, that Father of Lies will once again suggest that our relationship with You is satisfactory and we'd be fools to even think about making a deeper commitment to You. O Lord, once again he'll remind us that we can't go down front during the altar call to pray or make a public commitment—after all, what other people think is more important than what You think. O Lord, Satan is using a hundred schemes here to make sure You don't win the victory in our lives here this morning.

O Lord, we need Your help—big time. The Enemy is right here in our midst. Help us to praise You so much that Satan trembles. May Bro. A. proclaim Your Word so accurately and so boldly here this morning that it makes Satan sick. O Lord, we ask You very specifically: give us the desire and the strength to so resist temptation and Satan's lies here this morning that we send Satan packing.

O Lord, may the status quo fall by the wayside here this morning. May we give you permission to do Your thing in our lives this morning. May we be attacked by Your Truth. May we literally be overwhelmed by the fact that Jesus Christ is really who he said he was and how that information should affect our lives. May Your agenda be so accomplished in our lives here this morning that Satan ultimately has to cancel a host of those reservations—both here and throughout this community. O Lord, may Satan rue this day forever. And may Your name be glorified continually in this place until Christ returns.

Use these tithes and offerings for Your kingdom.

Amen

∞

At Monday Night Prayer Meeting.

Precious Jesus,

We're not here to tell You something You don't already know. We're not here to ask for something You don't already know we want. Lord, we may have come to listen to each other pray or to enjoy the fellowship or to support the pastor or to undergird the programs of the church or out of obedience, or we may have come for wrong reasons. But, Lord, now that we're here, let this not be another time when we just leave a message on Your answering machine. Grace us with Your presence in a special way. Let us feel You chiding us for our failures, let us feel You comforting our unrest, let us feel You challenging us with Your will.

Rather than being part of an earthly prayer meeting, Lord, allow us to feel like we're part of the ongoing prayer meeting You're leading on our behalf. Your Word indicates that You are always making petition to God as our high priest interceding for our continual salvation. O Lord, it pleases us immensely to think that You're interceding for us, intervening on our behalf—especially when we're faltering, asleep, or faithless. We're thankful that when we do not pray You're standing in the gap making intercession for us.

Likewise, we appreciate when You are joined by the Holy Spirit who helps us in our weakness when we don't know how to pray as we should, who intercedes with sighs too deep for words and God who searches the heart, knows what is the mind of the Spirit because the Spirit intercedes for the saints according to the will of God. (See Rom.8:26-27)

Lord, may we sense the words or things that You're praying for us at this very moment so we can imitate Your prayers. Lord, as we pray may we allow You to convince us of what we need and You are ready to give. Lord, lead us to pray for what You are more ready to give than we are to ask. O Lord, may we end this prayer session convinced You have communicated Your desires to us.

Lord, Satan keeps trying to tempt us to sin in little ways. We confess that we're so spiritually haughty because we haven't committed any of the big sins that we allow ourselves not to be concerned when we are tempted to commit a small sin. Lord, I confess to eating too much at times, to saying what is best left unsaid, to telling white lies, to exaggerating, to bringing pens home from work. O Lord, Satan has his way with me because he knows that if he can get me to do the little sins that it is just as effective, if not more so, as tempting me to do the big sins. It keeps me from being able to do any thing big for You.

And, Lord, when I do resist temptation, sometimes I feel guilty because I've been tempted. Instead of giving You the victory, Satan gets the victory because I have such spiritual pride that it makes me think I'm above being tempted in certain areas. O Lord, help me to give You the glory every time I resist temptation successfully.

Lord, I recently read that the revival that took place at the Southern Baptist Seminary started with confessions of the smallest of sins— things like a student telling his professor that when he was asked whether he had read his assignment and he said yes that he had really read only three-fourths of it. And one professor admitting to another that he was jealous of the other's success. Lord, is this what we need to do to start a revival in this place? O Lord, burden each of us with the importance of not submitting to even the smallest of temptations. May we confess all of our sins to You, no matter how small. May we confess to each other those sins that we should.

Lord, there's a verse over in 2 Samuel that tells how Shammah stood and defended a piece of ground full of lentils while the rest of the Israelites fled from the Philistines. He held his ground and killed many Philistines and the verse ends with "and the Lord worked a great victory." (See 2 Sam. 23:11-12) Lord, help us to stand our ground and not submit to even the smallest of temptations and allow You to gain a great victory.

To You be the glory both now and forever. (See Heb. 13:21)

Amen

∞

Prayed at Monday Night Prayer Meeting. Several national holidays are celebrated on Mondays, but Monday Night Prayer Meeting normally happened regardless—even when no member of the church staff can be there.

Lord of Abraham, Isaac, and Jacob,

We praise the work of Your Holy Spirit that has inspired this regular Monday Night Prayer Meeting. We praise You because there were not any serious thoughts of canceling this meeting just because today is a national holiday. Lord, may You get all the glory.

We praise You for inspiring the writers of old to record Your Word. We praise You for preserving Your precious Word for these many years. We praise You for using Your Holy Spirit to speak Your personal message to us as we read, study, and meditate on Your Word.

Lord, we especially thank You for the amazement and wonder and blessing we feel when we encounter words You had recorded thousands of years apart by different authors that all fit together as neatly as a jigsaw puzzle.

Lord, I pray for those of our fellowship who don't read Your Word outside the walls of this church building. And I pray for those boys I've had in Sunday School over the years for whom reading in an anathema. Lord, may this church preach and teach Your Word in such a way that Your living Word may reign in their lives.

Lord, I pray for Ding, Shan-ling, and Elaine, who when Lyle and I visited with them were so anxious to show us their Bibles, even though they were written in a language they couldn't read. Lord, may Your Holy Spirit speak to them in a mighty way in a language that they can understand.

Lord, You blessed Jacob with a dream in which he saw a ladder whose feet were here on earth and whose top reached to heaven—and angels went up and down and You stood above it.

Lord give us the spiritual discernment to recognize that You have, in effect, given each of us a ladder, too—that You are sending Your angels from heaven to remind us of Your many precious, magnificent promises. O Lord, so many of us are suffering defeat in our lives because we do not know or do not claim Your promises. O Lord, help us to stand at the foot of the ladder to receive and act on Your promises. O Lord, may we quit complaining and go to celebrating because we know and act on Your promises.

Lord, help us to see that Your angels also bringing protection—that we are watched over constantly while we sleep, that Satan is prevented from tempting us beyond what we are able to resist. O Lord, help us to recognize that You're almost always looking out for us, sending Your angels of protection as necessary. Make us so spiritually sensitive that we recognize Your handiwork in all the events of our lives—so that we can just stay in the praising mode.

Lord, help us to see that some of Your angels are bringing provisions— that they are supplying our every need. O Lord, help us to recognize that all blessings come from You.

Lord, Your Word says "I assure you, most solemnly I tell you, you shall see heaven opened and the angels of God ascending and descending upon the Son of Man." (John 1:51 Amp) O Lord, we pray for those we know who are not receiving Your provisions, Your protection, or reminders of Your promises. But even more we pray because they do not have ladders to get them to heaven. O Lord, there are no other ladders that reach to heaven but Your Son, Jesus Christ. O Lord, we pray for those who don't even know they need a ladder. We pray for those who are looking for a ladder. We pray for those who have ladders that don't reach to heaven. O Lord, may we Your church be diligent in praying for these.

And, Lord, may we as a church so trust in You that it puts Your power on display before these. May our lives demonstrate Your power and authority over the world, over the flesh and over Satan. May we show off our loving Lord. May we broadcast Your love and Your salvation far and wide.

To You be the glory and dominion forever and ever. (See 1 Pet. 5:11)

Amen

∞

Prayed at a Monday Night Prayer Meeting.

Sovereign Lord,

We are told that statistically each of us is due about one or two unbelievable coincidences in our life. I guess mine was several years back when I went to a baseball game in San Diego and ran into two people I knew from Tullahoma. And if that were all that happened we could rack it up to chance.

But, Lord, as we read Your Word, we encounter coincidence after coincidence, all of which seem to fit together to bring about Your plans. Joseph's brothers sold him into slavery, and he ended up as second in charge in Egypt just at the time when Your chosen people needed to escape the famine and be in a safe haven where they could become numerous enough and strong enough to go in and possess the Promised Land. O Lord, it had to be You—even Joseph told his brothers that You were at work in the events that happened.

Lord, the Pharisees unwittingly plotted to kill Jesus at exactly the time and place and in exactly the fashion that would fulfill all the prophecies You had already provided. O Lord, it had to be You.

Lord, I remember praying for a boy in my SS class, a boy who came less than once a month, to be saved the next Sunday. Lord, I remember being moved from praying the words to meaning the words more than

I ever meant anything in my life. and I remember it happened just the way I'd been praying. O Lord, it had to be You.

Lord, I remember a revival prayer that You gave me. And I remember shortly thereafter in a meeting to write a white paper on evangelism for this church being read the riot act by our chairperson for even suggesting that a series of revival meetings was a method of evangelism—as if I already knew that our preacher was against formal revivals. Then, Lord, events transpired that the preacher left shortly thereafter and we did have a set of revival meetings and in almost miraculous fashion that prayer got used, not once but twice. O Lord, it had to be You.

Lord, Brother D. and his wife enlisted one of the best real estate professionals in their former location to sell their home. After like a year they went back to try to sell it themselves. And when they returned they explained to us the coincidences that resulted in their house being sold. And we all had to say to ourselves, "Lord, it had to be You."

Lord, Lyle and I went visiting two Monday nights ago. We prayed very specifically before we left to the effect that we didn't feel that You wanted us to plant seeds that night, but that we felt that there was someone in Tullahoma that needed You and that we were willing to let You use us to tell them about Jesus. We also allowed as to how we didn't know where to go, that we wanted You to lead us, that we were depending on You to get us where we needed to be. Lord, it happened just like we prayed. As we left that young man, his wife said, "The prayer of my life has been answered tonight." I can imagine how she must have felt as two men appeared out of the blue, knocked on her door, and the prayer of her life was answered. But I know how I felt about what happened that evening: "O Lord, it had to be You."

O Lord, the Power Team© showed up at our door and we saw things we never thought we'd see in person. O Lord, it had to be you.

O Lord, we come tonight praising You and thanking You for the coincidences that You arranged that resulted in us accepting Jesus as Lord and Savior. O Lord, we come tonight praising You and thanking You for the times in our lives when we've been able to look back over what happened and had to say, "O Lord, it had to be You."

O Lord, help us to pray everything You want us to pray. Give us the faith to pray the prayers that when answered we can't help but say, "O Lord, it had to be You."

O Lord, when it was all over Job said, "Mine ears had heard of You, Lord, but now my eyes have seen You." (Job 42:5 NIV) O Lord, may we as a church and as individuals continually see, recognize, and acknowledge Your coincidences to the point where our faith brings others to faith in You. O Lord, may our faith in prayer grow by leaps and bounds. O Lord, may our faith know no bounds.

O Lord, it was You.

Amen

This was prayed during a Monday Night Prayer Meeting. My wife and I hosted a Southern Baptist agricultural Missionary to Rwanda at our house for the week of one of the World Mission Conferences which were an annual Duck River Baptist Association event. FBC, Tullahoma, is a member of this association. We consider that time with him at our house to be one of the major reasons our son dedicated his life to missions.

Lord of Salvation,

Bill Gates doesn't have enough money to buy his way to Heaven. In fact, You have said it is easier for a camel to go through the eye of a needle than for a rich man to go to Heaven. (See Matt. 19:24)

But, of course, all things are possible with You. Lord, we praise You because going to Heaven isn't a function of how much money we have.

Lord, we don't have any members of our local congregation who are members of the Mensa Society. In fact, Your Word says that You "will destroy the wisdom of the wise and the cleverness of the clever You will set aside. Where is the wise man? Where is the Scribe? Where is the debater of the age? Has not God made foolish the wisdom of the world?" (See 1 Cor. 1:19-20) Lord, we praise You because going to Heaven isn't a function of how smart we are.

Lord, we know that the entire Power Team© pushing together isn't strong enough to force open the door to Heaven. And we know that no one can work hard enough or long enough to get to Heaven. In fact, Your Word says that it is not of works lest any man should boast. (See Eph. 2:8-9) Lord, we praise You because going to Heaven isn't a function of our strength or accomplishments.

Lord, we know that being born into the right family isn't enough to get us to Heaven. In fact, David is described as a man after Your own heart. However, Jewish tradition states that Absalom, King David's third son, is in the furthest depths of hell. However, Your Word indicates that people who are adopted into Your family get to Heaven. Lord, we praise You because going to Heaven isn't a function of our family tree.

Lord, we know that we can't be good enough to get to Heaven. Your Word tells us that Adam took just one bite out of an apple and You kicked him out of the garden, that Moses committed just one little sin and he didn't get to go into the Promised Land, that for one sin Elijah's servant got leprosy, and for one sin Ananias and Sapphira were struck dead. Lord, we praise You because going to Heaven isn't a function of how good we are.

Lord, we praise You because You chose us, You sent Jesus to die for us, You put us in an environment where it was hard to do anything but choose Your love, You adopted us. You even gave us the faith that we used to put our trust in You. O Lord, we praise You because we're going to Heaven and we don't have any credentials for going except for the blood of Jesus.

O Lord, Your Word indicates that You have given the church the keys to the kingdom of Heaven. O Lord, we recognize that with authority comes responsibility. Lord, help us to give heed to our task. May we take the keys and unlock the door and hold it wide open. Lord, in my own way of thinking, I would say that the key to Heaven is Jesus. O Lord, may we as a church constantly give Jesus to the lost. I have also heard others say that the keys to Heaven are Bible study and prayer. Lord, may we as a church be about the task of standing in the gap and interceding for the lost we know about. Lord, may we regularly be about studying Your Word and involving others in studying Your Word. Lord, maybe the key is nothing other than carrying out the Great Commission. O Lord, may we as a church live in such a way that it causes others to glorify Your name and may we make concerted efforts to spread Your Good News far and wide.

O Lord, as we participate in the World Mission Conference events this next week may we be exposed to efforts being made to take the keys and open the door to Heaven. May we be so inspired it will move us to join in what You are doing.

O Lord, may we have the distinct privilege of being a tool in the hand of our loving God.

Amen

Prayed on a night we were taking loaves of home-made bread to those we were going to visit.

Father of Faith,

We believe in You. We believe You are the Father, infinite in love and power. As the Son, You are our redeemer and our life. And as the Holy Spirit, You are our Comforter and strength. We have faith that You came in the form of a man, died for our sins, and were resurrected. We have faith that You will share with us everything You want us to know about You and You will do everything that You have promised.

Lord Jesus, grow our faith. Encourage us to take enough time to worship You and to study Your Word and to wait on You in prayer that we absorb everything there is in You for us. In order that our faith might grow, let us recognize You in the big picture, working with almighty strength to accomplish Your will in the world and in us. In order that our faith might grow, let us recognize You working in the details of our lives. O Lord, we want with our whole heart to have unshakable faith in You. But, Lord, we confess that there are moments when we doubt. O Lord, fill our every moment with faith in You.

O Blessed Savior, how can we Your church glorify You in word and in deed and fulfill the work of intercessor unless we have steadfast faith. Blessed Savior, "speak Your word, 'Have faith in God' into the depth of our souls."[32]

O Lord, we pray for those on the periphery of our fellowship who have made a commitment to You, but haven't followed through with believer's baptism. Lord, grow their faith.

O Lord, we pray for those who have trusted You as Savior, but haven't trusted you as Lord of their lives. O Lord, grow their faith.

---

[32]   Murray, Andrew, *With Christ in the School of Prayer*, p. 95.

O Lord, we pray for those church members who are letting sin get the better of them. Give them faith to trust Your Word and to claim its promises.

O Lord, we pray for those church members who are not praying for at least one lost soul. Grow their faith in prayer.

O Lord, we pray for those that we know that are lost. Use us to pray for them and to reach out to them so that their faith grows, too.

May the bread we deliver tonight ultimately result in someone feasting at Your table.

Lord, thank You for bringing Bro. A. Please send many more workers to the harvest.

Amen

Prayed as an offertory prayer at an 8:30 Sunday Morning Worship Service.

Holy, holy, holy are You, Lord, of Hosts,
The whole earth is full of Your glory. (See Isa. 6:3)
We will sing of Your mercies forever, Lord.
With our mouths we will make known Your faithfulness to all generations (See Ps. 89:1)
We praise You for Your unconditional love,
for Your abiding presence,
and Your omnipotent power

We will not forget Your benefits, for it is You, Lord,
Who forgives all our iniquities,
Who heals all our diseases,
Who redeems our lives from destruction,

Who crowns us with loving kindness and tender mercies,
And who satisfies our desires with good things,
So that our youth is renewed and is strong like an eagle's. (See Ps. 103:2-5)

Lord, we could come just asking for the ordinary again this morning. We could just ask for another Band-Aid® to put on our wounds and enough oomph to keep us going until next Sunday. We could ask You to bless the gift and the giver here this morning and to use these tithes and offerings and this service for Your glory. And we do ask for these things. But, Lord, You are such a mighty king and so, so rich that we would be remiss and might insult You if we didn't ask for something big, something big that You want us to have. For that reason, Lord, I ask for an invasion from outer space. O Lord, may Your Holy Word and Your preached word so invade our minds and be so powerful here this morning that Your Holy Spirit finds so much submissiveness, so much willingness, so much fertile soil, so many open doors that He is able to invade inner space in our lives that He has never been able to occupy before. O Lord, may the invading forces be so overwhelming that we find ourselves confessing our sins and begging You to come and take complete control of our lives. O Lord, may we find ourselves praying for precisely what we have been scared to pray for in the past, but for which we know You want us to ask. O Lord, when we leave this place may we have a surreal sense that You are in absolute control of our lives, may we be in a mode where we are going to consult You to direct our every action, may we be so dedicated to You that we desire to do nothing in life but Your will, may we feel so much love for You and our fellow believers that we just can't contain it. O Lord, may the invasion here this morning be complete and may it spread like wildfire to other places. May Your Word spread quickly, run its course, be glorified and triumphant. (See 2 Thes. 3:1)

O Lord, in these moments ahead, while Neil and Julie sing, prepare our hearts for the first onslaught.

O Lord, I make these requests in the name of Jesus, not because it gives credence or power to these requests, but because Your Holy Spirit impresses upon me that I am asking for exactly what Jesus would ask for if He were standing here in my place.

Amen

∞

Prayed at a Monday Night Prayer Meeting. Monday Night Prayer Meeting has proven to be a good time to confess sins of the church.

Father Confessor,

Sometimes when it comes time to confess my sins I draw a blank. Lord, I don't think it's arrogance. I don't think it's denial. I think it has more to do with my sins not being as important to me as they should be. To some extent this results from our culture which limits sin to murder, stealing, drunk driving, dealing drugs, intolerance, pedophilia, child abuse, and one or two other newsworthy crimes. O Lord, help each of us who has allowed the world's definition of sin to blind us. But, Lord, the church is also not without blame. Homosexuality, abortion, drunkenness, doing drugs, and adultery are condemned from our pulpits, but aside from not being involved in these particular activities, we find ourselves living lives that don't set us apart from the rest of the world. The only members church discipline is ever performed on are our paid leaders. And like Bro. A. so ably illustrated we come to church all dressed up and pretend we don't have any problems or any sins. We all know the admonition to confess our sins one to another but no one will go first, so we think maybe we're the only one who has sins. And, Lord, I don't hear anyone confessing the sins of the church. Are we also drawing a blank as a corporate body?

Lord, so often when I'm feeling guilty because I can't think of any sins to confess You change my focus from sins of commission to sins of omission and cause me to shift from thinking about the Ten Commandments and start thinking about what You called the most important commandments. Lord, help me and us as a church consider the sin of not loving You with all our heart, all our soul, and all our might all the time. O Lord, we confess that our actions show that we are not fulfilling this commandment. We place other activities ahead of Your time. O Lord, our greatest sin may be how little our actions show we love You! O Lord, help us to worship and adore You. O Lord, help us to add or increase the element of adoration to our prayers. O Lord, help us to have an attitude where we just can't get enough of You.

Lord, help me and the church consider the sin of not loving our neighbors as ourselves. May we find ourselves asking have we loved our neighbors enough today that it cost us time? Have we loved them enough today that it cost us money? Have we loved them enough that we had to humble ourselves? O Lord, has our attitude remained one of love all day long for our fellow man? O Lord, help us to so interact with our fellow man so he is given no reason to think less of You and, indeed, is given reasons to glorify Your name.

Lord, help me and the church consider the sin of not obeying the Great Commission. Have we selfishly been keeping You to ourselves? Whom have we told about Jesus today? Why does the church visitation program primarily visit only people who have visited us? O Lord, we have made valiant efforts to try to get the world to come to us, but what efforts have we made to try to go. After all the command says, "Go." O Lord, give us a compassion for the lost like Yours.

O Lord, we have so much confessing to do in the area of sins of omission concerning these commandments, what seem to be Your most important commandments, that we all of a sudden go from being blank as to what sins we have committed to not having enough time to list all our shortcomings. O Lord, bring us to tears of remorse as a church and as individuals over our great sin in these areas.

Lord, cause us to spend so much time in Your Word and give us spiritual discernment that our sins are immediately recognizable to us. And may we confess them ASAP.

Amen

∞

Prayed at a Monday Night Prayer Meeting.

O Lord Who Spoke Creation into Being,

The true measure of someone's power and authority is if, when they speak, their desires are carried out. O Lord, Your power and Your authority are above all others because when You speak Your every word is always carried out even when it requires unbelievable miracles of incomprehensible proportions. O Lord, we praise You for Your magnificent power and Your unquestionable authority.

Lord, Your Word says, "This is what we speak, not words taught us by human wisdom, but in words taught us by the Spirit expressing spiritual truth in spiritual words." (1 Cor. 2:13 NIV) Lord, we find ourselves in a rather unusual position primarily because in true prayer You are putting Your words in our mouths—and what we ask ends up happening. Lord, we pray asking that, indeed, we may speak Your words as we pray, not because we are repeating words we know You have said or have recorded in Your written Word, not because we know what You want and ask for it, not because our will accidentally coincides with Yours about some issue, but because You have put Your desires in our heart and they have overflowed into our words.

O Lord, may the very process of prayer be used as a tool to change our hearts to yearn for the same things Your heart yearns for. May our study of Your written Word continually reveal Your heart and Your will and lay it on our heart. May our corporate worship major on moving us to be more like You in desire. Lord, when we look upon a crowd may it be with the same love and compassion that Jesus had when he looked

140

upon a crowd. When we see sin in our lives may it be with the same hatred that You have for it. When we consider the lost may they gain the same priority in our lives as they did in Jesus' life. When we look upon human need may it have the same effect on us as it had on Jesus.

Again, Lord, we find ourselves in an unusual position because Your Word indicates that we are raised up with Jesus and that Jesus is seated at Your right hand. Lord, You have purchased a place of honor for us and have offered us the opportunity to unite with Jesus in His spiritual rule seated next to You! Lord, if I understand rightly, You make the decisions and then wait for us to say the words in prayer from our heart which has to be in agreement with Yours and then in Your time what You have willed in Heaven will happen on earth. O Lord, it seems like You have given us power, not power to cause something to happen, but power to activate Your will. But Lord, it seems like great responsibility comes with that power—because if we fail to pray Your will may not get done. O Lord, how many souls have been lost eternally because we have not prayed for them with a heart like Yours. O Lord, help us to overcome that great burden by giving us a compassion like Yours and a sense of exactly whom we should be praying for.

O Lord, we simply open our lives to You, acknowledging our total dependence on You. May we live in Your constant presence. Lord, when we focus on ourselves, trying to effect positive change in our lives by our own efforts we usually seem to fail. But when our attention is focused on Jesus, we begin to absorb and reflect Him. O Lord, help us to make the commitment and spend the time and give up some of the activities that currently fill our time so that we may set our sights on You, bring You into clear focus, and follow Your every move.

Thank you for creating needs in our lives that cause us to pray. Replace our expectations with Your desires.

Amen

Prayed as an offertory prayer at an 8:30 Sunday Morning Worship Service.

Lord of the Harvest,

There is new ground here that needs to be broken this morning. Yes, we may sing our favorite songs, study familiar Scripture, and revisit old truths, but may we not be the same people when this morning is over. May Your Holy Spirit make new inroads into our lives here this morning.

Lord, there are seeds that need to be planted here. May we be careful to do our part. May we say what You want said and do what You want done. And may all of the seeds planted here this morning find fertile soil to grow in.

Lord, there are seeds and seedlings here that need to be watered. May we water them well with our prayers, and with our tears, if need be. And may Your Light shine upon them so they grow.

Lord, there are those here this morning that need to bear fruit. May Your Word and Your Holy Spirit prune them so that their fruit might be plenteous.

Lord, the fields are ripe unto harvest this morning. May our eyes be open to the great need and may our heartstrings be pulled. O Lord, may not one ear of grain be lost.

May Your word spread quickly, run its course, be glorified and triumphant. (See 2 Thes. 3:1)

And may we never stop glorifying You.

Amen

Prayed at a Monday Night Prayer Meeting. It should be noted that FBC, Tullahoma, as a gift to the community, provides an outdoor Living Nativity Scene every year at Christmas. This has grown into what is called Night in Bethlehem, an extravaganza put on December 21-23 every year.

Lord Who Created the First Living Nativity Scene,

As we reread the account over in Matthew, we encounter the verse that says: "...you shall call his name Jesus, for He will save His people from their sins." (Matt. 1:21 Amp) O Lord, we praise you because You keep Your promises big time. We praise You because all of our sins, past, present and future, have been forgiven through the death of Jesus on the cross. But, Lord, we have to praise You less than we could because we haven't claimed all the victory over sin that You have provided.

You see,
even though (Repeat this with indented phrases below or not.)
> Your Word says that love suffereth long; we are still impatient at times,
> Your Word says that love is kind; we have been less than kind with our words at times,
> Your Word says that love envieth not; we experience twinges of jealousy at times,
> Your Word says that love vaunteth not itself; we find ourselves boasting of things other than You,
> Your Word says that love is not puffed up; we experience self-pride all too often,
> Your Word says that love does not behave unseemly; we find ourselves doing just that at times,
> Your Word says that love seeketh not its own; we are selfish at times,
> Your Word says that love is not easily provoked; we are easily irritated.

Your Word says that love thinketh no evil; but our thoughts are not always pure,

Your Word says that love rejoiceth not in iniquity, but rejoiceth in truth; but we think certain sins are fun,

Your Word says that love beareth all things; sometimes we can be heard complaining,

Your Word says that love believeth all things; we sometimes choose not to believe the best about our fellow Christians,

Your Word says that love hopeth all things; Lord, we don't even set out enough chairs to seat our entire SS class,

Your Word says that love endureth all things; sometimes we lay out.[33]

Lord, athletes discipline themselves for the purpose of gaining a great victory on the field. Salesmen control their tempers and their demeanor so they may win a big sale.[34] And many people win the acclaim of their fellow men by living upstanding, moral lives within the laws of society. And, Lord, some of us Christians gain moral victories when we control our appetites and our attitudes and our activities in an effort to imitate Christ. But, Lord, convict all of us of the fact that what You hate most is not the acts of sin we commit, but the mutiny against You that self-government of our own lives represents.

Lord, Your Word indicates that we can attain a state where sin ceases to be a problem in our lives. We are admonished to be perfect even as our Father in Heaven is perfect. We are admonished to be holy and pure. 1 Cor. 10:13 assures us there is a way to resist every temptation that comes our way. Lord, the most impressive testimony I ever heard was from a man in his sixties who had been a homeless wino on the

---

[33] This list originally appeared in An Unknown Christian's *The Victorious Living* at the end of Chapter 3. I modified it significantly, but still many of his original thoughts pervade. An Unknown Christian. "The Victorious Life." *Bibleteacher. org.* Christian Digital Library Foundation, n.d. Web. 5 July 2013. <http://www. bibleteacher.org/VictoriousLife.htm>.

[34] Ibid, Beginning of Chapter 5.

streets of St. Louis. He had lost his job and his family because of his alcoholism. But he wandered into a Salvation Army center and found Jesus, and he experienced complete victory over his alcoholism. Not only did he say he'd never taken another drink, but he said he had never had another desire to take another drink. And the proof was that he was working as a bartender, telling his story to every patron that came in. Then when he had stayed long enough to tell his story to all the regular patrons, he would quit that bar and go to another one and do the same thing. Lord, that goes against conventional wisdom that says once an alcoholic always an alcoholic. That goes against everything that AA would tell us about how our only hope is a constant struggle with a network of others to help us.

Lord, I can only understand how he obtained total victory over his sin and I still struggle is if the difference is that he gave 100% of his life to Jesus where I've been holding back some. O Lord, I want to completely surrender to You. May we not just have the victory of having enough strength to refrain from sinning. But may we have the victory of not wanting to sin. Lord, remind us again and again that we become the person you want us to be not by struggling against sin but by completely submitting to You. Lord, help us to surrender ourselves completely into Your hands. Come and take complete possession of our being so we may be able to say with Paul, "I live, and yet no longer I, but Christ liveth in me." (Gal:2:20 KJV) May You have all there is of each of us. O Lord, may Your power be made perfect through our weakness. (See 2 Cor. 12:9) May perfect love cast out the great list of little sins in our lives and fill our entire being. O Jesus, make us holy and keep us holy. Give us the complete victory over sin. Lord, we're willing to be willing. O Lord, make us more than conquerors. (See Rom. 8:37)

Lord, may we have the mind of Christ in us and power from on high so that holiness becomes our very life. Lord, we know that victory over sin in our lives is not a one-time deal, but rather a moment-by-moment thing. Help us to demonstrate faith in You and submit to You moment by moment so that You can have that victory in our lives moment by moment. Lord, may this kind of victory over sin not just be in one or two of us, but may it become the norm here at FBC. And may we the people of FBC be so submissive to You that there is such an atmosphere of victory here that this community is affected. O Lord, we pray that we may get so submissive, so humble, so low, so hungry, so concerned, so passionate, so broken, so clean, so prayerful that that submissiveness becomes so infectious that it permeates this entire country. O Lord, may the devil's kingdom be shaken, may his power be broken, may his prisoners be released, may history be changed. May people who wait in darkness by the millions see the light.

O Lord, may we be known as a church whose meat is to do Your will.

Amen

Written after reading An Unknown Christian's *The Victorious Living* and Leonard Ravenill's *Sodom Had No Bible*.

Prayed at Monday Night Prayer Meeting. Of particular note is the name Kirk. This is a young man who grew up here at FBC, went off to college, and became a hardened atheist. He became the number one person on my prayer list when he was in my Sunday School class as an eighth grader. I prayed for this young man every day for very close to twenty years. I and many others spent many hours and shed many tears praying for Kirk's salvation. He gave his life to Jesus when he was in his thirties.

O God Who Hears Our Prayers,

You delighted in the prayers of Enoch who walked and talked with You and then was not. (See Gen. 5:24) You heard the prayers of Abraham and delivered Lot from Sodom and gave Sarah a child in her old age. You reveled to answer Elijah's prayers, raising the dead, sending fire from heaven, giving drought and then rain. You heard the prayers of Daniel in far-off Babylon and delivered him from the lions and revealed to him Nebuchadnezzar's dream. You answered the prayer of the Canaanite woman and the Roman Centurion. You heard the prayer of the thief on the cross. You heard the prayer of the sinful as well and the upright and godly. You heard the prayers of the publican and the sinner.

Lord, we thank you for answering the prayers of unworthy creatures at times and showing them mercy, for we were once unworthy creatures praying to You and You showed us mercy. O Lord, we praise You because it is part of Your unchangeable nature to hear prayers. O Lord, we praise You for whatever it is that You put in us to cause us to pray to You. Lord, we praise You because not only are You the prayer-hearing god, but You are the prayer-answering god. You are the rewarder of them who diligently seek You. O Lord, we praise You because You are not only a prayer-hearing god and a prayer-answering god, but because You work miracles in our midst. O Lord, may we be a church that gives testimony of the definite, miraculous answers to prayers that You work in our midst so that our young people will have no doubt that You are a prayer-hearing, prayer-answering, miracle-working god. May we be able to prove to the unbelieving world that You are indeed God by being able to show them the answers to our prayers. Lord, may people be saved as a result of seeing our prayers answered. May this church see the conversions of drunks and prostitutes and hardened atheists and agnostics that we pray for. May we see their lives changed and hear their testimonies. O Lord, save the most outrageous sinner in this town to bring testimony of Your saving power.

Lord, Your Word recounts a parable about a man who goes to a friend at midnight saying to him, "Friend, lend me three loaves for a friend of mine in his journey is come to me and I have nothing to set before him." (Luke 11:5 KJV) And Jesus said that this man longing to have bread for his friend got it by persevering. O Lord, we long to have the bread of life for some of our unsaved friends. O Lord, I beg You for the bread of life for Nathan, Josh, Kirk, Chris, and Stephen. Lord, I pray for some young men who I believe have given their lives to you but haven't followed through with public acknowledgment or baptism. I pray for Josh, Jackson, Hunter, and Brian. Lord, I pray for a young man named Austin whose dad limits Austin's involvement in church to Sunday mornings.

Lord, as we read last night, You promised the Israelites as they prepared to go in and take the Promised Land, that "every place that the sole of their feet shall tread upon, that have You given unto them." (Joshua 1:3 KJV) Lord, we are in a spiritual warfare whereby through faith and prayer souls can be won for Christ. Lord, grant to us a similar promise. Lord, for every soul we pray will You put feet to our prayers and give us every place that our foot shall tread. Lord, not only do we pray for individuals by name who need to be saved. We pray asking You for the same promise You gave the Israelites. May You give us all the territory our feet shall tread. Lord, we first claim the very confines of this church structure. May we be true to pray for every lost soul who darkens these doors. Lord, may we claim the halls of THS. In particular, Lord, may our Youth department undertake praying for every freshman at THS. Lord, may we claim the Freshman class at THS as our territory. Lord, may we claim Continental Apartments and Brandywine Apartments and Arnold Village and Tara and Abbott and Sharondale and Kaywood and Colonial Acres and Bel Aire and Kings Ridge. And Lord, will You put feet to our prayers and may we claim all the territory You want us to claim. And Lord, we pray for more feet—send more workers to the fields. Lord, may we your people at FBC feel the leading of Your Holy Spirit to understand what territory our feet should tread upon. Then Lord, may we assault the gates of Heaven until the victory of that territory is final. May our prayers be unceasing. Fill us with Your Holy Spirit. May we pray with an energy that never tires, a persistency that cannot be denied, and a courage which never fails.

O Lord, Samuel said to the Israelites something like "...far be it from me that I should sin against the Lord by failing to pray for you." (1 Sam.12:23 NIV) Lord, forbid that we as a church and as individuals should sin against anyone by failing or ceasing to pray for them. Lord, forbid that we Sunday School teachers should fail or cease to pray for our class members. Lord, forbid that any deacons fail or cease to pray for our deacon families. Lord, may we pray for our families as David did for Solomon that they have a perfect heart to keep Your commandments and Your statutes. (See 1 Chron. 29:19) May they not only obey You but delight in doing so.

May Your Word spread quickly, run its course, be glorified and triumphant. (2 Thes. 3:1)

Amen

∞

Prayed as an offertory prayer at an 8:30 Sunday Morning Worship Service. Our Sunday Morning Worship Service has been broadcast on the radio for over fifty years. Only recently have our services also been on TV.

Lord of Love,

We praise You because love is so much of Your character that Your Word even says that You are love.
We thank You because You love us even better than we love ourselves.
We thank You because You loved us while we were yet sinners. (See Rom. 5:8)
We thank You because You showed Your love for us by dying in our place on the cross.
We thank You because You love each of us as if we were the only ones You had to love.
We thank You because You call Your sheep by their names.
We praise You because You are like the shepherd who misses even one lost from his flock,
    You are like the housewife who searches diligently for the lost coin,
    You are like the father who grieves for one boy gone wrong.

149

O Lord, may we share Your grief for those boys and girls, some of whom are now men and women, who have been rebellious and are still lost. We know it is not Your will that even one of these should be lost. Open the door for Your message to these. When opportunity arises for speaking with any of these may we have courage to speak, not hesitantly or with shame, but powerfully with joy. Give us the boldness we need. Break hearts that are hardened; melt hearts that are cold. And, Lord, cause us to pray diligently for these and to send out a search party for those lost souls who are so lost they can't find their way to church.

Lord, will You open hearts and minds this Sunday morning that have been closed to Your Word. May some actually hear and understand something of the Gospel through the radio and TV and have their reliance in themselves shaken. May Your Truth be glorified here this Sunday morning. May your leaders and teachers stand on Your Word. And may there be a deep submission to it.

O Lord, embolden us to mobilize Your church to do Your will. Help us to develop the prayer habit so we can call Your will down from Heaven. O Lord, may we be a listening people, hearing Your voice and following Your leading. Empower us to carry out Your commands here on earth. May we have no desire but to accomplish Your will.

Lord, we pray for the leaders of this country and others. May they make decisions that result in an environment where Your Word may flourish and great numbers of people may come to a saving knowledge of You.

Lord, we pray for those who laugh and make fun of Christianity and Christians. Lay not this sin to their charge.

Keep us from the Evil One.

Amen

Prayed during Monday Night Prayer Meeting.

O Lord, is it I?

Is it I who am responsible for millions sitting in darkness just waiting for their time to begin spending eternity in a sinner's hell?

Is it I who sit around complaining about the whole nation going to hell, but am doing nothing to prevent even one individual from doing just that?

Is it I who spend more time organizing activities down at the church than agonizing over 5 billion lost people this world?

Is it I who judge my Christian walk by how well I play church and how good I am rather than by how much fruit I bear?

Is it I who have failed to shed even one tear for the lost this week?

Is it I who have failed to witness to even one lost person this week?

Is it I who have, in effect, robbed You of considerable glory by not doing my part?

O Lord, I confess.

O Lord, sentence me to focusing on why You really died on the cross?

O Lord, sentence me to spend hours looking at the lost from Your perspective.

O Lord, sentence me to loving the lost the same way You do.

O Lord, sentence me to praying for them with the same agony You have for them.

O Lord, sentence me to yield to Your every urging to spread Your Word and witness.

O Lord, may this church cease from being a refrigerator for the preservation of the saints and become a command center for the seeking and saving that which is lost. May we be the epicenter for a movement that will shake the world through prayer and concern for the lost and submissiveness to Your will.

Amen

∞

Prayed at Monday Night Prayer Meeting.

Lord of the Harvest,

I've heard of certain promotional schemes put on by radio stations where one of the announcers lived on top of a billboard or flag pole until the town's team won another game. O Lord, may we camp out on Your doorstep until revival comes in a mighty way in this place. May we be incessant in badgering You about it. O Lord, may we become the proverbial squeaky wheel that gets the grease. O Lord, may we assault the gates of Heaven with our petitions until Your Holy Spirit reigns in this place.

Lord, Paul referred to a problem in 2 Corinthians about how the gospel is veiled to those who are perishing, for the god of this world has blinded the minds of the unbelieving that they might not understand the gospel or see the glory of Christ. (See 2 Cor. 4:3-4) O Lord, we see the same problem in our little piece of this world. The god of this world has worked through the media and the government and individuals to produce a society in which the gospel is not allowed to be discussed in many places and is treated as some sort of mythology believed by the ignorant in other places. Lord, the god of this world has tricked many into worshipping the gods of knowledge and tolerance and personal development. Many are following their personal spirits. O Lord, would you bind the god of this world and overcome these gods of knowledge and tolerance and personal development and self?

Paul also addressed another problem in 2 Corinthians, arguments and pride. (See 2 Cor. 10:3-5) O Lord, arguments and self-pride are the very strongholds which set themselves up against knowing You. O Lord, would You pull down these strongholds and bind these gods so that once again the lost of this community would be open to Your message, be able to see Your truth, be able to recognize their own sins, and would be able to accept Your Son?

Then, Lord, there is one more piece of the puzzle that has to be put in place. Lord, there is an apathy here among Your people concerning the lost. Yet Your Word indicates that we must stand in the gap and intercede for these in order for them to be saved. And Your Word says: How shall they call on Him in whom they have not believed, and how shall they believe on Him in whom they have not heard, and how shall they hear without a preacher. (See Rom. 10:14) Lord, we confess that we have not done our part. Please, use Your Holy Spirit to convict us of the need to pray for the lost, to either bring them to church to hear a preacher or be one to them.

And, Lord, please bring many more laborers to the harvest for we are not willing that any should perish.

To You be the glory, both now and forever. (See Heb. 13:21)

Amen

Prayed as an offertory prayer at an 8:30 Sunday Morning Worship Service.

Gentle Shepherd,

You knock on the door of our hearts, but won't force Your way in.
You know our every weakness, but won't take advantage of us.
You know all our sins and faults, but won't broadcast them to the world.
You bind our wounds and tend to our hurts.
You caressed us as You knitted us together in our mother's womb and watch over us as we sleep.
You came in the form of a baby and walked on earth as a man so we might feel more comfortable with You.
You died on the cross so we wouldn't have to pay the penalty for our sins.

O Lord, we thank You for Your gentle love. We thank You for making the ultimate sacrifice for us. We adore You because Your Word says that no one can snatch Your sheep from Your hand.

O Lord, we confess that we have thwarted some of Your plans to make life for us abundant and free from the ravages of sin and free from anxiety and one that glorifies You through our every action. We have hindered Your purposes with our will and our hesitations and our doubts. O Lord, open Your arms wide and hug us tight and make us feel loved again. O Lord, we need to feel Your gentle chiding and reproofs. Use Your Word and Your Holy Spirit this morning to accomplish exactly that. Use them to prune our lives and excite us to Your work.

O Lord, the world is cruel and hurts us. Steady our hearts to meet whatever comes our way. And may we reflect Your gentle love as we deal with others. And may we spread that love everywhere we go. And may these tithes and offerings be used to spread it even further.

And, Lord, may any here who have heard Your gentle knocking and not opened the door hear Your gentle knock again this morning and open that door and dine with You.

Amen

∞

Prayed at a Monday Night Prayer Meeting.

Father in Heaven,

I confess to having been envious of those who have a better testimony than I—who have been drunks or on drugs, murderers, or adulterers and found You. I confess not only to being envious of their great testimonies, but also of how they can easily relate to the lost who have major problems in their lives, and how they are more thankful than I, and how they are more dedicated to You than I.

Lord, I thank You for a new perspective. Thank You for bringing to my attention the verses over in Matthew 22:37-38 (NIV) that read: "Love the Lord your God with all your heart and with all your soul and with all your mind. This is the first and greatest commandment." Thank You for letting me see that breaking the greatest commandment obviously results in the greatest sin. Thank You for letting me see from Your perspective no one has committed a greater sin than I.

Lord, I pray for all the people of this community who might come to their senses if confronted with the question: "Are you aware that you have committed the greatest sin that any person could ever commit?" and these verses.

First, I pray that we as a church, as a body of individuals, would become peacemakers by being confrontational with Your Good News when and where Your Spirit leads.

Secondly, I pray that You would make a holy visitation to each of these so that Your Holy Spirit might complement Your Word.

Amen

❧

Our church conducts a worship service at Life Care of Tullahoma, one of our local nursing homes, every Sunday. I have had the honor of filling in as the one bringing the message a few times when others have had to be away. I always begin with the prayer that follows. I'm also Chairman of our Deacon Hospital Visitation Team which supplements our church staff's visitation and our Deacon Family Care Plan visitation so that, hopefully, no church member misses being visited every day while in the hospital. And I usually use some form of this prayer when I visit in the hospital or make a pre-hospital visit. Plug in the name for the blank. I usually pray this prayer very powerfully (speak loud and resolutely).

Linda is one of my wife's very best friends. So naturally, when she fell and broke her hip we went to the hospital to visit. I knew Linda's favorite verse so I incorporated it into my prayer. Afterwards the Holy Spirit convicted me as to how this verse was not only the perfect verse for Linda and her situation at that time, but also apropos for just about any hospital visit.

Almighty Heavenly Father,

What a mighty God you are! There is nothing you can't do—no sickness you can't heal, no miracle you can't perform, no problem you can't solve, no life you can't revitalize, no need you can't provide for, no sin you can't forgive.

Lord, your Word says that
Even youths grow tired and weary,
and young men stumble and fall;

but those who hope in the Lord
will renew their strength.
They will soar on wings like eagles,
they will run and not grow weary,
they will walk and not be faint. (Isa. 40:30-31 NIV)

Lord, we know that _____ has put his/her hope and faith in you a long time ago and we know that he/she is relying on you to address his/her current problem. Lord, I claim the promise of that verse for him/her that you're going to once again restore him/her again and renew his/her strength so once again he'll/she'll be able to walk and not be faint and run and not be weary. And that's what I pray for—that you would heal him/her in accord with your will. Wrap Your loving arms around him/her and help him/her to feel your presence. Give him/her strength and perseverance and help him/her to know that we love him/her and are continuing to pray for him/her.

In Jesus' name,

Amen.

If this person has cancer or is worried about cancer, I add in something like the following:

Lord, we know in Your infinite wisdom and omniscience that when you knit _____ together in his/her mother's womb that every cell was designed to do a particular function and that's all it did. Lord, we're asking that by whatever means necessary, by surgery, radiation, chemotherapy, immunotherapy, or through Your miraculous intervention, You would restore him/her to the point where once again every cell in his/her body does only exactly what You originally intended for it to do and nothing else.

Note: I originally encountered the ideas found in this last paragraph in a prayer being offered up for Larry Burkett and his cancer in a book somewhere—but I don't know where.

∞

Prayed at Monday Night Prayer Meeting.

O Lord Who Sometimes Gives Second Chances,

We come confessing that we need another chance. You see, just as when You said to the disciples to put out into the deep water and let down the nets and Peter was skeptical and said, "Master, we worked hard all night long and haven't caught anything," (See Luke 5:5 NIV) we confess that when You have asked us to do the ordinary, sometimes we failed You in deed or attitude or both. O Lord, help us to follow Your every command.

Or, Lord, we've been like Peter and the other disciples who, when they first saw You walking on the water, thought You were a ghost. O Lord, our focus has been so much on other things that we, too, don't always recognize You when You come. Help us to see You in the hitchhiker and the down and out and in those who are in need—because You have said when we have done it unto these that we have done it unto You. O Lord, help us to recognize Your leading every time You try to lead us.

Or, Lord, we may not have argued out loud with our fellow Christians as to which of us is greatest as Peter did, but in our own minds we have justified ourselves by saying we're better than certain others. O Lord, we have allowed selfish pride to reign in our lives. Which of us hasn't thought our opinion so important it needed to be heard above all others. O Lord, help us to be humble.

Or, Lord, we have either questioned your eternal plan or had thoughts so out of tune with Your thoughts that we deserved, as Peter did, to hear the words: Get behind me Satan; You are a stumbling block to me. You do not have in mind the things of God, but the things of men (See Matt 16:13). O Lord, take our focus off of this world and put it on Your kingdom.

O Lord, we have, in effect, sliced off some servant's ear and need to feel Your rebuke because, like Peter, we have been pushing our agenda instead of Yours. O Lord, help us to work with You instead of trying to work for You.

Or, Lord, like Peter, we have promised You we were going to do something only to hear the cock crow and to recognize that we have done exactly the opposite. O Lord, help us to be as faithful to keep our promises to You as You are to us.

O Lord, give us another chance—but not just another chance to try to get it right, but a chance to turn it over to You. And, Lord, just as You saw the great potential in Peter despite his shortcomings, grow us to the point where You might use us to preach a sermon and three thousand be saved or to take the Good News to a Cornelius and his family or to offer the gift of the Savior to a blind beggar, or to do Your bidding whatever it may be.

O Lord, may we be remembered not for our failures, but for Your successes.

O Lord, help us to have the kind of commitment that Peter ultimately had—the kind that will follow You anywhere, do whatever You ask, love You intensely, and be willing to give up our life for You and then say we're not even worthy to die the same way You did. O Lord, may we have the kind of faith, rock solid, upon which You can build and grow Your church. O Lord, help us to become a church full of people with faith like Peter's.

Amen

Prayer at Monday Night Prayer Meeting prior to a Wednesday night rally for the all employees of the public school system in Tullahoma at the beginning of the school year

Father of Faith,

Your Word says that our thoughts are not Your thoughts and our ways are not Your ways. For as the heavens are higher than the earth, so are Your ways higher than our ways and Your thoughts higher than our thoughts. (See Isa. 55:8-9)

O Lord, we praise You because You have continually surprised and blessed us in ways we hadn't even thought of. We humans were surprised when David, the least likely of Jesse's sons, was chosen to be king. We humans were taken aback when You let Lazarus die. We humans were puzzled when You chose to speak to Elijah, not in the dramatic events of Mount Carmel, not in the earthquake, not in the storm, but in the still small voice. Most of us humans here on earth still choose not to believe in the incarnation, in Your humble birth in a stable, in Your simple life as a carpenter, in Your death on the cross, in Your resurrection, and in the gift of Your Holy Spirit. O Lord, who would ever have thought of such a plan? No one but You, o Lord. You answered the urgent prayer of the church to release Peter from prison in such a miraculous way that at first even those praying didn't believe it.

O Lord, I come tonight praying for things that my finite mind can comprehend, things Your Holy Spirit impresses upon me to pray for, but for which I have no understanding of how they can be accomplished. These are not things which man can accomplish. Lord, I pray that every employee of the Tullahoma School System who needs to hear Your Gospel message will hear it Wednesday night. Lord, I pray that as Brother A. preaches the message You've laid on his heart Your Holy Spirit will succeed in getting across to each person here the message You need to lay on their heart. O Lord, I pray that every person here will be receptive to Your message for them. Lord, I pray that somehow Your agenda might be accomplished here Wednesday night.

O Lord, I come tonight praying that You would work Your will through and in this church. O Lord, I can't imagine the number of people you want to bring to a saving knowledge of Jesus Christ through the efforts begun in this church. O Lord, I can't imagine the number of additional workers that need to be added to our number to reach all those that need to be reached. I can't imagine the depth of commitment that You want from us or how You can move us from where we are to where You want us to be. O Lord, we confess to being narrow minded, to being negative, to complaining, to not having enough faith, to not involving ourselves in Your Word or in prayer near enough. Lord, I can't imagine the persecution, the suffering, the tears that might need to be shed. But I would like to pray for Your desires for this church to happen. I can't express in words how that might happen because I can't even imagine how You might plan to get it done. But I know I believe You can do it. O Lord, I once again pray that this church would become that one church in all of history, past, present and future, that comes closest to being all that You want it to be. O Lord, would You require of us to do whatever it is that causes that to happen—and then help us to do it?

In the meanwhile, Lord,
Your will where You will when You will.

Amen

✺

Prayed at Monday Night Prayer Meeting.

Hey, Lord,

It's just us again. We ain't many. And what there are of us here ain't much. But for the moment, I guess You're stuck with just us.

161

Lord, we thank You for calling us here tonight and thank you for getting us here—most of us wouldn't have made it if it hadn't been for You.

Lord, we know You don't need our help. You were doing fine before we came along, and You'll do fine after we're long gone. But we sure appreciate You allowing us to have a little piece of the action anyway, even though we ain't hardly worthy. Lord, we know that You do whatever You please and can do it without our help.

But do know that, just like we told the preacher yesterday morning, we're available, just in case You've got something more in mind for us to do. Yeah, we'd like to tell You that we've already made up our mind to do whatever You ask, but You know better than that, You know where we draw the line. I hear tell that You can do more with one person 100% committed to You than You can with 100 people 80% committed. If that's the case Lord, You might consider bringing some more people on board 'cause most of us are more like 80%-ers. But in all seriousness, Lord, don't give up on us and leave us stuck where we are. Lord, it's kind of like You gave us a car when we were born. When we got saved we let You get in the back seat and ride around with us. Lord, You were such an irritating back-seat driver—always warning us of every curve in the road, always telling us "I told you so." every time we messed up, we finally let You come sit in the front seat and do a little navigating. And now You keep tapping us on the shoulder asking if You can drive. Lord, You know we're scared to let You drive—You might drive too fast or take us where we don't want to go. Or if we let You drive, You might not let us back in the driver's seat again. Lord, we just don't trust You enough—not that we don't want to because our brains say that You would be the perfect chauffeur and take us to all the best places. Therefore, if'n You don't mind, grow our faith, Lord, so we won't be so scared to step up to that next level of commitment?

Lord, I was hoping that with me out of the way for a couple of weeks on vacation that You'd get all the problems down here at the church house solved. But now that I've been back for a while it's obvious one of two things have happened: either I brought 'em back with me or else some of these other folk are part of the problem, too. Could You help us out a little bit, Lord? First off, we don't all seem to be tuned into the same channel. If You go to business meeting or deacon's meeting—and, of course, some of us wonder whether You even get an invitation sometimes, it's obvious that some of us are tuned into different channels than others. And all those who speak do so as if they're getting a 50,000-watt, clear channel signal straight from Your transmitter. Lord, could You help us fine-tune Your station. Could You help us discern between the real thing and the cheap imitations we sometimes hear. Lord, help us to tell the difference between Your voice and the voice of our gut. Lord, help us to tell the difference between Your voice and the voice of Old Scratch. Lord, help us lock into Your signal.

Lord, another problem down here at the church house that hasn't gone away is that some of us are narrow-minded, critical, or negative. And, Heaven forbid, some of us are all three. Lord, we know that when a baby is raised by parents who are harsh, abusive, and angry it grows into a harsh, abusive, angry growed-up person. That's why we know that when we see narrow-minded, critical, negative Christians we know they haven't spent enough time with their positive, affirming, broad-minded Father in Heaven. Lord, we know that it was Your intent that every person be saved and loved by You. But a lot of us got saved but we didn't allow ourselves to experience the love that follows. O Lord, I plead with You that You would cause Your Holy Spirit to work overtime in our lives to cause us to take the effort and spend the time to get to know You and experience You to the point where our attitudes are a reflection of having spent so much time with You.

O Lord, we praise You because You love us just the way we are. O Lord, we praise You because You love us too much to let us stay that way.[35]

---

[35]   I don't know where I first heard this, but when I searched for it on the Internet,

O Lord, we celebrate Your gift of prayer because we know that You didn't invent it so we would get better—even though we will. O Lord, we celebrate Your gift of prayer because we know that You didn't invent it so we would become holy—even though we will. O Lord, we celebrate Your gift of prayer because we know that You didn't invent it so it would make us more like Jesus—even though it will. But You invented it because You love us and want to spend time with us—Lord, may Your gift of prayer do everything you intended for it to do in our lives.

Lord, we pray for a healthy dose of Your concern for others.

To You be the glory and dominion forever. (See 1 Pet. 5:11)

Amen

Prayed at a Pre-Service Deacon-Pastor Prayer Time on Sunday morning.

Lord and Master,

We ask You to keep the problems within this fold to a minimum so that our shepherd can concentrate on catching Your vision, sharing Your vision and sharing Your Gospel message.

Continually give Him Your sense of urgency.
Continually let his prayer time maintain priority in his life.
Let his love for Jesus grow every day.
May he only get marching orders from You.
Keep him Kingdom oriented.
Encourage him by fulfilling Your promises.

I found it as Ford, Leighton, Leighton Ford Quotes, www.searchquotes.com/quotation/God_loves_us_the_way_we_are,_but_too_much_to_leave_us_that_way./1005/.

May we Your sheep hear his voice this morning and follow You.

And may You receive all the glory.

Amen

❧

Prayed at Monday Night Prayer Meeting.

Holy Father,

You didn't call us to be super salesmen who can sell snowballs in Alaska. You didn't call us to twist arms and trick people into accepting You as Lord and Savior. But You called us to pray to release the strongholds Satan has built up in the hearts of people, to pray to remove the spiritual blinders he has put on their eyes, to pray to prevent Satan from snatching the seed of the Gospel planted in their hearts. And You called us to lead holy lives such that others might see Jesus in us. And You called us to take Your Word unto the uttermost parts of the world. O Lord, may we be true to our calling to pray for the lost, to lead holy lives before them, and to tell them about Jesus.

Lord, You didn't call us to hire mercenaries to fight the battle that rages for the hearts and souls of men and women in this world. But You called us to put on the belt of truth, the breastplate of righteousness, the shield of faith, the helmet of salvation, and to have feet shod with the preparation of the Gospel, (See Eph. 6:11+) and to join Your army and fight with Christ as our captain using the strategies of prayer and love, not that men might die, but that they might live. O Lord, may we, the people of FBC, be true to our calling to accept our sacred role as the army of God and to join in the intercession for the lost so that there might be a great harvest of souls.

Lord, You didn't call us to hire orators to thank You or musicians to praise You. But You called us to make a joyful noise unto You. O Lord, may we be so true to our calling to make a joyful noise unto You that the rocks and trees are in tears because they can't be heard above us and can't ever find a time when we're not loud and vocal in praising and thanking You.

Lord, You didn't call us to build ornate church buildings or magnificent structures to honor You. But You called us to be Your church, to be Your people, to love one another, to be united and to edify Your church with encouraging words, and to do only those things that are beneficial. O Lord, may none of us ever be guilty of tearing down Your church by complaining or by being negative, but may we be true to our calling to build up Your church with encouraging words and by doing only that which is beneficial.

Lord, You didn't call any of us to be loners. You didn't call any of us to try to save the whole world all by ourselves. You didn't call any of us to do our own thing. But You called us to be part of Your church, part of the body of Christ, a body in which if the big toe hurts the whole body suffers, a body in which if the tongue tastes something sweet the whole body enjoys it, a body in which each part has its own function and is not jealous of any other part. O Lord, may we, Your body at FBC, be true to our calling to be a well-trained, well-conditioned, growing, living body whose members work in perfect concert to do Your every desire.

Lord, You didn't call us to be in charge down here at the church or even to take the reins of our own lives and lead. You didn't call us to have our own way or to lead lives of ease. But You have called us to give up our right to be right, to give up our worldly desires and to put You on the throne of our lives. O Lord, may we be true to our calling to abandon ourselves into Your hands, to be submissive to Your will, to humble ourselves before You and others and to let You reign. O Lord, let Your will be done in us—and in all Your creatures. We desire nothing more than this.

Lord, You didn't call any of us to worry about what other people think, or to be perfectionists, or to be workaholics. You didn't call any of us to be slaves to the guilt trips our parents may have burdened us with or to be slaves to any past sin. But, Lord, You have called us to bask in Your unconditional love and to accept the freedom that You want us to have. O Lord, may we be true to our calling to be in constant fellowship with You. O Lord, may it move us to the point where we delight in You and You delight in us.

Lord, You didn't call any of us to be Martha's who never take time to sit at the feet of Jesus. You didn't call any of us to be valued by what we do. But You called us to feed upon Your Word and to pray without ceasing. O Lord, help us to be true to our calling to love You with all our heart, with all our soul, and with all our might.

Lord, You didn't call any of us to be legalists, trying to live up to the Ten Commandments and church doctrine and making sure that everybody else does, too. But You set us free by the redemptive work of Jesus on the cross. Lord, just as You didn't call us to continue to live under the bondage of sin, You didn't call us to continue to live under the bondage of a set of rules. O Lord, may we be true to our calling, not to focus on a set of rules, not to focus on being good, not to focus on good deeds, but to focus on Jesus. And Lord, may we be true to our calling to extend the grace and love of Christ to all those we come into contact with. May we see to it that no one misses out on Your grace.

O Lord, may we run in the path of Your commands, for You have set our hearts free. (See Ps. 119:32)

Amen

∽

Prayed at a Monday Night Prayer Meeting.

O Lord Who Called Us to Righteousness and Desires to Hold Us in His Hand and Keep Us Forever,

We come confessing. We confess to being smug. After all, once saved, always saved! We know we're Your children and going to Heaven. We're involved in Your work and just voted to do two construction projects, and we're members of the fastest growing church in town. O Lord, we've planted ourselves beside Your living water and have put out roots so we'll never be parched. But, Lord, make us so we can't live with ourselves until that river of living water flows right through us.

Lord, we confess the sins of self-righteousness and self-pride. O Lord, for the vision to see ourselves through the eyes of others! O Lord, for the vision to see ourselves through Your eyes!

O Lord, we confess to letting our minds continually drift toward worldly and secular things. We find ourselves thinking thoughts we don't even want to think. We find ourselves in conversations we are not using for Your glory. O Lord, the average conversation between two church members isn't about Your work or Your Word or Your things, rather it's about the weather or sports or politics or stuff on the evening news. O Lord, make Your Kingdom so important to us that conversations are all aimed at bringing You glory. O Lord, currently we find ourselves saying things that are better left unsaid. Move us to the point where we find ourselves saying the things that need to be said—and You get the glory.

Lord, we seem to have a preconceived idea of what is right and wrong. And we confess that we're trying to live by a set of rules instead of in relationship with You. You see, when it comes time to vote around here, so many of us are voting based on what we think or what our opinion is because we don't know how to discern the will of God because when we pray, if we pray, we don't let You get a word in edgewise. And some of us have said no to Your will so many times You've quit communicating to us anyway. O Lord, correct the mindset that some of us have that we were saved by grace but we are kept by works. O Lord, help us all to experience You.

Lord, we confess to putting our families ahead of You. Lord, we've become a church where it is accepted that if Little Johnny has a soccer game on Sunday in Chattanooga that the whole family goes—never giving You a second thought. If the Vols play a night game in Knoxville on Saturday that the whole family makes a weekend of it—never giving You a second thought. If we haven't seen the kids or Mom and Dad in three weeks, take the weekend and go see them—never giving You a second thought. Lord, whatever happened to people taking a stand for You and saying, "No, Sunday is the Lord's Day, and I'm going to be in the house of the Lord come Sunday no matter who's got a game?"

Lord, we come confessing that our enthusiasm shows we're more attached to our favorite team than we are to You.

Lord, our actions show that we're more interested in pleasing others than we are in pleasing You.

Lord, we confess that we spend more time watching TV than we do in Your Word.

Lord, we confess that if You did try to tell us what Your will is for our lives we wouldn't recognize Your voice—but probably we aren't expecting You anyway.

Lord, we confess that we don't trust You enough to turn all of our problems over to You—we'd rather worry about most of them ourselves.

Lord, we confess to spending more time grumbling about the music than we spend praying about it.

Lord, we confess that we fall into one of two categories: either we forgot to give You the glory for our success or we say we give You the glory but we take the credit.

Lord, we confess that we've failed to invite one person to church this week, much less invited one to accept You as Lord and Savior.

Lord, we confess that we trust in our bank account or 401(k) plan to provide for our future more than we do in You.

And, Lord, the list could go on and on—and what's so bad is that we've had these sins in our lives for years—and the situation hasn't been improving. Lord, we ask not that You would discipline us, but would You empty us?

May we no longer be so attached to our families that they take priority over You. But may we turn their care and protection over to You. May we be ready to yield them to Your purposes—whether here on earth or in heaven.

Empty us of our attachment to worldly things. May our prize possession be You. May no material possession possess us.

May no earthly activities keep us from our appointments with you and for You. May we not be so attached to any earthly process or methodology that it blinds us to Your truth.

Amen

Prayed at a Sunday Night Worship Service.

Jehovah Raffa, God Who Heals,

We could make our first priority to lift to You those who are physically ill, but when we remember the story of the paralytic who was lowered through the roof by four friends and set before Jesus, we recall that Your first concern was his spiritual condition—as apparently was the case with all the sick who were brought to You. For that reason, Lord, I first lift to You every lost soul whose name appears on the prayer lists of the people who are here tonight. Lord, I very specifically ask that You would raise our level of concern for them to the exact same level that You have for them.

Then, too, Lord, Paul asked three times that his thorn in the flesh be removed but You chose to use it as a humbling device. But there is never recorded any prayer for spiritual healing that You denied. For that reason, Lord, I specifically pray that You would heal each of us here tonight of our spiritual handicaps and illnesses. O Lord, some of us, even though we're saved and going to Heaven, are standing in the need of much prayer. We can't pray for the sick effectively because we have distanced ourselves from You.

Lord, we know that before our prayers can be answered we must confess our sins. O Lord, we first confess that we haven't been confessing our sins regularly. O Lord, give us the desire to keep short accounts with You.

O Lord, Your holy anger is an unchanging part of Your nature. You are eternally angry at sin and unrighteousness and injustice. But You are never vindictive, never get mad, never lose control. But, Lord, we confess that we are guilty of unholy anger—anger that comes suddenly, that is vindictive, and sometimes causes us to lose control. Lord, sometimes we pretend that our anger is holy anger by couching it in the term 'righteous indignation,' even when it wasn't. O Lord, help us to have sudden feelings of love rather than sudden feelings of anger.

O Lord, we also confess that we don't have enough faith. Even as we pray some of us don't believe what we are praying for will come to pass. Some of us don't believe You have the ability or desire to intervene in our daily lives to bring about what we pray for. Lord, some of us express lack of faith by failing to claim Your promises. Some of us express our lack of faith by worrying about things even though You said to be anxious about nothing, to just turn it all over to You. O Lord, we pray very specifically that You would increase the faith of every believer here tonight.

Lord, Your Word says that You forgive our debts and we should forgive our debtors. Lord, some of us have said the words, "I forgive," but we still remember. And that memory affects our actions. O Lord, give us the love to forgive and forget.

O Lord, Your Word says to seek first Your kingdom and Your righteousness. (See Matt. 6:33) We confess that there are many times lately when we haven't put You first. We've been doing our own thing, satisfying our own desires. O Lord, help us to make You the lord of our lives on a moment-by-moment basis.

O Lord, Your Word says to go into all the world and preach the Gospel to every creature. (See Mark 16:15) We confess that we've been quietly staying close to home. O Lord, convict us of our need to be more involved in spreading Your Good News.

O Lord, Your Word says that all men shall know that we are Your disciples if we love one another. (See John 13:35) O Lord, we confess to thinking less of some of our fellow Christians than we should and of even saying things about them that we shouldn't. O Lord, we confess that we deliberately slight certain people in our congregation for one reason or another. O Lord, help us to see our fellow church members through Your eyes.

O Lord, Your Word says that it is more blessed to give than to receive. (See Acts 20:35) But, Lord, some of us have robbed You by keeping part of what we should have given to You. O Lord, help us to be so thankful for what You've done for us that we want to give You everything.

O Lord, Your Word says that our bodies are the temples of the Holy Spirit, (See 1 Cor. 6:19) but some of us have overeaten or overtaxed our bodies or partaken of things that are harmful. O Lord, help us to be holy even as You are holy.

O Lord, Your Word says that whatever we eat or drink or do, do all for Your glory. (1 Cor. 10:31) O Lord, we confess that we have taken credit for what You have done. Help us to reflect all praise to You and to lift You up instead of ourselves.

O Lord, Your Word says that we should put away all bitterness and wrath and anger and clamor and evil speaking, (See Eph 4:31) but some of us have complained and found fault and have had a critical attitude toward certain others or things. Some of us are irritable and cranky. Some of us have been impatient. O Lord, help us spend so much time with You that You rub off on us.

O Lord, Your Word says that You resist the proud and give grace to the humble. (See James 4:6) O Lord, we confess to having selfish pride, to being stubborn, to insisting on having our way. O Lord, help us to humble ourselves before You decide to humble us Yourself.

O Lord, Your Word asks whether a fountain sends forth at the same place sweet water and bitter. (See James 3:11) O Lord, we confess that we have dishonored You and hindered Your work by being critical of Your servants. We have not been praying regularly for our pastor. We find ourselves more concerned with what other people think than with pleasing You. O Lord, may Your river of living water flow right through us to bless others on a continual basis.

O Lord, we confess these sins not just to get them off our chests and to feel our forgiveness, but because we sincerely hate them, Lord, and don't want to repeat them. Lord, some of us got so much confessing to do we don't need to turn over a new leaf but we need a whole new life. O Lord, do whatever it takes to come and take complete control. We just make a mess of things when we try to drive. O Lord, bless us with such a sensitivity to and so much remorse for sin in our lives that it literally brings us to tears every time we sin.

Lord, we now bring to You those who are sick, those we named and those whose names we didn't say aloud but whose names or faces came to mind. Remove everything in us which makes our prayers ineffective or prevents us from being channels of Your healing and comfort and love. Just as the four men brought the paralytic through the roof to set him before You, we bring these through prayer and set them before You because we know that all healing is with You. We can only bring them to You and offer ourselves in love and tenderness and sincerity. Grant them healing if that may be, but above all grant them peace and joy that they may know that You are with them, that they are safe, and that nothing can snatch them out of Your hand and defeat Your purposes. We ask it for Your name's sake.

O God the Father, Lord of Life, from whose strong and loving hands we cannot be snatched, and who has called us to be Your fellow workers, we lift up to You those You've brought to our minds. Be with their doctors and show them how to cooperate with Your healing powers to maximize the healing process for these. And, Lord, when there is no relief in sight, when any of these must suffer and those who love them can only look on, save both from any anxiety or despair. Show us that for those who trust in You, no pain can be in vain, that all things find a place in Your purposes at last. So we ask for patience and endurance and a quiet mind. Lay Your healing hand on those who feel they can bear no more until they can feel Your everlasting arms around them and underneath them.

O Lord, we came tonight expecting the ordinary—a typical Sunday evening service where hymns and choruses are sung, where a good Bible-based sermon is preached, where there is good fellowship, and where our comfort zone isn't threatened. But Lord, even though we're scared to ask, we ask You to do the extraordinary here tonight—even the supernatural. Grant, O Lord, that Your Holy Spirit would challenge those of us who don't or can't sing to make a joyful noise unto You tonight. Then, Lord, help Bro. H. preach with such power and such authority and so true to Your Word that Satan is stymied, his strongholds in our lives torn down, his spiritual blinders on our eyes removed, and Your truths hit us smack between the eyes. Then, Lord, may Your Holy Spirit come in and take control. Then, Lord, may we find our hearts burning within us with love for You and our fellow Christians. May we find ourselves so energized and excited to do Your will that we really are ready to do whatever You say—no matter what it is. O Lord, may we literally be throbbing with desire to study Your Word and to pray often and much, and to do Your every request. O Lord, may Christ our Lord really end up being glorified here tonight, but not really so much in the music and the preaching, as in our subsequent actions.

Amen

❧

Prayed as an offertory prayer at an 8:30 Sunday Morning Worship Service.

O Lord Who Answers Prayer,

We come confessing—confessing that probably the greatest sin we have committed since accepting You as our Lord and Savior is that we have not prayed near as much as we should. O Lord, the souls that would have been saved, the lives that would have been changed, the bodies that would have been healed, the extents to which Your Kingdom would have grown in our lives if we had been but praying as we should.

O Lord, we come in great distress assaulting Your throne with our pleas to change us. But don't just make us a people who pray more, but completely remake us into a people whose prayers shake this world, whose prayers keep your angels busy transporting Your Kingdom and Your will from heaven down here to earth, whose prayers result in miracles day in and day out. O Lord, may we not be a people who strive to live by a set of rules found in Your Book, but may we be a people who have Your law written on our hearts. Create in each of us a clean heart, o Lord. (See Ps. 51:10) But may our hearts not just be sprinkled on the outside with the blood of the Lamb. Rather may the very blood of Jesus be coursing through our veins cleansing us from the inside day and night. May we not be a people who pray out of duty and habit, but may we be a people whose souls pant for You like the deer pants for water. O Lord, may we be a people who delight in You and in whom You take great delight. O Lord, may we be a people whose very lives give off an aroma that wafts its way to your nostrils and You smell Jesus.

May our prayers be unceasing. May we become known as a people after Your own heart.

O Lord, may we be known as a people of prayer and may this place be known as a house of prayer. (See Isa. 56:7 & Matt 21:13) O Lord, may the world beat a path to our door trying to understand this unusual phenomenon that takes place when a people completely dedicate themselves to You and to prayer. And may Your reputation know no end.

O Lord, may these tithes and offerings we're going to put in these plates be but a pittance compared to the offering of our lives we make to You this morning.

May Your Word spread quickly, run its course, be glorified and triumphant. (See 2 Thes. 3:1)

Amen

∞

Prayed at Monday Night Prayer Meeting.

O Lord Who Rains on the Just and the Unjust Alike,

When we look out and see the raindrops falling we are reminded of Your great provision and, even though we might not see a rainbow, that You keep all of Your promises.

I am also reminded that someone once told me that the raindrops are the tears of God falling from Heaven. O Lord You have great reason to grieve. You grieve because there are 4-5 billion people walking this earth who do not call You Lord. You grieve because there can be found no one to stand in the gap and continually offer the names of each of these up to you until Your will is done in their lives. You grieve because so many of the very people here on earth who call themselves by Your name, who worship You regularly, who are heavily involved in the work of Your church only give lip service to serious intercessory prayer.

O Lord, the rain also reminds us of the seeds that have been planted, the watering that must be done, and the harvest that needs to take place. O Lord, we ask that You would bind the demon spirits that hinder the planting of seeds in the hearts of the people of this community. We ask that You would use Your Holy Spirit to draw the lost of this community to Christ. We ask that You would dispatch holy angels to do battle against the forces of Satan that are trying to prevent the watering. We ask that You would send more laborers to the harvest. (See Luke 10:2) O Lord, would You run Your combine up and down the streets of Tullahoma and let us drive or grease the wheels or do whatever needs to be done?

O Lord, would You tear down the strongholds that remain in our lives so that we might not only pray with faith, but that we might pray and intercede for these with a clean heart?

O Lord, there is a battle going on here. While the defeat of Satan was assured by Jesus' death and resurrection, Satan has not yet been destroyed. His strongholds are legion. O Lord, You have commissioned us to participate in the mop-up operation. May we make use of the appropriate warfare weapons. May we make significant use of prayer and fasting. May we invoke the name of Jesus, use the word of God, rely on the blood of Jesus, and put on Truth, Righteousness, Faith and Salvation. (See Eph. 6:11+)

Thus armed, may we engage the enemy and claim the victory. May we take every thought captive to the obedience of Jesus Christ. (See 2 Cor. 10:5) May we resist every temptation. May we claim every inch of our own lives for Your Kingdom. May we pray every prayer that You want prayed. May we stand in the gap and claim every soul You ask us to pray for for Your Kingdom.

O Lord, as we think of the rain, we think of the showers of blessing. I pray for the blessing of Your moving us from praying what we want or what we think we're supposed to be praying for to praying exactly what you want us to pray for. I pray for the growth in faith that comes from praying for something that we know is Your will and watching it happen right before our eyes. I pray for the growth in faith that comes from praying for something again and again we know is your will and knowing that when all things that are fulfilled for that to happen then it will happen.

I pray for the day that all those slots are filled in the intercessory prayer room. I pray for the day when the folk we're praying for start taking up their places in the activity of intercessory prayer. I pray for the day that You lay someone on our heart so much that our tears match Yours. I pray for the day that You not only move us from praying what we want to what You want, but then You move us to doing exactly what needs to be done to bring it about. O Lord, I pray for the day when Your glory will know no end. To You be the glory forever.

Amen

∞

Prayed at a Monday Night Prayer Meeting.

O Just and Righteous Father,

Although the world as a whole does not know You and has failed to recognize You and has never acknowledged You, Jesus knew You, and the Disciples knew You sent Him. And Jesus made You known to them. And they, with the help of the Holy Spirit and generations of new disciples, have imparted that knowledge to us. And now may our goal be to continue to make You known in order that the love You have for us may be in those of the world who currently know You not and that Jesus himself may be in them also. (John 17:25-26, my rendition)

O Father, with that in mind, and because Your Word says that we should earnestly seek the greater gifts, and because despite all the seed we've planted and all the watering we've done all too often the harvest still rots on the vine or is consumed with fire, and because You are burdening us so much with the lost, o Lord, would You gift some of us with the gift of evangelism? O Lord, I'm not talking about the ability to get up and preach an evangelistic message, I'm talking about the all-consuming passion to win every lost person we come into contact with to Jesus and the Holy Spirit power to witness in every circumstance. I'm talking about giving us the knack of moving conversations to spiritual things, the boldness to constantly ask the all-important questions, the wisdom to know exactly what to say, the sensitivity to understand exactly what needs to be done, the wherewithal to know how to move to a point of decision, and the mastery to close the deal, and the submissiveness to do it all under Your control.

O Lord, lest this church and ultimately You, Lord, get a bad rap because we expend a lot of energy interceding for the lost to little or no avail, lest it is Your will that almost every soul You impress upon us to pray for remain in Satan's clutches, spread the gift of evangelism among the membership of this church. O Lord, may some of us who have a hoe or a hose in our hand be given a scythe.

O Lord, may we not be a church run by the 15% who are overcommitted and overworked. But may we be a church where everyone's gift or gifts are recognized and employed for Your glory. O Lord, just as the deacons were set aside to enable the Apostles to dedicate themselves to prayer and preaching, may those sitting on the sidelines take up their place of service so that all may exercise their gifts for Your maximum glory.

And may the world never be the same again.

Amen

∞

Prayed at a Monday Night Prayer Meeting.

O Lord Who Sees from Beginning to End, Who Has No Match in Heaven or on Earth, Who Entertains No Fears, Who Has No Ignorance, Who Has No Needs, Who Has No Limitations and Always Knows What's Best, Who Never Makes a Mistake, Who Possesses the Ability to Bring Everything to a Purposeful Conclusion and Ultimate Good, Who Is Invisible, Immutable, Infinite, and Self-sufficient, Whose Judgments Are Unsearchable, Whose Ways Are Unfathomable, (See Rom. 11:33) Who Directs Rather than Wishes, Who Fulfills Rather than Dreams, Who Is Full of Wisdom and Knowledge,

Those attributes don't even begin to fill out Your résumé to qualify You as Sovereign of the entire Universe. O Lord, You are the Master and the Mover, the Giver and the Creator, the Enforcer and the Provider.

O Lord, Your plans are not only beyond our comprehension; they are beyond our ability to alter and hinder or stop. They cause adversity and prosperity, tragedy and joy. They include illness and health, safety and danger.

O Lord, even though we can't understand why at times, You know. Even though we can't explain the reason, You understand perfectly. Even though we can't see the end, You see all things perfectly.

O Lord, You never cool off in Your commitment toward us. You never break a promise. You never lose Your enthusiasm. Your loving kindness never ceases. Your compassions never fail. They are new every morning. Great is Thy faithfulness. (See Lam. 3:22-23)

O Lord, help us to present our bodies, including all our members and faculties, as living and holy sacrifices to You. May we be Your avenues of kindness. May we be Your messengers of love. May every bead of sweat from our brow glorify the Son. O Lord, help us so resist the world's attempt to squeeze us into its mold, help us to be so true to take every thought captive to the obedience of Jesus Christ (See 2 Cor. 10:15) that we may literally be transformed into a person who not only knows what is Your good and acceptable and perfect will but who actually does it and does it for Your glory. (See Rom. 12:2)

Lord, Your sovereign will decrees that each of us is free to choose between good and evil. But would You give us the desire and the will and the strength to choose good every time? But we also know it is Your personal desire that none should perish. Therefore, would You also give us the desire and the will and the strength to exert whatever influence needs to be applied to those who have not yet made that final choice between good and evil—between the person of Jesus Christ and personal selfish desires, so that the odds lie heavily in Your favor?

O Lord, may we not worry—because You are sovereign. May we be properly humble—because You are sovereign. May we be properly submissive one to another—because You are sovereign.

And may Your glory know no end.

Amen

∞

Prayed during a Monday Night Prayer Meeting.

O Lord, God of Heaven, the Great and Awesome God Who Keeps His Covenant of Love with Those Who Have Had Their Sins Washed Away with the Blood of Jesus,

Let Your ears be attentive and Your eyes be open to hear the prayer of Your servant who is praying before You day and night, night and day for the lost folk of Tullahoma.

First, Lord, I confess the sins that Your people at FBC, including myself and my family, have committed against You. O Lord, we spend hours in idle chatter and watching TV every day, but only a few minutes meditating on Your Word or in quiet prayer listening for Your voice every week. We recognize that almost half of our membership hasn't been to church in over a year, but we don't ever pray for them. We make out our date books or Franklin planners or computer calendars establishing our schedules and agendas such that when You try to schedule an appointment we have a good excuse so we can't work You in. O Lord, we get so busy that we don't have enough time for the One Who Gives Us the Time to Start with. We've already established in our minds the limits of what we will or will not do so that when You ask us to stretch those limits we feel justified by explaining that we just can't or don't do that. We fulfill our obligation to the Great Commission over in Matthew by writing a check at Christmastime so that we don't have to go anywhere. We recognize Acts 1:8, but based on the amount of intentional witnessing we do, we apparently don't recognize Tullahoma as our Jerusalem, and we certainly don't recognize the Judea's and Samaria's right here in Tullahoma. O Lord, we are a proud people, outwardly giving You the glory but inwardly taking the credit for the good things that have been happening here, and at times using those good things as a reason to feel smug. But, Lord, the greater sin is that we treat all these sins as acceptable. O Lord, move us to not only acknowledge these sins but to feel remorse for them.

Lord, I remind You that even though we have sinned and even though we may not have confessed all our sins or repented of them that You look at us through the blood of Jesus and see us as righteous. Therefore, I pray with confidence that You will hear my prayer and answer it. Lord, I specifically pray for the lost people of Tullahoma. I remind You that You desire that none should perish. I remind You of the great sacrifice You made when You took the first step to see that these might not perish. Now at our insistence, Lord, would You, for the sake of the lost folk of Tullahoma, move in our lives to cause us to stand in the gap and pray for these folk? Then cause us to stand on our heads, do a tap dance, live holy lives, actually go out and witness, or do whatever it takes to confront every one of them with Your Good News in a manner which results in Your Holy Spirit getting at least a level playing field. O Lord, may we forget about our own desires and, in mass, establish Your desires as our goal. Then,

Lord, may we get so lost in You and in Your desires that the lost get a desire for You.

And may You get all the glory and all the credit and all the praise.

Amen

∾

This was prayed during a Monday Night Prayer Meeting. Most prayer requests in the prayer room are filled out by church members who come to pray. Additional prayer requests are called into or e-mailed to the church office. Some are called in by the public directly to the prayer room. Prayer requests remain in a stack on the desk in the Prayer Room for a period of time then placed in notebooks based on category. The Salvation Book contains the names of individuals for whom the prayers have been asked to pray that they be saved.

O Lord,

We are poor and needy—poor because we are powerless in this business of salvation. We know that our salvation didn't depend on how smart we were, how good we were, how rich we were, or upon whom we knew. We know that the major player in our salvation was Your Holy Spirit. And we're needy because You have not granted our heart's greatest desire. O Lord, we plead for Your mercy.

O Lord, we are in great distress because we cannot command the Spirit, and yet we can do nothing without Him. He does as You will. O Lord, we know that every lost soul that has been saved has been the result, not of the efforts of man, but of Your Spirit. But, Lord, if we could, we'd do our part.

O Lord, if he could, Monroe would weep the tears of confession and repentance for Roy, Charles, and Clyde. Lord, if he could Virgil would die on the cross for his son, Kirk. Lord, if they could, Donna, Ruth,

Florence, and Terri would believe that Jesus died on the cross, not just for themselves, but for their husbands, too. Lord, if I could, I'd walk down the church aisle and yell to the Heavens for Lee, Jonathan, Josh, Hunter, William, and Casey that they've accepted Jesus as Lord and Savior and want to be baptized. Lord, if he could, Lyle would take that step of faith for George.

But, Lord, our hands are tied. We can do but the Spirit's bidding. O Lord, grant our great request that each of these may be saved so that Your name may be glorified in all the earth. O Lord, grant our request so that our faith and belief in prayer may grow by leaps and bounds. O Lord, we add to these the names of every individual whose name is in the "Salvation Book" in the Prayer Room. O Lord, grant that Your Spirit would bid that we do whatever You need to answer our prayer. O Lord, if You need us to intercede both day and night for these; o Lord, if you need us to go and visit these; o Lord, if You need us to go and plead with these; o Lord, if You need us to lead exemplary lives before these; o Lord, whatever You need us to do, use Your Holy Spirit to convict us to do it.

O Jehovah Jireh, Great Provider, our need is to see these folk saved. O Lord, if our desire is not enough, grow our desire. O Lord, we're not asking for a snake, but for the very desire of Your heart.

O Lord, we plead for You to work in the lives of those whose names we've mentioned because if You don't work, the mightiest and most zealous of us are wasting our time. O Lord, You are the one who has laid these on our hearts and asked us to pray for them. Now honor Your own request by working mightily in their lives. O lord, our barley loaves are so little and our fishes so few, but we know You can feed thousands with them.

O Lord, at times we feel as if we're casting the net on the wrong side of the boat. O Lord, show us which side of the boat to cast the net over so the boat can be filled with fish.

O Lord, we are of such little faith that we must be convinced again and again that there is no way we can win any of these in our own power. Must we come to the point of practically giving up in despair before You act so You can convince us that You and You alone bring faith in people's lives? Must we wait as Elijah did until there is no possibility that any person could claim any responsibility for helping to save these before You act? O Lord, may we, in effect, pour water over these three times just as Elijah did at Mt. Carmel to prove that only You can start the fire in their lives? O Lord, we will give You the glory—You who works all things according to Your will.

Lord, You told us to intercede for these. Can You now deny the very request You asked us to ask? Lord, we remind You that we make this request based on the very blood of Jesus and in the name of Him who died and rose again.

Amen

Prayed at Monday Night Prayer Meeting.

Lord,

We praise You because (Repeat with each indented phrase or not)
- You designed prayer to be the primary tool to communicate between the spiritual world and the physical world, between us and You,
- You are a prayer-seeking god,
- You are a prayer-listening god,
- You are a prayer-answering god.
- When it comes to prayer we know what You look like. You are all ears.
- You don't say, "un-hunh" to our prayers. You don't listen to us like I listen to my wife sometimes when I get home from work

and am ready for some peace and quiet and all she wants to do is talk and I keep saying "un-hunh, un-hunh, un-hunh."

- We have your absolute, 100% undivided attention when we pray to You.

Lord, I'd like to focus all of Your attention on several requests You have caused Your Holy Spirit to compel me to bounce back to You. Lord, these requests initially came from You—so I'm expecting You to do whatever needs to be done to bring these about.

1. Lord, would You grow our faith from believing that You can make the mountains tremble, that You can move mountains, to having the faith to believe our prayers can cause You to move mountains?

2. Lord, move the mountain of shyness that is preventing William, Josh, Sarah, and numerous others in our midst from stepping forward to make known a decision for You in this church.

3. Lord, move the Mt Everest of disbelief that resides in the lives of so many of the immediate members of our church family, just as Bro. D. mentioned yesterday. Lord, specifically coming to mind are Roy, Jason, John, Steve, Charles, Jeff, Philip, Clyde, and Kirk.

4. Lord, I pray for the USA. Would you give me and this congregation the heathen of the USA for our inheritance? Lord, would you use us to spread Your Good News next door, down the street, around the bend, over the river, through the woods, up to the top of the skyscrapers, and in every household in these United States until every person You died for in these United States knows that You died for them?

5. Lord, I pray that You would get an invitation from every member of FBC to change Your role from being the God we worship to the God whose every command we obey. O Lord, set up one of your earthly headquarters, one of Your command centers, in the heart of each of Your children here at FBC. Lord, may we spend so much time thinking about what You did

for us and who You really are that it makes us properly humble. And, Lord, may we spend so much time meditating on Your Word and communing with You that Your attitudes infiltrate our being. O Lord, may the thoughts we have originate from You, may our actions result from what we hear You say and see You do.

6. Lord, I pray that our commitment to prayer would mimic that of Jesus. May we be so caught up in prayer that we can see ourselves as You see us. May we be so caught up in prayer that we can see others as You see them. May we be so caught up in prayer that your Kingdom becomes the most recognized, most powerful nation here on earth.

7. Lord, I pray once again, believing with all of my heart, that You can and will do this: O Lord, will you please require of us to do whatever it takes to become the one church in all of history, past, present and future, that comes closest to being all that You intended for it to be.

Amen

∞

Grace Alone was an effort to raise $975,000 to support a building/remodeling effort. This was prayed during Monday Night Prayer Meeting.

O Great Prayer-hearing God, O Great Prayer-answering God, O Great Prayer-desiring God,

I remember some time back that we were praying for Joe because he wasn't able or couldn't bring himself to pray. And I know one of our strongest prayer warriors who firmly believes that one should pray only to God the Father—and not to Jesus or the Holy Spirit. And I recognize that some of us choose not to pray out loud in public. O Lord, please remove all hindrances that keep us from praying freely.

Lord, Your Word indicates that unbelief hinders prayer. O Lord, help us to believe that You really want to give us what we are about to ask. And help us to believe that the things we are about to ask are certainly not too great or difficult for You.

Lord, Your Word indicates that unconfessed sin hinders prayer. O Lord, we confess the sin of loving something or someone greater than You. Just as we have over a thousand fellow church members who at this very moment have chosen to be with someone other than with You tonight, we also at times find ourselves demonstrating that You are not number one in our lives. O Lord, we confess the sin of being in control of our lives at times instead of allowing you to be in control of our lives—and when we are in control we seem to lose control: we think sinful thoughts and do things we regret. It's as if someone else were in control. O Lord, we confess that we have been less than responsive to the needs of others. Lord, we have friends and relatives and coworkers who are dying spiritual deaths right before our eyes, and we won't even attempt to share the Living Water with them. O Lord, we confess that we have been hypocritical—we have had fleeting thoughts of how others might think more highly of us because of activity that we're supposed to be doing primarily for Your glory. O Lord, we confess that we don't believe Your Word as is evidenced by the fact that we continue to worry about things rather than just turning them over to You. O Lord, we confess that we have an unforgiving spirit. Some of us say we forgive, but we've not forgotten. And some of us haven't forgiven ourselves for some past failure. And, Lord, we confess that our relationships are less than they should be because we haven't been working on them hard enough. O Lord, may our sins of omission be brought to light so that we might recognize Your will for our lives. O Lord, we agree with You that all these sins are despicable and we really don't want to repeat any of them again. O Lord, may we recognize the forgiveness for these sins that we received when we accepted Jesus—so that as we approach Your throne with our requests not only will You look at us through the blood of Jesus but that we will ask with the boldness and confidence of one who has every right to ask and expect our requests to be fulfilled. O Lord, since we're going to pray what Your Holy Spirit leads us to think Jesus would be praying if He were walking in our shoes, may our prayers be as unhindered by sin as the prayers that Jesus prayed while he was on earth.

O Lord, some of us are guilty of praying with wrong motives. (See James 4:3) O Lord, I am reminded that if we pray for the right thing for the wrong reason that You know it and probably we're wasting our breath. And I know that when we pray for the wrong thing for the right reason that if we stick with it long enough You'll change what we're praying for to what we should be praying for. O Lord, may our motive for praying be to bring about Your Kingdom here on earth.

O Lord, having made attempts to remove all hindrances to prayer I come tonight not praying for myself, not praying for others, but praying for Your great needs. O Lord, may Your great need to have fellowship with us be met. May it be a constant, deep, intimate relationship in which lives are constantly brought closer to Your will. O Lord, I pray that Your great need to have Your Gospel message and Your great love conveyed to every living human being in a way that is timely, in a way that is understandable, in a way that is extremely difficult to resist be satisfied.

O Lord, may Your Word be honored and valued and loved and used for Your great purposes throughout this land.

O Lord, I have been reminded that some of us are still trying to live under the stigma of trying to live by a set of rules. O Lord, we have folk that are trying to live good lives rather than being in love with you. We have folk who have depended on You to save their afterlife, but haven't turned over their present life to You. Lord, we have folk who come every Sunday who think their ticket to Heaven is based on how good they are rather than on Jesus paying their freight. O Lord, I ask that your need to have every member of this church be brought to the blessed assurance that they are saved through the blood of Jesus and that no one can snatch them out of Your hand be satisfied. O Lord, may Your need that each of us understand that we have perfect freedom in Jesus, but at the same time that we are not to put a stumbling block in our brother's way, or in any way exercise our freedom in a way that will offend our brothers in Christ be satisfied.

O Lord, may Your great need to have unity in this church be satisfied. May those who have critical spirits become critical of themselves. May those who are just filling up a pew be filled with Your Spirit. May those who are playing devil's advocate become Your greatest proponents. May every person in this church get behind Grace Alone. May every member of this church feel nothing but love for his fellow church members.

O Lord, may Your needs be our needs.

Amen

∞

While this prayer was designed to be a morning prayer during a Sunday Morning Worship Service, it was ultimately prayed during Monday Night Prayer Meeting ('morning' was changed to 'evening') Morning prayers are almost always prayed by ministerial staff members at FBC.

O Lord, if I could, I'd climb a ladder up to Heaven and take everybody here with me. We'd find Your throne high and lifted up. And we'd see the seraphim flying around singing, "Holy, holy, holy is the Lord of Hosts. The whole earth is filled with Your glory." (See Isa. 6:3) And we'd be so in awe of You that we'd fall prostrate at Your feet and worship You with every ounce of our being. And, Lord, we'd listen so intently to everything You had to say, and we'd do precisely what You told us to do without any question or hesitation. But, alas, Lord, my ladder is too short.

O Lord, if I could, I'd pray so eloquently that it would transport all of us into Your very presence. And we'd all join the celestial choir; and everyone of us, even those of us who haven't ever sung a note in church, would sing praises and thanksgiving to You all day long. But alas, Lord, I don't have a silver tongue.

O Lord, if I could, I'd fill both the church buses and the van with the folk here this morning and we'd all go to Heaven and pay Jesus a visit. We would sit at His feet and learn from Him. We would see the nail prints in his hands and the spear wound in His side and constantly be reminded of His great sacrifice that paid the price for our sins. O Lord, not one of us would be able to resist telling Jesus that we love Him and that we want Him to not only be our savior but also the Lord of our life. But, alas, Lord, I don't have a celestial chauffeur's license.

O Lord, even though most of us won't be going to Heaven at least for a while, would You help us to begin experiencing Heaven right here on earth? Even though we can't lay prostrate before Your throne and worship You with all that we have, would You help us to prostrate our hearts to Your will and worship You right here with every ounce of our being? O Lord, even though we can't hear Your voice audibly here on earth, may we begin experiencing Heaven right here on earth by listening intently to Your earthly shepherd here this morning and recognizing what You are saying to us this morning as You speak through Your Holy Word and Your preached Word. And may we obey your every command without question or hesitation.

O Lord, even though we've not put on our heavenly choir robe yet, may we practice for Heaven here this morning. May those who are normally silent at least hum a little this morning. May those of us who can't carry a tune in a bucket have such a need to praise You that we can't be silent. And, Lord, may there not be a one of us here this morning that doesn't truly mean the words that are being sung.

O Lord, even though we can't sit at Jesus' feet and learn from Him, would You help us to develop a mindset that continually strives to learn everything You have for us in Your written Word and would You help us to keep ever aware of Jesus' great sacrifice for our sins? O Lord, may none of us be able to resist Your call upon our lives here this morning to love You and to not just trust You as our savior and let You take us to Heaven but to trust You as Lord and let You take control of our lives, hook, line and sinker.

O Lord, Your Word indicates that Jesus didn't die on the cross just so we can go to Heaven, but rather He died on the cross so that we might also have life and have it more abundantly right here on earth. And we know that about the only things we can't do in Heaven that we can do here on earth are to sin and to tell nonbelievers about Jesus.[36] If my thinking is right that indicates that the only reason you've not already taken us to Heaven is that we're here to tell Your Good News to the rest of the world. O Lord, use this service to excite us to Your work. O Lord, help us to share some of this heaven on earth we have with others.

Amen

∞

Prayed at a Monday Night Prayer Meeting.

Invisible, Invincible, Incredible Lord,

I praise You because (Repeat with the indented phrases below or not)
- You're not some statue that can't answer my prayers.
- You're not some god whose prophet can't even do a miracle much less raise someone from the dead.
- You're not one of 10,000 gods, none of which can touch me with a healing hand.
- You're not some philosophy that can't forgive my sins.
- You're not some religious system that can't even give me peace.
- You're not some New Age thing that can't deliver me from myself.

---

[36]   Warren, Rick, The Purpose-Driven Church, p 116.

- You're not some set of written-down rules that can't walk and talk with me.
- You are the One and Only, the Living God, the God who created the Universe and also created me.
- You're not just someone I believe in, but You are someone that I know and experience in my life.
- I feel You daily in my life.
- I've seen You work in my life and in my church.
- I've experienced Your deliverance in my life.
- I was dead in sin and You raised me to new life.
- I've been touched by Your healing hand.
- my prayers have been answered time and time again.
- I've heard You speak through Your Word time and time again.
- You hold me in Your hand and will never let me go.

Lord, I pray for those who do not have this precious gift of knowing You. I pray that you would use me as You need to bring enlightenment. And I pray for those who know You but don't realize that they are experiencing You in their lives. I pray that You would give them spiritual eyes to see Your activity in their lives.

Lord, I come confessing that I have at times resisted what You wanted to do in and through me. I now give You permission to have your way with me.

O Lord, we love You so much that we want more of You. O, please Lord, give us more of Your Holy Spirit. Give us more spiritual wisdom and discernment. Give us a more intimate relationship with Jesus so You may be more glorified.

O Lord, we praise You because You are the One and Only.

Amen

Used as an offertory prayer at an 8:30 Sunday Morning Worship Service.

Lord God Almighty,

We've come to what may just be the most important part of this service, the ingathering of tithes and offerings. If one looks at the order of worship, one might think that it's the least important part or that we almost forgot. But Lord, you know the reason we've placed it last isn't because it's not important or that we almost forgot or that we get more money when we take up the offering at the end of the service. It's in order to try to get the entire sermon on the radio.

Lord, there were times in your Word when You rejected people's sacrifices and offerings. You rejected them if they didn't bring the first fruits. O Lord, we come bringing you the first check we wrote after we got paid or else monies that were designated as the first line item of our budget.

Lord, I had a friend here at the church who told me that he was very careful to bring his tithe because he thought that if he didn't he might get sick or someone in his family might get sick. O Lord, help us to give out of love instead of fear.

Lord, Your Word indicates that the Israelites' offerings were rejected at times because they were unjust in their dealings with others— especially the poor. Lord, please accept our offerings here this morning because we have been kind to others this week.

Lord, some of us put money in the plate because we know others are watching. O Lord, may the reason we give to You not be because of what other people think, but because we honestly want to be a part of advancing Your Kingdom here on earth.

Lord, we know that You accept our offerings based on our inner attitude. We ask that if our attitude is not what it should be that You would chide us, discipline us, and prune us.

And, Lord, as we go here in just a minute, may each of us have You in our heart, Jesus in our focus, and the Holy Spirit on our case.

Amen

∞

Prayed at a Monday Night Prayer Meeting. Anytime one prays confessing the sins of the church it makes some people uncomfortable. Some people think you should never say anything negative about the church! How can one confess sins without identifying something that was done wrong?

Lord God,

You know me. I'm one of those Christians who thinks it's inappropriate to ask for Your forgiveness again—that when I invited You into my life and asked for forgiveness that You forgave all my sins—past, present and future, at that time and that 1 John 1:9 was written for the benefit of non-Christians. But, Lord, I very much believe I'm supposed to confess my sins and repent of them and keep short accounts with You.

Lord, I confess the sin of saying to myself, as I hear fellow church members pray asking for forgiveness, that they are being glib about it because I don't sense the repentance that has to go with it being present and at the same time having to confess the same sins over and over in my own life. Lord, You must get kind of bored hearing the same confession in my prayers day-in and day-out year after year. O Lord, move me from the want-to-get-rid-of-it stage to the I'll-do-anything-to-get-it-out-of-my-life stage, even to the point of putting You in charge 24-7. O Lord, make me that desperate.

But, Lord, I don't have an opinion about whether a church as a whole should only confess sins and repent or whether it's appropriate to ask for forgiveness, too. But I guess that is a moot point since I don't hear anyone confessing the sins of the church, much less asking for forgiveness or attempting to repent. I see in the letters to the seven churches over in Revelation that churches definitely sin and experience judgment, but see no evidence of any confession on any of the churches' part. I hear words from the Roman Catholic Church admitting that they have a pedophile problem among its priests—but really only after trying to hide it and having it become such a large problem exposed by the media that they couldn't deny it anymore. And it seems that the only reason that they are addressing the problem now is not because it's a sin but because it's hurting them financially. O Lord, make the best of that bad situation.

And, Lord, I don't hear the sins of FBC being confessed from the pulpit very often—in fact, more often than not I hear the positive that's going on here being emphasized. And if you're not a homosexual or an abortionist, you probably don't get your toes stepped on as an individual very often around here.

So, Lord, I want to take a stab at confessing the sins of FBC. If it makes any sense to stand in the gap and intercede on behalf of FBC to forestall judgment, Lord, I'm here to do it. Lord, give us another chance.

First off, Lord, we are two-faced. We vote one way with our ballots and another way with our wallets. Lord, aren't You tired of watching us waste Your money paying architects to draw up plans we never use? Lord, some of us keep most or all of Your tithe and say, "Charity begins at home." Similarly, Lord, a couple of years back we cut the percentage of our budget that we give to the Cooperative Program and said, "Missions begin at home." O Lord, we are a people who puts more faith in our bank accounts than we do in You. We are a people who trusts more in our 401(k) to take care of us in the future than we do You. O Lord, we are a people who bow down to the god of materialism six days a week and come to church on Sunday and worship You with our lips.

O Lord, we claim to be a church with a heavy emphasis on prayer, but usually we could hold Monday night prayer meeting in the baptistry we have so few people show up. And when was the last time we had ten Deacons show up for pre-service prayer meeting on Sunday mornings?

Lord, we are very much a fat and happy church. Fat because we have a wait problem. We like to wait around and see who, if anybody, is going to volunteer to fill those teaching positions down in the children's organizations. And happy enough to sit on the sidelines and complain while a few overworked souls do all the work. Why, Lord, more and more we pay people to get them to do the jobs that were formerly done by volunteers. One of these days we're not only going to be paying someone to babysit our kids, clean our floors, play the piano, pray for us and visit us, we're even going to be paying the piper.

Lord, we like to sit on our padded pews in our air-conditioned sanctuary and listen to piped in music and then complain because Bro. D. asks us to stand up to sing.

Lord, we are a church some of whose members spend countless hours putting on evangelistic endeavors in which scores make decisions for You. We then proudly quote the numbers but can't find the time to spend even one hour to follow up on any of these folk even though Your Word indicates that it is better that they never started following You than to have started and then given up. And, Lord, we are a church who ignores our inactive members. We not only don't have a plan for reactivating them, we don't even pray for them.

O Lord, we are a people who worship our children. We sign them up for baseball and soccer and dance and cheerleading and combine all that with school and church activities so that we're constantly transporting them somewhere or watching their games so that we don't have time for You. We miss church on Sunday because the travel squad has a game in Chattanooga. Our weekly schedule is so full there's no time to schedule a quiet time for ourselves much less a family devotion time. Some of us don't even go to church on Sundays saying it's the only time we have to be together as a family.

Lord, we are a church that likes to complain and grumble. And to make matters worse we like to complain and grumble to non-church members. The ministerial staff have found it's better to get forgiveness than permission—so they just do what they want rather than get church buy-in first because they know that getting this church to agree on anything that's not written in red ink in the Bible is like pulling teeth. Lord, in the name of church unity we compromise our goals because some of us are so out of touch with You we don't even know what frequency You're on much less how often You like to transmit.

Lord, we are a people who packed the pews shortly after 9-11. We got scared and ran to You. But, alas, Lord, we bought into a military solution and beefed-up security. So we don't need You anymore. We can rely upon ourselves to solve the problem. We've lost our wholehearted devotion and dependence upon You. Everything is okay again. The stock market is recovering. Lord, we're back to being complacent and apathetic. We don't want You to solve our problems—after all You might expect us to make some sacrifices or change our routine. We're back to coming to church when it is convenient and relying upon ourselves. Lord, we're spiritually comfortable—why we haven't changed much in umpteen years and don't want You or anyone else upsetting the apple cart now.

O Lord, we confess the sin of having a mind of our own instead of the mind of Christ. We do our own thing, satisfy our own desires, come to church to have our needs met and let our hang-ups limit our lives and cause us to miss opportunity after opportunity to witness for You. O Lord, we confess that FBC has failed to be a church that has 2000 in SS every Sunday, baptizes 250 every year, and sets the world on fire for you because we are holding back—we just won't turn everything over to You.

O Lord, we confess all these sins to You acknowledging that we need Your Holy Spirit's help. You see, I can't ask for forgiveness, even if it is appropriate to ask for forgiveness for a church, because we're not repentant, as a whole or as individuals. Those of us who hear these sins and don't take credit for any of them personally are at least responsible for allowing them to happen at FBC. Lord, I ask You to use Your Holy Spirit to convict us and bring us to the point of repentance. And then build Your church here.

And may You receive all the glory.

Amen

Prayed at an 8:30 Sunday Morning Worship Service as the offertory prayer. We have several bankers in the congregation.

Lord of All,

We praise You because You don't keep banker's hours. O Lord, we praise You because You are a 24-7, full-service god. We praise You because we can always bank on You.

Lord, we praise You because You don't give a paltry 2 or 4% on our investments with You. Rather when we invest in Your Kingdom You reward us according to Your riches in glory.

Lord, we praise You because You don't inflict hidden charges on us or charge us for checking or for ATM transactions. O Lord, we praise You because Your every move is in our best interest.

O Lord, we praise You because when we messed up and got in debt way over our heads, You didn't foreclose on us. Rather, when we came in tears and told you how sorry we were, You showed how You had personally paid the price and forgave our every debt.

O Lord, we praise You because You'll never file a Chapter 11 or go bankrupt or close Your doors. We praise You because our treasures are always safe with You in Heaven.

O Lord, we praise You because You aren't bugging us about getting long-term care insurance or starting a Roth IRA or adding to our 401(k). O Lord, we praise You because You have built a fancy retirement home for Your customers—and it's free of charge.

O Lord, I hate to have to admit it but some of us are more in debt to financial institutions than we are indebted to You. Some of us can't even give as much as the widow who had only two mites because we trust more in our bank account than we do in You. O Lord, some of us have put more faith in our 401(k)'s and pension plans and Social Security to take care of our future than we have in You. O Lord, some of us have taken money we could have easily given to You and bought material possessions that have ended us possessing us.

O Lord, we confess that there are areas of our lives that we're still trying to manage on our own that we should have turned over to You long ago. O Lord, may we resolve to do precisely what Your Holy Spirit is telling us we need to do right now.

And, Lord, when the plate reaches each of us and You examine our heart, may You find a new or strengthened resolve. Then, Lord, keep nudging us until we follow through.

May Your earthly kingdom know no bounds.

Amen

∞

Prayed at Monday Night Prayer Meeting. There is a fountain across the street in a small park that is part of the church campus. We have baptized a few people there.

Omnipotent Father,

The Israelites couldn't swim across the Red Sea, but at exactly the right moment You put a dry path through it.

They couldn't penetrate the walls of Jericho, but at exactly the right moment You leveled the walls.

Eight hundred and fifty prophets of Baal and Ashterah couldn't pray down fire from heaven, but at exactly the right moment you consumed not only the sacrifice but the altar and the water, too.

The leper and the blind man and the lame man couldn't be healed, but at exactly the right moment You healed them.

O Lord, you are always working miracles. You are always intervening in the routine of nature to work out Your sovereign will. You are still casting down thrones and dominions. You are still elevating peoples and establishing nations.

For the right reason, You will cause the sun to stand still or raise the dead from the grave.

O Lord, Your great power stands at the ready awaiting the prayers of Your people.

O Lord, through prayer, Moses was able to forestall Your judgment on his people.
O Lord, through prayer, Joshua was able to win victory after victory on the battlefield.
O Lord, through prayer, Elijah was able to prove that You are the one and only god.
O Lord, through prayer, Daniel was able to shut the mouths of the lions.
O Lord, through prayer, David became a man after Your own heart.

O Lord, we Your people come to You at this time acknowledging that up to this point we have just been playing at praying, else we would be seeing Your great miracles regularly. We know we have not because we ask not or we ask awry. (See James 4:2-3) O Lord, based on the spent blood of Jesus and on Your great promises to answer the prayers of Your people who pray in Your will, I pray first that just as Moses interceded for his people and You forestalled Your judgment, You would forestall the judgment for every person that we intercede for here at FBC. Lord, I pray that just as You won victory after victory for Joshua on the battlefield that You would win victory after victory in our lives and the lives of the folk that you ask us to intercede for. O Lord, just as Joshua ended up conquering the whole land by winning one battle at a time, may You win the war here by winning one battle at a time in our lives and the lives of the people we're praying for. O Lord, just as Elijah proved that You are the one and only god, may the evidence be so strong here that You are the one and only god because so many come to know you and testify how You worked in their lives. O Lord, just as You proved You are the one and only god by consuming even the water, may so many folk be baptized in our fountain that the water gets consumed. Lord, just as Daniel prayed and shut the mouths of the lions, we pray that the lying mouths of Your critics who blaspheme Your name and belittle Your abilities and Your bride here on earth would be shut forever because of the great horde of changed lives that screams to the world that those critics were dead wrong. O Lord, just as David prayed so much he became a man after Your own heart, we pray that we too may pray so much and in such a way that the end result is that we become men and women after Your own heart. And, Lord, just as the disciples prayed and the Holy Spirit came, we pray asking for Your Holy Spirit to come in such a mighty way that every person hears Your Good News in a language so that he completely understands and that no life remains untouched by His convicting and convincing effect.

And, Lord, may all this happen at exactly the right time so that You receive all the glory.

Amen

∞

Prayed at a Monday Night Prayer Meeting.

Father in Heaven,

That phrase brings to mind two misconceptions. First, a lot of people think that because You are Lord of the Universe and their Creator and their Sustainer that You are their father and they are Your children. In fact, many of them think that all people are Your children. But Your Word only refers to two groups of folk as being Your children—first the Israelites, then those redeemed by the blood of the Lamb. Your Word also says: "to all who received him, to those who believed in his name, He gave the right to become children of God—children born not of natural descent, not of human decision or a husband's will, but born of God." (John 1:12-13 NIV) O Lord, I pray for all those who mistakenly think that they are children of God and are not. O Lord, may Your Truth set them free. (See John 8:32) And may they be free indeed. (See John 8:36) O Lord, use us to convey Your truth to every one of them. And, Lord, may every one of them exercise their right to become Your children.

Secondly, a lot of people think that because You are in Heaven that You have a laissez-fair or hands-off policy with respect to the affairs of men on earth. O Lord, Your Word said that You walked and talked with Adam in the garden and later Jesus walked and talked with the Disciples and others and now Your Holy Spirit is actively working in the lives of men to convict of sin and convince of the need for Jesus and to lead men to recognize and do Your will here on earth. O Lord, I pray for all those who acknowledge You as Lord of the Universe but don't see You at work in their day-to-day world. O Lord, I pray that we would so walk the walk before their eyes and so talk the talk within their hearing so they can encounter You. And Lord, we pray that

that would be a life-changing encounter so that forever after they are walking and talking with You, too.

May Heaven come down and Glory enter into the lives of each and every one.

Amen

∞

Prayed at a Monday Night Prayer Meeting.

Lord of Salvation,

At Philippi, Paul and Silas had their clothes stripped.
Then they were beaten with rods again and again.
Then they were imprisoned in a dungeon.
Then they had their feet shackled in stocks.

And about midnight, they were praying and singing hymns of praise,

When the foundations of the prison were shaken,
And all the doors flew open,
And everyone's shackles were unfastened,
And Paul and Silas spoke Your Good News to the jailer and he and his family were saved. (See Acts 16:25-34)

O Lord! We've had our enthusiasm for sharing Your Good News stripped.
We've been beaten down by the outside world saying no again and again and being tolerant of everything but Your Good News.
We've been imprisoned by our own indifference and apathy and a worldly mindset.
And our feet have been shackled by our reluctance to share Your Good News anywhere except inside the church.

O Lord, the world is in a dark like midnight outside and we're praying and praising You.

Please, shake the very foundations of this church.
And throw open the doors so wide we've got room to take Your Good News with us as we go.
And unfasten the shackles that are keeping us from sharing Your Good News far and wide.
Then use us to speak Your Good News to whomever you put in our path. And, Lord, may those who are prisoners of darkness and their families be saved.

Amen

∞

Prayed at a Monday Night Prayer Meeting.

Yours, O Lord, is the greatness, and the power, and the glory, and the victory, and the majesty; for all that is in the heavens and the earth is Yours; Yours is the kingdom. O Lord, and Yours it is to be exalted as head over all. (See 1 Chron. 29:11)

Both riches and honor come from You, and You reign over all. In Your hand are power and might; in Your hand it is to make great and to give strength to all.

Now therefore, our God, we thank You and praise Your glorious name and those attributes which that name denotes. (1 Chron. 29:11-13)

Lord, give us strength to do more for You and the intimacy to know exactly what it is that You want done.
Give us the strength to be Your hands and Your feet and Your voice and the presence of mind to reflect all the glory Your way.
Give us the strength to resist even the thought of evil in our lives and a recognition of that way of escape that You provide for every temptation.

Give us the strength to be a person of integrity and honesty and the backbone to stand unashamedly for Your truths.

Lord, give us the honor of lifting to You the very words that Jesus would be lifting to You if He were here in our stead.
Give us the honor of being able to give You so much more than mere money.
Give us the honor of being able to spend so much time with You and in Your Word that You and Your Word abide in us.

O Lord, give us the riches that come from kingdom work that stores treasures in heaven. Give us the riches that come from the fellowship and relationship of fellow believers who are working together to build your kingdom here on earth.

O Lord, I humbly request that You would make us great by keeping us properly humble. O Lord, keep our sins ever before our eyes. We seek your reproof, Your correction, Your hand upon our lives. Scourge us, discipline us. May earthly comforts fail us so that we more and more rely on You.

O Lord, may You receive the honor and the glory and the greatness and the riches that come from our attempting to be properly thankful for what You have done for us. May we be ever mindful of Your call upon our lives to be totally committed to You.

O Lord, put people in our path who need to hear Your Good News. Put people in our path who need to experience Your grace. And may they never be the same.

Amen

Prayed at a Monday Night Prayer Meeting.

Lord God,

We're guilty—every one of us. We're guilty of categorizing our sins.
And to make matters worse, we're guilty of using society's standards
to be our guide in
- defining what is sin and
- determining which sins are serious.

Why, Lord, did you know that it's okay to
- cheat on our income tax return,
- cheat at school as long as we don't get caught,
- commit homosexual acts or fornication or adultery as long as
  its between two consenting adults,
- have an abortion as long as it's in the first two trimesters,
- be vindictive and revengeful if we've been wronged?

Did You know that pride is one of the highest virtues? And did You
know that it's a sin to be intolerant of anyone or any act and that it's
a sin to tell someone he's a sinner or that Jesus is the only way to the
Father?

And Lord, did You know that unless we
- commit a hate crime against Jews, homosexuals, or blacks,
- molest a child sexually,
- commit an act of terrorism,
- sell drugs to a minor
- or commit premeditated murder
that our sins really aren't that bad?

O Lord, what succumbing to society's views of sin has done to us is
making us fall prey to the 7:47 Principle.[37] As You recall, the last part
of Luke 7:47 (NIV) says, "He who is forgiven little, loves little."

---

[37] Lucado, Max, *A Love Worth Giving* by Max Lucado, p.1-10.

Lord, our love comes up way short because we use society's definition of sin instead of Yours. We haven't committed any of society's big sins; therefore, we don't need a lot of forgiveness. Why, many of us were nurtured into a relationship with You at a young age when our biggest sin may have been not sharing our toys with the other kids.

O Lord, when I hear the testimonies of folks here, I usually don't hear any remorse for the sins of the former life. I hear no crying. I see no tears. We don't see great love for You because we don't see that we have been forgiven of all that much.

Also, because we use society's definition of sin, we don't experience that sense of forgiveness as often as we should—because we don't keep short accounts with you. In fact, we tend to pray every once in a while and ask for blanket forgiveness of our sins—because we can't even bring to mind any sins we've committed recently. Or we pray for the sick when we are more spiritually sick than the ones we are praying for are physically sick. Or we are perceived as having a holier-than-thou attitude because we rank the sins we recognize in other people's lives as being much worse than the sins we identify in our own lives—which we don't even take seriously.

O Lord, use Your Holy Spirit and Your Holy Word to cause us to recognize Your definition of sin. Help us to listen to Your Holy Spirit instead of our own consciences. O Lord, help us to keep a close eye on our rearview mirror so that we see the sin in our lives every time it rears its ugly head. Help us to keep short accounts with You. Lord, help us to recognize that we are the greatest sinners who have ever lived because we have broken and continue to break, even at this very moment, Lord, the greatest commandment that was ever given—to love You with all our heart, and with all our soul, and with all our might.

O Lord, help us to turn off the TV and the radio talk shows and our computers and smart phones and I-pads and help us to tune into Your frequency.

O Lord, we desire to be a people who know we have been forgiven much and therefore love much—and because we have been forgiven much and love much, may we be a thankful people—a people so thankful that we share Your message near and far.

And May Your Word spread quickly, run its course, be glorified and triumphant. (See 2 Thes. 3:1)

Amen

∞

Night in Bethlehem is the name FBC gives to its yearly living nativity expanded to include Bethlehem and choir presentations etc. This was prayed at a Monday Night Prayer Meeting.

O Lord Who Inspired the Written Word and Who Is the Living Word,

We praise You because we know You have the final word.
We praise You because we know Your Word is true.
We praise You because Your Word is living and powerful and sharper than any two-edged sword, piercing even to the division of the soul and spirit, and of the joints and marrow, and is the discerner of the thoughts and intents of the soul. (See Heb. 4:12)

Lord, as we settle into the season of the year in which Your Written Word proclaiming the arrival of Your Living Word should be on the lips of everyone, what we see is disturbing—because Your message has been diluted, compromised, squelched, ignored, defamed, kept in a manger, or turned into Santa Claus. O Lord, there is a great injustice out there. Folk are dying out there and going to a sinner's Hell because we have distorted Your message, Lord. We confess. We of the church are guilty of stifling Your message with legalism and rituals and traditions, of confusing folk with religious language, of keeping the message to ourselves, of failing to take a stand when others have insulted Your message, and of failing to live lives through which others could see Your Living Word through us.

Lord, we know that exciting things happen when we pray. Unleash Your power. May Your Word spread quickly, run its course, and be glorified and triumphant. (See 2 Thes. 3:1)

Lord, may Your Message come through loud and clear in the upcoming children's musical and in the Night in Bethlehem and in the preached word and in our lives as we walk before others. May misconceptions be corrected. May our celebration of the birth and new life of the babe in a manger turn into a celebration of new births and new lives of babes in Christ. Lord, may not only seeds be planted and watered, but may a crop be harvested.

And may Your kingdom increase here on earth.

Amen

∞

Prayed at Monday Night Prayer Meeting.

Lord of Salvation,

I've got a question burning in my mind. What is supposed to be the number one motivator for me to have enough evangelistic fervor so that I follow through on every witnessing opportunity Your Holy Spirit draws to my attention?

Is it supposed to be the thoughts that sometimes run through my mind of non-Christians I encounter spending eternity in excruciating agony in a place of fire and brimstone, in a sinner's Hell? If that's it, Lord, send those thoughts more frequently.

Is it supposed to be the vision I sometimes have of how some of those I encounter could be rejoicing and praising Your name because they're enjoying victory over sin in their lives, experiencing the peace of forgiveness, and feeling the joy of knowing that You hold them in Your hand and no one or no thing can snatch them away? If that's it, Lord, send those visions more often.

Is it the image that comes to mind sometimes of these folks experiencing Heaven—of being constantly in Your presence, of experiencing no pain and no problems and feeling Your love all day long? If so, Lord, better send that image a lot more.

Or is it merely the last words that Jesus spoke before he ascended into Heaven, what we call the Great commission, to go and make disciples of all nations combined with James 4:17 which says: Whoever knows to do right and fails to do it, for him it is sin? If so, Lord, help me to hate sin in my life more.

Or is it the remembrance I have of the joy I get when basking in the thought that Your angels in Heaven are rejoicing because a soul was brought into the fold and I had some small part in it? If so, Lord, let me remember it more.

Or is it the thought that I sometimes get that one of my loved ones might be killed or led astray by the person that I was supposed to win to Christ but didn't? If so, Lord, send the thought time and time again.

Or is it that I'm supposed have a love just like Yours for these and therefore can't help but shed tears for their lostness and take advantage of every opportunity to change that? If so, Lord, grow my love.

Or is it supposed to be the natural result of my standing in the gap for these folk, interceding for them over and over again so much and so often that You change what I'm praying for and what I'm doing with respect to these folk to what You want me to pray and to what You want me to do? If so, Lord, move me to pray more fervently and more often for them.

O Lord, whatever the answer, whichever of these is to be the prime motivator, would You cause that to present itself more forcefully and more often in my life? And, Lord, if there's anyone else here that needs to be further motivated to be Your intentional witness, would You do that in their life also?

Amen

∞

Prayed at a Monday Night Prayer Meeting.

O Lord,

If the Mayor of Tullahoma's secretary were to phone us to set up an appointment for us to have a personal one-on-one session with the Mayor to discuss the future of Tullahoma, we'd be flattered, we'd feel honored, and we would comply with his wishes.

If Governor Bredesen's office called saying he needs us to come to Nashville so he could get our personal opinion on how to fix TennCare, we'd spend time organizing our thoughts, put on our best suit, and head to Nashville.

If President Bush's office called saying he needs us to come to Washington so he can get our opinion on the Iraq situation, we'd cancel our other appointments, buy a new suit, and head to DC. And we'd be properly humbled by the experience.

But, alas, Lord, none of these folks even know we exist. But You, Lord, God of the entire universe, the one who holds the sun and the moon in Your hands, the one who elevates kings and deposes them, the one who spoke creation into being, have provided us with a personal standing invitation to come into Your presence and make our requests known to You.

O Lord, we praise You not only because You are not only the only one who truly cares about our opinion and who truly listens and the only one who is willing to give us all the time we need to express our opinions and needs and concerns, but You show your great love and trust in us by giving us great responsibilities.

O Lord, we acknowledge what an awesome task You have given us to be good stewards of this planet we live on and to have dominion and authority over all the animals. We confess to being wasteful at times and to being ineffective in getting the rest of the world to get serious about our environment. O Lord, give us wisdom and direction.

But even more mind boggling is the fact that You have put us in charge of the family business now that Your Son is back in Heaven. O Lord, you have shown total confidence in us to get the job done. And we feel humbled. Lord, we're down here struggling to run the business properly. We acknowledge that parts of the business are doing better than others. In particular, two facets of the business deeply concern us: procurement and recruitment.

In terms of procurement, we're not getting near enough of Your will brought down from Heaven and done here on earth. Your Word indicates that it requires prayers to bring Your will down here to earth from up there in Heaven. Lord, we're sending our orders up to Heaven, but the goods only seem to be trickling in and some of them are a long time coming. Lord, help us to speed up the process and increase the throughput. O Lord, if it requires more prayers, more desperate prayers, or more prayers, use Your Holy Spirit to communicate that to us and others who need to know. Then use Your Holy Spirit to cause it to happen.

Additionally, Lord, we have recruitment problems—big time. First off, we're having a problem just getting the Word out. So few people even know about Your business here on earth. And many of those who do know seem to have some misconceptions that keep them from buying in. O Lord, may Your Word spread quickly, run its course, be glorified and triumphant. (See 2 Thes. 3:1) O Lord, help us to overcome our internal problems that keep us from getting the Word out the door. Be with our agents out in the field and bless their efforts. And, Lord, bring more workers. There is too much to be done with so little time to do it. Lord, apparently this is a job we can't do by ourselves. Help us to be totally reliant on You.

And may the business thrive.

Amen

∞

Offertory Prayer prayed at an 8:30 Sunday Morning Worship Service. Baptists and Presbyterians are the only denominations that believe 'once saved, always saved.' The strongest passage supporting this doctrine is John 6:37-40,44,50. However, the one I like the best is John 10:27-29.

O Lord Who Is on High,
O Lord Who Reigns over All,
O High and Lofty One Who Inhabits Eternity and Revives the Spirit of the Humble and the Heart of the Penitent, (See Isa. 57:15)

We praise You because (Repeat with the indented phrases below or not)
- the tomb is empty and You are the Captain of our salvation.
- the only hell we can experience is right here on earth.
- all our sins—past, present, and future, have already been forgiven.
- we couldn't lose our salvation if we tried.
- we don't ever have to sin again.
- Your river of Living Water flows right through us.
- You've already prepared a mansion for us in Heaven.
- there's no fine print in our contract with You.
- we don't have to worry about thieves because our treasures are safe with You up in heaven.

- we don't ever have to worry about anything now that we've put our burdens on you.

O Lord, we know that if we also worship the god of materialism or status that our tithes and offerings would be as offensive to You as was the smell of the burnt offerings that wafted up to You in the Temple when the Israelites were worshiping Baal and Ashtoreth in the night at the same time. O Lord, we know that if we're merely giving out of habit or duty or obedience the experience is pretty hollow and we're failing to feel the joy that can truly be ours from giving out of love. O Lord, we ask that You would move us closer to being like You—so that we give generously because it's our nature, so that we love You and our fellow man so much that Your work here on earth is our all-consuming passion—as is evidenced by how we spend our time and our money. O Lord, may these offerings be used to comfort those who mourn, to delight those who have given them, to grow Your Kingdom. May Your Word spread quickly, run its course, be glorified and triumphant. (See 2 Thes. 3:1)

And may Your glory know no end.

Amen

❦

An offertory prayer prayed at an 8:30 Sunday Morning Worship Service. Approximately twelve Deacons are given assignments for each morning worship service. So each Deacon ends up giving the offertory prayer about once every three months.

O Lord,

We praise You because while You are the Lord of Abraham, Isaac, and Jacob, You are our god, too.
We praise You because just as You worked in the lives of Abraham, Isaac, and Jacob, You work in our lives, too.

We praise You because when Abraham was tempted to keep the spoils of victory, You sent Melchizedek. You provided an opportunity for Abraham to tithe and to acknowledge that You provided the victory.

Lord, we confess that we, too, are tempted to keep of the produce of the labor of our hands, the spoils of our victories, for ourselves. And we praise You because at this very moment You are providing an opportunity to tithe and acknowledge that we receive no gain but what it doesn't ultimately come from You.

Lord, we praise You because You helped Abraham see that he couldn't be made rich by even a thread or a shoe lace that belonged to someone else. And he gave it all back. Thus Abraham gained a victory greater than over four kings—he conquered self and surrendered it to God.

Lord, we confess that we're tempted to say that now that we've given You Your ten percent, the rest is ours to do with as we please. Thank You for helping us see that we're to return any ill gain and be good stewards of the ninety percent. Help us also conquer self and surrender it to You. Lord, just as the arrival of Melchizedek helped Abraham understand that he shouldn't be beholding to the King of Sodom, may our High Priest in Heaven intercede on our behalf so that we are reminded at just the right time that we don't need the friendship of unbelievers, that we don't need to be popular, that we don't need to participate in anything shady, that we don't need to tolerate the evil practices of the world, that we don't need to water down our testimony for fear of offending anyone, because we have You.
O Lord, thank You for being You.

Amen

Written after reading *Hebrews* by R.R. DeHaan.

Prayed as an offertory prayer when the offering was taken up at the end of an 8:30 Sunday Morning Worship Service.

Father of Faith,

We come acknowledging that just as You are the creator of the entire universe and You created it out of nothingness, so too You are the creator of our faith and You created it out of nothingness. For where there was no faith, there is now faith; and we were not responsible for creating it.

Lord, we pray for any here who have no faith, who don't believe that You are the creator of the universe and that Jesus was God Incarnate and died on the cross for our sins and was resurrected after three days. Create faith in their lives.

Your Word indicates that if we don't have enough faith we should pray for more. Lord, we do exactly that. Your Word says that if we have faith the size of a mustard seed that it can grow to the size of a tree. Lord, we pray that You would grow our faith, no matter how small, to the size of a tree—a tree that bears much fruit in our lives and for Your Kingdom.

Lord, we use the expression "seeing is believing." But we weren't there. We didn't see Jesus do any miracles, die on the cross or be resurrected. Your Word indicates that those who believe without seeing are blessed. Bless us more because we believe and did not see.

Lord, we ask that every penny given here this morning be used to grow our faith and the faith of fellow Christians around the world—and to spread Your Word so that some who have no faith today may find faith tomorrow.

And, Lord, as we leave this place in just a few minutes, may each of us go with the grace of our Lord Jesus, the love of God, and the fellowship of the Holy Spirit.

Amen

Prayed at a Monday Night Prayer Meeting.

O Lord Who Is Always There,

Help us to throw aside every encumbrance, every burden and worry that slows us down, and every sin which so easily besets us so that we may run with patient endurance the race that is set before us—looking to Jesus as the author and finisher of our faith. (See Heb. 12:1) O Lord, help us to run our race so that we may lay hold of the prize and make it ours.

O Lord, we're not running the race for the cheers and applause, to be seen or admired, or for the cups of water along the way, or for a runner's high. Nor are we running the race to finish second. But only, Lord, so that we might receive the ultimate prize—the prize of being in Your presence forever and ever.

O Lord, we praise You because you invited us and encouraged us to run—even though we weren't qualified.

We praise You because You paid our entry fee when there was no way we could.

Thank You for allowing us to wear Your colors and be on Your team.

O Lord, help us to keep it up—help us keep our oil lamps continually full with anticipation and preparation for the coming Bridegroom.

O Lord, we pray for those who began the race, but aren't making any progress now. Help us to pick them up along the way and to return their focus to Jesus.

Lord, we pray that many others would join the race. May Your will be done in their lives.

O Lord, grow our hope for the hereafter, our desire to be with Jesus, our longing to know You more and more into an obsessions. May our eyes look neither to the left or to the right, but may they stay focused on Jesus. O Lord, we thank You for the instances when we've experienced a small piece of Heaven right here on earth—for those foretastes of glory divine.

Fascinate our minds with Christ. Keep our feet on the path. And encourage us with Your love.

Amen

∞

Prayed as an offertory prayer at an 8:30 Sunday Morning Worship Service.

Lord, we come asking for Your blessing,

Yeah, we know that You make Your sun to rise on the evil and the good and send rain on the just and the unjust, but we're not asking for that type of blessing—'cause the evil folk get it without asking and we suspect we do too.

And, yeah, we know that we received the blessing of salvation and, for that matter, every spiritual blessing when we believed. We realized that You showered us with certain blessings just because we put our faith in Jesus Christ. But, Lord, we're not asking for a blessing we've already received even though some of us have not availed ourselves of some of those blessings.

And, yeah, we're familiar with some of those promises You made—like if we hunger and thirst after righteousness, You're going to satisfy us. But we're not asking you to keep Your promises here this morning, because we know You always do.

And, Lord, we're not asking that You bless us when we die—because we know that we're not only going to get a mansion in heaven but also rewarded for those good deeds we did here on earth for which we didn't get any reward.

But, Lord, we come asking You to bless us, not because we're numbered among the just or the unjust, not because we accepted Jesus as our Lord and Savior in the past few moments, not because we've just satisfied our end of one of Your promises, not because we're fixing to die in the next few moments, but only, Lord, because we are Your children and we're asking and because You are who You are: a compassionate, loving God who loves us beyond measure.

Lord, we ask You to bless us with a church family that loves us, encourages us, cries when we cry, laughs when we laugh, overlooks our shortcomings, visits us when we are sick, checks on us when we aren't there, meets our needs when we're needy, and provides an environment in which we are continually challenged to grow in the Lord.

And bless these tithes and offering to the furtherance of Your Kingdom.

Amen

∞

Prayed at a Monday Night Prayer Meeting. The Lottie Moon Christmas Offering for International Missions is an offering Southern Baptists give around Christmas time to support about five thousand missionaries around the world. Lottie Moon was a missionary to China from 1873 to 1912. When my wife and I went to the Olympics in Atlanta a number of years back, we parked quite a distance north of the city and were shuttled in. We were let off several blocks from our venue. As we were walking to the venue, we saw it: a church with a big sign on it that said 'The Perfect Church.' We naturally laughed because we knew we couldn't join because then the church wouldn't be perfect anymore. So if your church is like mine, whether it has pedophilic priests or bats in the belfry, you should confess the sins of the church, all of which you are at least partially responsible for and ask God to help.

Lord of Love,

I come confessing that we are a church that is more concerned with image than with people.

We put on a façade about being a great evangelistic church. We've been placing great emphasis on the FAITH Evangelism® Strategy for almost two years now—a program designed to win folk to the Lord left and right. But, Lord, the number of baptisms is down so much that it should be treated as a crisis—to the point where the entire church should be on its knees every Sunday begging you to end the drought. Yet, Lord, it's not even mentioned since it puts the church in a negative light.

And, Lord, we've remodeled the old Sears building inside and out to create our new Ministry Center specifically so our youth would have a place of their own. Lord, we spared no expense to make it one nice facility. Yet if You look closely, Lord, you won't find a basketball goal anywhere—we took those down and refuse to put them back up; apparently they attract the wrong crowd or don't look pristine. And you'll see signs on the doors that tell all skateboarders to stay away else we'll call the police on them. O Lord, those boys are going to think that You don't love them—and I guess You don't through us!

And, Lord, we say great things about our Deacon Family Care Program practically every time someone joins the church—but You and I both know that there is a large number of people who either don't know who their Deacon is or haven't ever heard from him. O Lord, reality seems to be different from the impression we give.

And, Lord, I remember a young man and his grandmother who used to come to church here a few years back and sat close to the front. Each Sunday evening at 7pm sharp, he'd get up and go out the front to get a drink of water to take with his pill. One of our ministerial staff didn't like it and asked him to stop. They've never been back; and when I see them around town occasionally they go out of their way to say something bad about the ministerial staff member. And the preacher and the other ministers continue to get up and go out the front to get drinks of water for the speaker if they feel like he needs it.

And recently, Lord, a man told me how one of our ministers visited his wife when she was in the hospital in Nashville. He went out of his way to make a good impression on the doctor, nurse, and social worker who were in the room at the time, then proceeded to announce in front of all of them that if this man or his wife needed anything, financial or otherwise, just to let him know down at the church. A few weeks later this man went to the minister to see if he could get some financial help and the minister refused him, telling him he needed to do a better job supporting his family.

O Lord, we used to have a place set aside for collecting aluminum cans to be recycled for the Lottie Moon Christmas Offering. But somebody decided that area didn't look as nice as it could. So they tore it down— and now we have to collect cans on the sly.

O Lord, we used to have a nice graveled area for parking right next to the entrance to the Prayer Room so folk could get in and out without getting wet or being accosted. But somebody decided it looked tacky so they did away with it, planted grass there and blocked off the driveway. And now we only have about a third of the slots filled in the Prayer Room.

O Lord, at first glance this is a great church, but on closer inspection, we don't love the lost enough to win them to the Lord, we don't love the boys of this community who carry skateboards enough to allow them on the property, we don't love our own members enough to pay them a visit every once in a while, we're more concerned with having our worship services go according to plan than we are with folk's physical health, we're more concerned with leaving the impression that we meet our members every need than we are with meeting any of their needs, and we're more concerned with winning the city beautification award than the safety and comfort of our own members.

O Lord, I pray for the day when we quit being concerned with what other people think and are only concerned with finding and doing Your will.

Amen

Note: The signs about skateboards are gone; a basketball goal is up; and our youth department went out of its way to engage and involve the skateboarders. Sometimes God answers our prayers quickly.

FAITH Evangelism® is a registered trademark of LifeWay Christian Resources.

∞

Prayed at Monday Night Prayer Meeting.

Lord Jesus,

Over in Luke it is recorded that the Disciples asked You how to pray. After what we call the Model Prayer, there is no "amen," apparently because You weren't through teaching them how to pray. Rather, You told the parable of the man who had a friend on a journey show up late at his house to spend the night. He didn't have anything in the house to feed his friend, so he went to his neighbor and asked for bread for his friend. And he had to ask more than once. Lord, I take this to mean that it's just as important for us to ask for the bread of life for our friends as it is to ask for what sustains our very physical existence. Then, Lord, You tell us to ask and keep on asking, seek and keep on seeking, and knock and keep on knocking—and then the door will be opened. (See Luke 11)

Lord, we're here to do exactly that. We're here to ask for salvation for our friends. And this isn't the first time we've asked, and it won't be the last. But, Lord, as we examine Your Word, we recognize that asking over and over again was accompanied by a strong, strong desire. Esther prayed for her fellow Jews to be saved from Haman as if her life depended on it. Moses asked God to blot his name out of Your Book rather than destroy the Israelites who made the golden calf. And Daniel interceded for the whole nation of Israel by prayer and supplications, with fasting, sackcloth, and ashes. And Paul, with bitter grief and incessant anguish, wished he could be cut off from Christ rather than his countrymen and kinsmen. (See Rom. 9:2-3) And You agonized in the garden for the sins of all mankind.

So, Lord, we come with deep concern and heavy hearts asking that Charles, Jay, Steve, Jeff, and John be saved. And if, perhaps, our desire isn't strong enough, would You grow our desire to the point where it is so strong we keep asking until the door is opened?

Lord, when You fed the five thousand it was the Disciples who carried the bread and fishes to thousands who were hungry. Likewise, use us, Your current disciples, to carry Your Living Bread to the thousands who are without.

Amen

Written after reading a section in John Rice's *Prayer: Asking and Receiving* called "Praying Bread for Others—Christ's College Course in Prayer" (pp. 82-85).

Prayed at Monday Night Prayer Meeting.

Father of Salvation,

We thank you for the love which drew salvation's plan. We praise You because it is Your desire that all men be saved.

But, Lord, we come confessing that, while Your plan is perfect, we're failing miserably with one of the parts we are to play. We must repeat a confession we find in Your Word: "A friend of mine who is on a journey has come and I have nothing to set before him." (See Luke 11:5) Lord, there is not a one of us who does not have a loved one—a spouse, a child, a parent, a sibling, a close kinsman of some kind or else a dear friend who is lost. And, Lord, while You have placed us on the banks of the very river of their lives in which they are floundering, we're not able to throw them a life preserver. We say, "It's easier to witness to someone we don't know than to lead our loved one to Christ." Yet we're not leading someone we don't know to Christ either. O Lord, in truth, our cupboard is bare. And You have a whole bakery full of bread.

Therefore, Lord, our request is twofold. First, would You bring our loved ones to Christ? And, Lord, help us to be faithful to lift them to You day and night, night and day, over and over, again and again until Your will is done in their lives.

Secondly, Lord, would You use Your Holy Spirit to cause us to move to a position in our lives where we can offer them the Bread of Life? O Lord, grow our concern for them so that it matches Yours. And put us in the right spot at the right time and give us the strength and the desire and the impetus to pick up the life preserver and throw it to them.

O Lord, may Your will be done in their lives because Your will is done in our lives. And may You receive all the glory and credit.

Amen

Prayed during a Monday Night Prayer Meeting.

Omnipresent Lord,

Your Word says that if I ascend up to Heaven, You are there;
If we make our bed in hell, behold, You are there;
If we take wings of a morning and dwell in the uttermost parts of the sea,
Even there Your hand will lead us, and Your right hand shall hold us.
(See Ps. 139:8-9)

Lord, we praise You because even though You're there, You're hidden. You don't stand there visible all day long like a policeman looking over our shoulder watching our every move—but You provide an environment in which we truly have freedom of choice.

And we praise You because even though those that are for us are greater than those who are against us, we can't see them with our eyes as Elisha and the servant did at Dothan—therefore we can truly live by faith.

Lord, some folk say that You are never more than a prayer away, but we, Your children, know that You set up Your tent in our hearts—and, indeed, sometimes we hear you in there thumping around.

But, Lord, we can't see You, even though we acknowledge that You are there all the time, we desire a constant recognition of Your presence in our lives. We know You sometimes bless us with rainbow days—days in which evidence of Your miracles and promises just explodes in our face. And we pray for more 'rainbow days.'[38]

But more often than not, we experience ordinary days—days in which we get caught up in other activities and don't make conscious recognition that You are there—even though You are.

O, Lord, help us to get in the habit of recognizing Your handiwork in every creature and creation that You've made and in every blessing and

---

[38] Ortberg, John, *God is Closer than You Think*, pp. 32-34. This whole prayer was heavily influenced by the first two chapters of this book.

trial that comes our way. And then, Lord, move us from recognizing Your presence all the time to practicing Your presence all the time—to carrying on that intimate conversation with You all day long.

O Lord, we acknowledge that at times while in Your presence we have allowed our focus to wander and have deliberately sinned—stepping out of that intimate relationship with You. O Lord, give us such a sense of Your presence that it keeps us intimate with You all day long.

O Lord, I pray for all those who have no sense of Your presence in their lives. Help them to feel and acknowledge that You are there. And I pray for all those who are not intimate with You. May Your Holy Spirit convince them of their need.

May Your presence fill our hearts and may we walk and talk with You all day long.

Amen

Prayed during a Monday Night Prayer Meeting.

O Lord Who Said, "I AM WHO I AM,"
  We praise You because You Are Who You Are,
  Not some invention of the human mind as some would suggest,
  Not some vague abstraction that we need to pretend exists.

O Lord, we praise You because You Will Be Who You Will Be,
  Not some idol created by human hands,
  Not some made-up god limited by the limits of the human mind.

O Lord, we praise You because You are the Great I AM,
  The one and only True and Living God,
  The god who spoke the word and the whole universe came into existence,
  The god who breathed the very breath of life into our nostrils and can take it away in an instance,

The god who spoke to Moses in the burning bush,
The god who is found by all who diligently seek Him.

O Lord, we thank You because You have grown our faith in You
Through the faith and testimony of fellow Christians and those
who have gone before us,
By giving us minds that say if there is a creation there had to
be a Creator,
By using Your Holy Spirit to speak to us as we pay attention to
Your Holy Word and Your spoken word,
By keeping Your every promise.

O Lord, we thank You for growing our faith from the size of a mustard
seed to the size of a tree.

O Lord, You call us into account. To those who have been given much,
much is required. You have given us much and we come up short. You
gave us Your written Word and we put it on a shelf and drag it out on
Sunday to take to church. You have given us the ability to speak Your
Word yet we're reticent to speak it when you send a lost person to cross
our path. You've given us the gift of prayer, yet we've never taken it
seriously. You've blessed us with Your presence, yet we're too busy to turn
around and bless the needy and hurting with our presence. You've given
us Your love, yet we find ourselves unable to love our fellow man to the
point where we must make a sacrifice. You've given us Your promises,
but for the most part we can't even name them much less claim them.

O Lord, use Your Holy Spirit to chide us and to make us feel more
guilty. Lord, make us make Your priorities for our lives the only
priorities in our lives.

And may Your Kingdom know no end.

Amen

Prayed at a Monday Night Prayer Meeting.

Hound of Heaven,

We praise You because You are the big dog who doesn't stay on the porch.

We praise You because You are like the bloodhound that never loses the scent.

O Lord, we thank You because You hounded us until we finally submitted to You. We praise You because You hounded us not like a pit bull hot on our heels ready to pounce any moment, but like a determined suitor who wouldn't be denied—who respected us and loved us unconditionally and only wanted the very best for us.

O Lord, we thank You for following us until we followed You.
Lord, we pray very specifically that You would follow some others until they follow You:
Charles, John, Steve, Jeff, and Roy.
O Lord, we pray for all the folk who are running from You.

Also, Lord, we praise You because You didn't stop hounding us just because we started following You, but You are continuing to hound us about certain sins we still struggle with and about certain areas of our lives where we are still not following You. O Lord, we praise You because You are relentless.

Let the chase continue.

Amen

This prayer was written after reading Francis Thompson's *The Hound of Heaven* and David Jeremiah's *Captured by Grace.*

Baptist Churches are known for committees. This prayer was prayed at the initial meeting of an ad hoc committee.

Lord God,

I know a little ditty that goes: "Committees of twenty deliberate plenty; committees of ten act now and again; but most work is done by committees of one." That's exactly what we want—only we want that one to be You.

If there is any leg work to be done, use our legs. If there is any manual labor to be done, use our hands. If there is any paper work to be done, use our skills. If there are any presentations to be made, user our voices. If there are any lives that need to be changed, use our prayers.

But, Lord, may You be the only one here with an agenda.
We don't want to make any decisions; that's Your job.
We don't want to come up with any ideas; that's Your job.
We don't want to vote and make democracy work.
We want You to let us know Your will and make theocracy work.

Lord, unfortunately, in order to communicate and accomplish your will You will probably use our hands and feet and mouths. Lord, may we not speak unless it is as You lead us. May we act only as You lead. May the only attitude we have come from you. May we give up our right to be right. May it be Your way or no way.

Lord, don't let us get in Your way with our ideas; just overwhelm us with Your plan. May we not get ahead of You, but wait patiently for Your leading.

Lord, work Your perfect will here in spite of imperfect us.

Lord, give us a heaping helping of humility so that we are not here to get our egos stroked. May each member's inputs be treated as if You are talking—because You are.

Lord, when we make our report to the church may You get all the glory and honor and take all the credit too. May we as committee members fade into the background.

And may Your will prevail.

Amen

∞

This prayer was prepared, ready to go, and delivered on the Sunday morning we had somebody from the Creation Museum delivering our sermon. The Lord plans ahead!

Mastermind of the Universe,

We praise You because, while not one scientist down through the ages has come up with even one theory on how to make something from absolutely nothing, it was a piece of cake for You to form the whole universe from exactly that. Lord, we lift to You those present-day scientists who don't worship You as Creator. May they see the light.

Lord, there are Christians and others who treat the Genesis account of Creation as symbolic or a fable or a myth. O Lord, may we never have a perception of You as being a god who is too weak or too small to do exactly what You said You did or to do exactly what You said You will do. O Lord, may we never doubt You.

Lord, there are folk who say they see God in a sunset or that there is a god in each of us or that Mother Earth brings the storms and the rain. O Lord, may we never confuse creation with You, the Creator. May we never be guilty of worshipping self, human potential, or any created thing.

O Lord, we praise You because You do marvelous things. (See Ps. 86:10 NIV) We praise You because, while You are the God who created more than four billion stars in the Milky Way and in the process also created over one-hundred billion other galaxies, You are also the God who wipes away the tear running down our cheek, takes us in Your warm embrace, and heals our wounds.

O Lord, You are so awesome that every head should bow,
every knee should bend,
every mind should worship,
every will should yield,
every hand should serve,
and every heart should love.[39]

O Lord, we pray for exactly that to happen.

Amen

∞

Prayed during a Monday Night Prayer Meeting.

O Lord Who Hears Our Prayers,

I'm here to put together words that form sentences, sentences that form a prayer, a prayer that is to glorify You and edify the Church. But, Lord, words alone should not make up a prayer. Words alone are as hollow as ping-pong balls. Strip away the words, Lord, and feel our passion, feel our love, feel our yearning, feel our faith.

---

[39] Lotz, Anne Graham, The *Glorious Dawn of God's Story*, (Dallas, 1997) p. xxxi.
She writes "How unbelievably awesome is the One Who Created Everything!
our heads should bow,
our knees should bend,
our wills should yield,
our hands should serve,
our minds should worship,
our hearts should love

O Lord, feel how much love we have for you and feel loved. O Lord, sometimes we feel so much love for You there are no words to adequately express it. O Lord, it says in the Bible that sometimes the Holy Spirit must pray to You with groanings when we try to pray but can't find the words. (See Rom. 8:26) May His groanings express how much we love You.

O Lord, sometimes we look about and see so many lost in sin and our whole world seemingly mired in sin; and we desire so much to see Your will done. The tears well up in our eyes for the lost and because we know You grieve for them. O Lord, sense our strong desire for Your will to be done. O Lord, just as Jesus prayed, "Thy Kingdom come, Thy will be done." and then went out and brought it about, we ask You to bring about Your Kingdom and Your will through us. May You act disguised as us.

I'm not here to heap up empty phrases as the Gentiles do; for they think they will be heard for their many words. (See Matt. 6:7) I'm here to ask You to sense our faith—faith that says we believe in You and we believe in prayer. O Lord, we lift to You every circumstance, every need, every desire in our lives. Use them as entry points into our lives. Help us remember that before a need occurs, You've already fully prepared the supply and all we have to do is ask. Help us to remember that every circumstance or problem in our lives is first and foremost an opportunity for You to get involved and grow our character and faith and draw us closer to You. Help us to remember that every desire we have that we express to You in prayer is a desire You can take advantage of to work Your will in our lives; and we pray for exactly that to happen. O Lord, grow our faith.

O Lord, ignore our words and read our hearts.

Amen

Prayed as an offertory prayer at an 8:30 Sunday Morning Worship Service.

O Lord Who Doesn't Leave Things to Chance,

We praise You because You never roll the dice or play the odds.
We praise You because there has never been a cosmic accident.

O Lord, we praise You because on purpose You created the entire universe and the earth we stand on.
We praise you because on purpose You created each of us.
We praise You because on purpose You loved us.
We praise You because on purpose You sent Jesus to die on the cross for our sins.
We praise You because on purpose You put a need in us that can only be satisfied by finding You.

O Lord, on purpose we came here this morning to show You we love You.
O Lord, on purpose we bring you tithes and offerings to show You we love you.

O Lord, on purpose I am going to pray a little prayer that I sometimes pray. O Lord, would You require of us that we do whatever it takes to become that one church in all of history that comes closest to being all that You want it to be?

O Lord, may Your purpose become our purpose.

Amen

Prayed during Monday Night Prayer Meeting.

O Lord of the Bible,

We praise You because You are not just the Lord of the Bible, but You are the Lord of the genome and the atom and the cosmos.

O Lord, we praise You because while we worship You in the church house we are in awe of Your great love which drew salvation's plan, saved us from ourselves and the ravages of sin, and gave us new life, abundant life, and eternal life with You. There are geneticists who worship You in their laboratories because they are in awe of the complexity and intricateness they see as they explore the more than three billion base pairs of the human genome. There are astronomers who worship You in their observatories because they are in awe of the ten billion observable galaxies which each average ten billion stars while the universe just goes on and on beyond what they can observe. And there are quantum physicists who worship You in their laboratories because they are in awe of how everything fits together and holds together at such an infinitesimal level.

O Lord, we praise You because no matter where our scientists look, Your fingerprints are everywhere.

O Lord, we lift to You all those who diligently seek truth. We pray for the day when all true seekers of truth worship the same Truth. For Your Son said that He is the Way, the Truth and the Life and that no man comes to You except through Him. (See John 14:6) May all who find the Truth be free indeed. (See John 8:36)

O Lord, we thank You because You decided what six billion chromosomes we needed and just where they needed to be placed to make up our DNA and because You put together the quarks and leptons that make up the neutrons and protons that make up the atoms that make up the molecules that make up the cells that make up us.

O Lord, we acknowledge You as Creator Lord. Let us also acknowledge You as Sovereign Lord—the one who reigns in our life and whom we should allow to control our every thought and deed.

May Truth reign and may every cell in our body be used to honor and glorify You.

Amen

∞

Prayed during a Monday Night Prayer Meeting.

O Lord Who Drew Salvation's Plan,

We have the confidence in approaching You, that if we ask anything in accord with Your will, You will hear us. And we know that if You hear us, whatever we ask, we know we have what we asked of You. (1 John 5:14-15)

I therefore ask, knowing that it is in Your will, that You would fulfill all that Your sacrifice on the cross and Your resurrection was supposed to provide for me and for all born-again Christians here at FBC.

O Lord, it's embarrassing to us and to You, it's a blurring of our witness to the world, that some of us still don't feel like we're forgiven. Lord, some of us are still suffering from guilt from past sins. Some of us are still unable to forgive others of the hurt that they have caused us even though you forgave us of a million times more. Some of us claim to have forgiven but can't forget. Some of us still allow new sins to steal our sense of salvation. O Lord, does Jesus' death on the cross enable us to have our every sin—past, present, and future forgiven once and for all or has Satan just got us believing lies? O Lord, may we feel so forgiven that we can forgive anything.

O Lord, some of us, even though we were baptized in a fashion that symbolized the death and burial of the old life and the being raised to new life with Jesus, are basically still living the old life. We try to live the new life in our own power and we fail miserably time and time again. Others of us are not experiencing the companionship and the empowerment of the Holy Spirit. We're living lives of mediocrity and even of depression rather than experiencing the abundant life. O Lord, does Jesus' death and resurrection enable us to have new life, abundant and free, or has Satan just got us believing lies. O Lord, may we give over to you every decision and every moment so You can give us victory over temptation every time it rears its ugly head and give us peace like a river even through the darkest times.

O Lord, some of us are living as part of the world. We try to live according to the world's idea of success and live according to its rules. O Lord, does Jesus' resurrection mean that we are part of Your Kingdom, part of Your family, that we should live according to Your rules, that we are just passing through this world with a permanent home in Heaven or has Satan just got us believing lies. O Lord, may we be so set apart for You that everyone knows that we're Yours.

O Lord, some of us are so busy doing our own thing that we are missing out on the blessing of doing the good works which You have prepared in advance for us to do. O Lord, does Jesus' death and resurrection mean that we are his workmanship created in Christ Jesus to do good works or has Satan just got us believing lies? O Lord, may we experience the blessing of doing Your will and knowing it.

O Lord, I pray that each of us will realize and experience every ounce of forgiveness and every moment of abundant life and every hope for an afterlife with You in Heaven and every other blessing that Your sacrifice on the cross and Your resurrection was meant to bring about in our life.

Amen

Prayed as an offertory prayer during an 8:30 Sunday Morning Worship Service.

Father of the Groom,

We could honor FBC and its membership for giving almost $50,000 to the Lottie Moon Christmas Offering; we could honor them for paying off the church debt, His Vision Our Passion. But, Lord, I haven't finished my unofficial survey yet, but it's a shame that it even crosses my mind that maybe, just maybe, we had more folk get divorced last year than we baptized. And Your Word says You hate divorce!

O Lord, we have become a people who, if we give our tithe, don't have an abortion, and aren't a practicing pedophile probably think we're okay. O Lord, we've become a people who are comfortable with a little sin in our lives. O Lord, use Your Holy Spirit to convict us of even the smallest sin in our life.

O Lord, I ask You to purify us through our prayers. May we be cleansed to be a Bride suitable for Christ's perfect purity. May we be a church that comes under the unconditional lordship of her Head, Jesus Christ. May we be a church that is not led by her pastor, but by Jesus Christ Himself. May we be a Bride that truly loves her great Bridegroom.

And, Lord, we plead that You would help us stop glorifying man and to only glorify Jesus. I pray for the day that only Jesus' glory is perceptible in this church. I ask that no name, no individual, no group be exalted except for Christ. O Lord, do exalt Jesus' name as it has never been exalted before. And help us to exalt it higher than we ever have before. Let it be high and holy in this body. Give us that much of a taste of Heaven here and now.

O Lord, fulfill Your purpose in this church body.

Lord, almost nowhere in Scripture do You ever give the church a command. All Your commands are to individuals. Nowhere do You tell the church to give. But You have told us each to give as we have purposed in our heart. O Lord, may that take place here and now. May each of us give as Your Holy Spirit has caused us to purpose in our heart.

And may Jesus get all the glory.

Amen

∞

Prayed during a Monday Night Prayer Meeting.

All Powerful Lord God Almighty,

We praise You for Your great power.
We praise You even more for Your great goodness.
We praise You because, while You have the power to do anything, You choose to do only things that are in our best interest.
We praise You because Your will for our lives is all about our best interest.
We praise You because Your power is perfect.
We praise You because Your goodness is perfect.
We praise You because Your will for our life is perfect for us.
We praise You because You care so much for us that You didn't just get Your will for our life off the rack; You custom designed one for each of every one of us.

O Lord, we confess that we have substituted our personal will for our lives for Your perfect will for our lives. O Lord, society is going to Hell, and we are watching the same TV programs, going to the same movies, having the same divorce rate, laughing at the same jokes, lusting after the same material possessions, setting the same priorities and goals, going to the same parties, and buying into the same values. O Lord, we're not holy and set apart—rather we're wholly involved in the world's activities and we've set You apart from most of our life.

O Lord, we need a wake-up call. O Lord, we've had enough 'feel-good' sermons. We've gone home "affirmed, approved, and applauded"[40] rather than "confronted, convicted, confessed and cleansed."[41] O Lord, may Your Holy Word and Your preached word hit the mark in our life. May the difference between Your perfect will and the way we're living be held in such stark contrast that we recognize our sin for what it is. May the tears flow, the aisles fill, and life-changing commitments be made. O Lord, we pray for Your perfect will to reign in our lives, for Your great goodness to be accepted by all here, and for Your great power to be demonstrated.

O Lord, send a great revival for our soul.[42]

Amen

∞

Prayed as an offertory prayer during an 8:30 Sunday Morning Worship Service.

O Lord Who Gave Us Jesus,

We thank You for the gift.

I remember a good friend of mine who confided in me that the real reason he was so careful to give his tithe so faithfully was that he felt that if he didn't he might get sick—or someone in his family might get sick. Lord, just a few weeks back, his pride and joy, his only son got sick and after only a couple of days in the hospital died. I wonder what he is thinking now. Be with him. O Lord, we bring You a gift

---

[40]   Drace, Jerry. "The Work of the Evangelist." *Uu.edu.* R. G. Lee Society of Fellows, n.d. Web. 6 July 2013. <http://www.uu.edu/centers/rglee/fellows/FALL97/Drace.htm>.

[41]   Ibid.

[42]   Baptist Hymnal. Nashville: Convention Press, 1975. Hymn 271.

this morning, a portion of what You have enabled us to earn. But we give it not out of fear.

O Lord, there is a bunch of people, preachers, and churches here in the US that are part of what is called the Faith Movement. They're also known as the "name-it-claim-it" folk. Basically they believe that if they give generously to You and if they have enough faith or believe hard enough that you'll return that money ten or a hundred fold. O Lord, we bring You a gift this morning, a portion of what You have enabled us to earn. But we give it not because we think it will make us rich.

O Lord, Dave Ramsey says that You don't need our money—and that the church doesn't need our money either, but that we should give to the church because it turns us into givers—it makes us better people. O Lord, we bring You a gift this morning, a portion of what You have enabled us to earn. But we give it not because it will make us better people.

O Lord, there are legalists out there who preach that we're sinning if we don't give at least a tithe to the church. But, Lord, we Christians are to live by grace not by law. We're not required to obey Your Old Testament law or live by any set of rules; rather we're just supposed to live in a close relationship to You. O Lord, we bring You a gift this morning, a portion of what You have enabled us to earn. But we give it not out of obedience to You or some law or some set of rules.

O Lord, Your Word says that You love a cheerful giver. O Lord, we bring You a gift this morning, a portion of what You have enabled us to earn. But we give it not as we force ourselves to be happy about it so that you'll love us.

O Lord, there are business men who join a big church and give generously to it because they know it's good for business. O Lord, we bring You a gift this morning, a portion of what You have enabled us to earn. But we give it not for any earthly gain.

O Lord, there are those who dig into their wallet or purse every time the offering plate is passed because they know others are watching. O Lord, we bring You a gift this morning, a portion of what You have enabled us to earn. But we give it not out of concern for what others might think.

O Lord, we bring You a gift this morning, a portion of what You have enabled us to earn. And we give it for the same reason You gave us Jesus—we give it out of love. And it's the very least we can do considering what Jesus did for us.

Amen

∽

This offertory prayer was delivered right before Valentine's Day at an 8:30 Sunday Morning Worship Service.

Lord of Love,

We praise You because You love us like an only son—and then some.

We didn't bring a box of chocolates or a dozen roses, but we come with confession and a contrite heart. O Lord of Love, will You be our Valentine.

It is said that anticipation is the greater joy. We confess that in our case You probably got more joy anticipating what it would be like when we loved You than You've gotten from us actually loving You.

O Lord, we sing love songs and songs of adoration and hymns of praise to You every Sunday, but then we go all week and don't spend so much as even one minute meditating on Your Word so You can speak to us.

O Lord, we claim to love our neighbors as ourselves, but don't even know the names of some of them just down the street and haven't picked up a hitchhiker in years.

O Lord, we claim to love You with all our heart, soul, and might, but then sometimes we don't give You anything more than a tithe.

O Lord, we claim to love You but we spend most of our time with ourselves on the throne of our lives and doing our own thing.

O Lord, we claim to love You but we spend more time agonizing over our favorite team than we spend agonizing over even one of the five billion lost people in the world.

O Lord, send us to our room with no TV for a healthy dose of Your Word.

O Lord, sentence us to focusing on what Jesus did on the cross for us.

Sentence us to grieving about every new sin in our lives the same way Your Holy Spirit does.

Sentence us to a new realization that the penalty for every sin no matter how small is death.

O Lord, bless us with Your presence. Bless us with an encounter with you like Moses had at the burning bush—that changed the direction of the rest of his life. O Lord, bless us with an encounter with You like Moses had on Mt. Sinai that changed his countenance so that everybody could see that he had been in Your presence. O Lord, bless us with an encounter with You like the Disciples had—such that they walked and talked with Jesus all day long for years to come.

O Lord, please accept everything that is put in these plates above the tithe as part of our Valentine's present to You, because it is a love gift from us.

O Lord, comfort the disturbed and disturb the comfortable.

Amen

∞

This offertory prayer was prayed after the invitation of an 8:30 Sunday Morning Worship. Some in the church thought this prayer was inappropriate; others thought it was very appropriate. Be aware that when you pray what God wants prayed it often makes somebody uncomfortable and anytime you imply that the church is less than perfect or suggest sin has been committed it makes some people uncomfortable. While the Holy Spirit is called the Comforter, one of His primary jobs is to make us uncomfortable with our sin.

Lord Most High,

I would like to extend a personal invitation to You to come join us next Sunday. We missed You here this morning. Where were You? Oh, I know all about You being omnipresent so that technically You are here all the time. And I'm aware that You inhabit the praises of Your people and that Your Holy Spirit resides in the hearts of the Christians here and that Your Word says that where two or more are gathered in Your name, You are there; but let's be honest—each of us ignored or resisted those few tugs on our heart we felt during the sermon and the invitation so the end result was exactly the same as if You hadn't been here in any form, shape, or fashion.

I hear tell that You only go where You are invited. You'll have to forgive us, Lord. You see, we got busy doing something else that I guess we all forgot to invite You into the building or else we just assumed somebody else was going to do it. O Lord, we got so caught up in singing that we didn't realize that You weren't really here. And then the special music was so good that we just assumed that You were enjoying it as much as we were. Although, maybe that's not true 'cause a bunch of folk applauded the musicians rather than praising You; and I'm 100% sure that they wouldn't be doing that if You were really here and they could feel Your presence. And then the preaching, Lord—You have truly blessed us with one of Your anointed prophets. Once again he took some of Your truths of old and enlightened us and warmed our hearts as he gave fresh understanding of Your Word. But, Lord, we don't need another 'feel-good' sermon we can say 'amen' to and turn into a conversation piece at the dinner table. O Lord, we need a sermon that ushers in Your presence and ushers in Your Kingdom in our lives. O Lord, we don't need more of what we've been getting—we need You. We've got too much man here and not enough You. O please, Lord, overwhelm us with your presence next Sunday. And may Your presence be so thick and cause so much tension in this room that it scares the devil out of us and causes each one of us to invite You into all those rooms of our heart we haven't opened up to You yet.

O Lord, please accept these tithes and offerings as a down payment on what we owe You in hopes that next Sunday You're going to really show up and we'll be giving You our everything.

Amen

❧

Prayed at a Monday Night Prayer Meeting.

Author of the Universe,

We praise You because as author You have author-ity over Heaven and Earth.
And, Lord, we thank You that You gave that authority to Jesus Christ. And, Lord, we thank You because Jesus has delegated some of that authority to us.

O Lord, it is an awesome thing to recognize that I can pray to change the weather just as Elijah prayed for it not to rain and it didn't rain for three or three-and-a-half years; and then he prayed for fire from heaven and You granted his request.

And, Lord, it is awesome to recognize that I can pray to change the fate of entire populations just as Moses interceded for the Israelites and prevented them from being destroyed at the base of Mt. Sinai.

But, Lord, it is especially burdensome to recognize that I can fail to intercede for an entire population and they can be destroyed or taken captive like the Hebrews were over in Ezekiel.

O Lord, by the authority invested in me by Jesus and with the deep impression that this is what You want me to do, I lift to you the entire population of Tullahoma, TN. O Lord, would You stay Your hand and give these folk another chance? O Lord, I pray that Your Holy Spirit might work in a mighty way in the lives of the saved of this town to cause them to saturate the town with Your Word and Your love. Please, Lord, may neither Your Word nor Your love return void, but may they produce the effects for which You produced them. (See Isa. 55:11) And may You receive all the glory.

Amen

∞

Prayed as an offertory prayer during an 8:30 Sunday Morning Worship service.

O Lord Over All,

I understand that there won't be any atheists in Hell—which is consistent with that verse which says that "every knee shall bow, every tongue confess that Jesus Christ is Lord." (See Phil. 2:10-11) It also brings to mind that old STP commercial whose punch line was "You can pay me now or you can pay me later." Lord, we praise you and thank You because Jesus already paid for our sins so that we won't have to pay for them later. And we're thankful that we already are confessing by word and by deed that Jesus Christ is the lord of our lives—while it still is not too late.

O Lord, we pray for a whole passel of folks in this community who haven't put the additive in their tanks yet. Each of their engines is still running, but it might blow up at any minute. O Lord, don't give up on them. We lift them to You as Moses did the Israelites and as Abraham did the Sodomites. O Lord, give us another chance to get the Good News to them. Clear the airways of any static, help us to tune into their wave length, help them get their ears on, and help us make it as obvious as the nose on their face. Then, Lord, may Your Word not return void, but may it accomplish what You intended. (See Isa. 55:11)

O Lord, use us for Your glory.

O Lord, we praise You because You are able to save us from the penalty of sin.
O Lord, we praise You because You are able to save us from the power of sin.
O Lord, we praise You because You are able to save us from ourselves.
O Lord, we praise You because You are able to save us forever.

Now to Him who is able to keep us from stumbling and to present us blameless in the presence of His glory in triumphant joy and exultation, to the one and only God, our Savior through Jesus Christ our Lord, be glory, majesty, might and dominion, and power and authority, before all time and now and forever (See Jude 24-25).

Use these tithes and offerings so that Your word might spread quickly, run its course, and be glorified and triumphant. (See 2 Thes. 3:1)

Amen

∞

Prayed at an 8:30 Sunday Morning Worship Service.

O Lord of Second Chances,

We are a program-driven, meeting-going, committee-run church doing most of the good things a good church is supposed to do. And one of those things is what we are doing right now—getting together to worship You on the Lord's Day. But, Lord, in a lot of ways we've just been going through the motions here this morning.

You see, we cultivate the cult of the comfortable around here. We have our comfortable pew cushion which we sit on in our comfortable spot. We have our comfortable circle of friends and sing the songs we're comfortable with. We come to get entertained. At times rather than a worship service we have a production. We actually pay people to come and entertain us. And sometimes we clap for our musicians instead of praising You. And we have our comfortable pastor who usually preaches 'feel-good' sermons—the kind where we don't get our toes stepped on. Lord, I heard the two most obvious sins in Southern Baptist churches are divorce and obesity. In fact, just a couple of weeks back, one of our church members, a 27-year-old man died of a massive heart attack due to his obesity. But I've never heard the preacher mention those things, but rather we are continually warned about abortion and homosexuality while more and more of our church members are getting divorced or having gastric bypass surgery. And then we've got our comfortable god—a god whom we say has saved our soul and is going to take us to Heaven, a god who is also letting us keep our list of things we won't do for Him—a list that hasn't gotten shorter over the years but has actually grown, a god who is letting us get away with the status quo. O Lord, is that god You?

O Lord, we've demonstrated a smug self-righteousness for so long around here that we must stink in Your nostrils and sometimes even in our own. You apparently are so embarrassed to see Your children misbehaving the way we are that You've abandoned us to our sin. That's why our aisles are still during the invitation and why we didn't have any expectation this morning that You were actually going to show up in a manner in which we could actually feel Your presence here.

O Lord, we confess.
We have gravitated to our comfort zone.
We have gotten comfortable with our sins.
We come to church to seek Your benefits, not to seek You.

We say all the right words but we get them in the wrong order: we say, "O Lord, bless my soul." instead of "Bless the Lord, o my soul." (Ps. 103:1 KJV)
Instead of coming to church to talk to You, we come to church to talk about You.
We've come to church to attend a revival meeting rather than to seek the Reviver.[43]

O Lord, can we have a do-over? May we come again. Only this time may we come with the expectation that You are going to show up and do the impossible here, that You're going to speak through Your servant words that are going to be used by Your Holy Spirit to convict us of the very sins that we have gotten comfortable with and we're actually going to repent of them in tears as we run down the aisle and rededicate our lives to You. O Lord, instead of coming to place our burdens on You, may we come to receive Your burdens.

O Lord, make us uncomfortable with our comfort with our sin.

Amen

∞

Prayed at an 8:30 Sunday Morning Worship Service.

O Lord,

I know You're in here somewhere, but there's got to be more to You than this. Our hunger exceeds our grasp. We keep getting glimpses of where You have been, but we want to experience You in the here and now! We're not happy just following Your tracks. Didn't You hear us baying this morning? Slow down and let us catch up.

---

[43] Praying God's Heart in Times Like These! "A Covenant to Seek the Reviver Not Just Revival, © Dr. Gregory Frizzell, 2009,www.frizzellministries.org, www.masterdesign.org/frizzell.html.

Lord, Your Word indicates that no man can see You and live. Nothing alive can stand in Your presence. O Lord, You gave Moses and all the Israelites the opportunity to step into the cloud and go up on the mountain and be intimate with You, but everybody thought they would die if they stepped into that cloud. O Lord, we're like Moses; we're willing to step into that cloud.

We know that if we're dead, then You will make us alive. Paul said he died daily. O Lord, we know we can't seek Your face and save face. O Lord, we're willing to lay our egos on the cross, crucify our wills, lay our bodies on Your altar, and die to self to be able to be intimate with You. But, Lord, we don't just want a visit; we want Your continuous presence.

And, Lord, 1500 years after Moses' request to see Your face, his request got answered on the Mount of Transfiguration when he saw Jesus. We humbly request that we, too, might see the face of Jesus one day.

In the meanwhile, Lord, we understand that we won't see Your face in our lifetime, but would You help us stay so close to You by dying to self daily that we continually see the evidence of Your actions right where we are? Help us to do Blackaby's idea of seeing where You are at work and joining You there[44] one better by being so close to You and so sensitive and responsive to Your needs that where we are You are always at work.

O Lord, set our hearts a-dancing with evidence of Your presence.

Amen

Written after reading Philip Yancy's *Prayer.*

∞

---

[44] Blackaby, Henry T. & King, Clause V., *Experiencing God: Knowing and Doing the Will of God*, p. 8.

This was an offertory prayer at an 8:30 Sunday Morning Worship Service.

Lord God,

If You'll look around, you'll notice that we didn't carry any lame or sick sheep in here this morning to give to You. Nor did we drag any blind lambs in here for You. Nor did we go out to the barn and find the scrawniest, sorriest-looking critter we had to give to You. Oh, sure, I know that Jesus was the blood sacrifice to end all blood sacrifices— so that if we really did sacrifice an animal to You this morning, we'd probably be insulting You. But I was speaking figuratively. Maybe a slightly better way of saying it is "we didn't pay all our bills, buy groceries, fill up our tank, go to Mickey D's and then look in our wallet or check book to see what we had left so we could decide what we could comfortably give You."

No, Lord, we didn't bring You leftovers here this morning.
No, Lord, we didn't even bring You our second best.
Rather, Lord, we brought You our very, very best.

You see, Lord, You blessed us with enough common sense to recognize that it never was those animal sacrifices that You were so interested in long ago, just as today it's not 10% of our money that You are all that interested in.

O yes, we did bring You some money, some tithes and offerings, to put in these plates—after all we know this church has expenses and ministries to support. And we have a responsibility to a part of that. But what we really bring to You this morning is the one thing that You desire every Christian to eventually give You.

O Lord, the sacrifice we bring to You this morning is not some animal, not some amount of money, not any material possession we have.

O Lord, by the mercies of God—in other words, because of what Jesus did for us on the cross, we each present our body as a living sacrifice, holy (both "h-o-l-y" and "w-h-o-l-l-y"), acceptable unto You, which is our reasonable service and worship. (See Rom. 12:1) That's not to imply that what we've done up until this point this morning is unreasonable, but rather that if we don't do this—if we don't present our bodies as living sacrifices we are being unreasonable—considering what Jesus did on the cross for us.

O Lord, we give it all to You—all 100%. Take it and don't let us take it back.

Amen

∞

Prayed at a Monday Night Prayer Meeting.

O Lord Who Works to Draw People to Himself,

I ran across an old adage recently that got me thinking. It said: "When I work, I work; when I pray, God works." That kind of makes me think I should pray all the time. O Lord, move us closer to praying without ceasing.

It also reminds me that all the great mission thrusts came out of prayer meetings and all the great revival movements came out of prayer meetings. And it brings to mind a belief I've had for many years that I can't back up scripturally but have been convinced by experience that no one gets saved unless someone is praying for them.

Lord, we're striving to make Christ known to those who know You not. And maybe we need to do less striving and more praying.

O Lord, would you open doors for Your message—doors in buildings, yes, but doors in people's hearts and minds, too—so that we may proclaim the mystery of Christ, that we may proclaim it full and clearly as we should and as is our duty?

Help us to be wise in the way we act toward non-Christians. Help us make the most of every open door. Let our conversation be full of grace, seasoned with salt, so that we may know how to answer everyone. (See Col. 4:6) Put the words in our mouths. Move us to the point where we're daily praying for those open doors with non-Christians and for You to work through us to go out of our way to initiate those non-Christians in conversation so that seeds may be planted, seedlings may be watered, and the harvest reaped.

And then, Lord, let us stand in awe of what You have done because we prayed.

May our prayers bring about Your work,

Amen

Written after reading Colossians 4:3-6 and the last chapter of Bill Hybel's book *Just Walk Across the Room.*

Prayed at a Monday Night Prayer Meeting.

Father of Faith,

We look at You and see the very epitome of faithfulness.
You are 100% faithful to Your Word.
You are 100% faithful to Your promises.
You are 100% faithful to Your commitments.
You are 100% faithful to us, Your children.
O Lord, we praise You for Your faithfulness.

O Lord, we look at Jesus and see the very epitome of faith.
He had so much faith in You that He was perfectly obedient to You.

Lord, our faith, at most, is the size of a mustard seed compared to the faith of Jesus.

O Lord, even on the cross, when His body was saying no, Jesus said yes to Your will.

O Lord, grow our faith so that we can respond positively every time we encounter Your will—so we, too, can be perfectly obedient to You. O Lord, help us to say yes to Your will even when our body is saying no.

O Lord, we confess to committing some sins of omission. Specifically, there are folk we didn't pray for that we should have been praying for.

O Lord, cause us to spend time in prayer for every church member who we know needs our prayers. And help us to be so sensitive and concerned with all those in our midst that we find out who needs our prayers even when they aren't forthcoming with the information.

But, also, Lord, help us to see each person we come in contact with through Your eyes so that we might see their needs. O Lord, may no one we know go to Hell because we failed to pray for them.

Amen

∞

Prayed at a Monday Night Prayer Meeting. This prayer is based on Rev. 3:14-19.

Lord,

You don't *really* love us, do You? Oh sure, You loved us enough to send Jesus to die on the cross for us. But Your Word says that those whom You dearly and tenderly love (those whom You *really* love), You tell them their faults and convict and reprove and chasten them; that is, You discipline them. And You didn't say those words to non-Christians; rather You said those words to the church at Laodicea. You said that they said they were rich, had prospered and grown wealthy and were in need of nothing.

O Lord, instead of praying for our daily bread, we just run down to Kroger's and buy it. Instead of relying on You to take care of our future, we have Social Security, our 401(k), and our retirement plan. Instead of relying on You for our health, we take daily vitamins, get the flu shot, have Medicare or a health insurance plan and access to the best doctors and medical care in the world. Lord, the reason we don't worry about being clothed properly isn't because we know You clothe the flowers in the field and the birds of the air, but because we have Dillard's and Goody's right here in Tullahoma and can get anything we want whenever we want.

They say that money doesn't buy happiness, but it buys enough of the necessities of life that we don't recognize how much we really need You. O Lord, just like the Laodiceans, we are neither hot nor cold and we, too, do not realize how wretched, pitiable, poor, blind and naked we are.

O Lord, instead of buying from the local merchants, help us to buy of You gold tried in fire that we may be truly rich. Help us to buy eye salve from you to anoint our eyes that we may see our sin and our condition. O Lord, help us to repent. Just as You told the church at Laodicea to buy their clothes from You, may we buy from You white clothes to cover the shame of our nakedness. O Lord, may we not only wear the garments of salvation, but the robes of righteousness. Cleanse us of our sins. And may our garments be washed anew every day.

And, Lord, may we not be all dressed up with no place to go. Send us out into the world with such an enthusiasm, such an earnestness, burning with so much zeal that You can't be resisted.

Amen

Prayed at a Monday Night Prayer Meeting.

Holy Father,

You know me. You know I claim I have a fat man living inside me who is trying to get out. To some extent, I blame it on my momma since she made me eat everything on my plate even when I wasn't hungry. Lord, I confess to the sin of eating too much.

Lord, the world says, "Here's a potato chip. Bet you can't eat just one." The Devil says, "Go ahead. One potato chip won't hurt anything." My fleshly nature says, "Mmm, that was good, let's eat the whole bag." But Your Holy Spirit says, "Don't take that first bite; never eat more than is necessary."

O Lord, it's three against one and they're piling on.

Lord, the real problem isn't that I'm a few pounds overweight. It isn't that this is a struggle that I have to continually deal with. The real problem is that anytime any sin of any variety or any size is not dealt with immediately by me, the believer, it continues to act like leaven until the whole is corrupted. Galatians 5:9 (NASB) says, "A little leaven leavens the whole lump." If I don't deal with sin, it deals with me. Good apples never change bad apples, but it never fails that bad apples eventually make the good apples bad. Taking that one bite potentially corrupts my whole life.

Unless I immediately confess taking that one extra bite and repent of it, I suffer death. No I don't physically die, but I go into a temporary state of death before You. I don't lose my salvation, but I break fellowship with You. I can no longer worship You properly, I can no longer serve You properly, I lose victory in my life, I no longer experience the abundant life. O Lord, I wonder why I don't hear from You when I pray and it's because I have sinned and haven't repented of it.

Lord, this is a problem I can't handle by myself. I tell myself over and over again that I am going to go on a diet or am going to not eat one bite more than I should. And time after time I fail to do what I told myself I was going to do. I need You to pull out all the stops to help me. Help me to become so focused on You and Your Word and Your work that I don't have the time or inclination to take that extra bite.

But, Lord, the reason I bring this before You at this time and in this setting isn't because I need to spill my guts before some of my fellow Christians, but because this is a problem that permeates the church. In practically every group setting at church I am in, I look around and I see folk who have a few extra pounds. And we don't get those few extra pounds by taking one extra bite and immediately falling on our knees, confessing the sin and repenting of it. No, we get them by not confessing for some period of time during which time we are out of fellowship with You, eat the rest of the bag of potato chips, allow other sins to creep in, and are almost useless for Your Kingdom.

Lord, change our mindset here at FBC. A good many of us don't think we've committed a sin unless it is a big sin. Use Your written Word and Your preached Word and Your Holy Spirit to convict us of the fact that a sin is a sin no matter how small. Help us to recognize that so often eating that first potato chip leads to eating the whole bag. Help us to recognize that taking that one extra bite causes us to break fellowship with You until we get it confessed and repented. Lord, help us to bring good, healthy food to our pot luck dinners instead of three tablefuls of decadent desserts. We don't need to be tempted at church. Lord, help us to be holy even as You are holy. Help each member of this church to so focus on You and Your Word and Your work that none of us have the time or inclination to take that extra bite.

And, Lord, may each of us give You the credit and the glory for our improved health.

And may Your Kingdom know now bounds.

Amen

Prayed at the beginning of a Deacons' Meeting.

O Lord,

I lift to You the Deacon Fellowship of First Baptist Church. Help each of us be true to our calling as a Deacon.

May we be so true to our calling that the 'Greek widows' of our church get taken care of so our apostles, our ministerial staff, can devote themselves to prayer and to preaching.

O Lord, help us to be so true to our calling that we find ourselves caught up in the Spirit, as Philip was, witnessing to the Ethiopian eunuchs of our present day world.

O Lord, help us to be so true to our calling that we find ourselves glorifying You the same way Stephen did in his death. May we, too, witness to a Paul.

O Lord, help us as Deacons be so true to our calling that it enables our staff to do their jobs effectively, that our church members are ministered to properly and their needs are met, and that You are glorified to the extent that the Paul's of this world are converted.

O Lord, help us to be the Deacons You want us to be.

Amen

∞

Prayed in early December as an offertory prayer at an 8:30 Sunday Morning Worship Service.

O Lord Who Put Together the First Living Nativity,

Help us to have a holy Christmas instead of a secular one.

Help us to be truthful to our children about Baby Jesus instead of lying to them about Santa Claus.

Help us to sing, "Glory to God in the Highest" instead of "Grandma Got Run Over by a Reindeer."

Help us to experience the miracle in the manger instead of "The Miracle on 34th Street."

Help us to worship the new-born Babe instead of bowing at the altar of materialism.

Help us to celebrate with fellow believers and get drunk with the Holy Spirit rather than celebrating with our workmates and getting drunk at the office Christmas party.

Help us take time to find and worship the King like the Wise Men did instead of being so busy with the preparations for Christmas we don't even see the star.

O Lord, instead of getting our Christian spirit out of a bottle, may we get it as a result of receiving the Christmas gift you wrapped for us 2000 years ago.

O Lord, help us to celebrate Jesus' birthday instead of Santa's return.

And, Lord, in deepest gratitude we thank you by putting money in these plates in hopes that next year many others will also experience a holy Christmas.

Help us to bless others with Your presents.

Amen

∞

Prayed at a Monday Night Prayer Meeting.

O Lord,

We praise You because You are our Shepherd and we are the people of Your pasture, the flock under Your care.

260

We praise You because You forgave all our sins and Your love is better than life.

We praise You because You are the Father of compassion and the God of all comfort who comforts us so that we may comfort others. (See 2 Cor. 1:3-4)

O Lord, the Holy Spirit has impressed upon us our need to pray to You. That's why we have set aside this time every week. This prayer meeting isn't one of those that's really a Bible study. Rather, ninety percent of the time here is spent in prayer. Lord, we're here to show You how important You are to us and how important spending a significant amount of quality time with You is to us.

Lord, since we became Your children You have grown our prayer life. You have taught us to ask and keep on asking. You have taught us how important it is to praise and adore You in our prayers. You have taught us to confess our sins and to express our thanks to You in our prayers. You have let us experience You changing over time what we asked for initially to what You wanted us to ask all along. You have grown our faith through our prayers not only when they've been answered with a 'yes', but also when they haven't been answered. O Lord, we want to thank You for the great gift of prayer. We thank You for the times when we have been amazed when You answered our requests in seemingly miraculous fashion. We thank You for those times when we prayed with a problem or a question and came away with an answer. We thank You for those times that we sensed You were right there with us when we prayed. And we thank You for the times when we were scared or crying and we felt better after we prayed.

Lord, I have two specific requests regarding this prayer meeting. First, would You cause us to pray what You want prayed here? I do know that most important is that we pray—because I know the Holy Spirit can change those prayers so that by the time You hear them they're asking for what we really need rather than what we might have asked for. But would You use Your Holy Spirit to help us so attune our hearts to You that what we ask is exactly what Jesus would have asked if he were here in our stead?

And, secondly, would You accomplish Your will through our prayers? My understanding is that Your will which is always accomplished in Heaven doesn't usually happen on earth unless some of us pray it down? Use our prayers to bring about Your will here on earth.

O Lord, we pray for Your plans and Your purpose to come to pass on earth. And would You give us this day our daily bread—not the kind that's baked in an oven, but the Bread of Life as is revealed in Your Word? O Lord, cause us to spend so much time meditating on Your written Word and focusing on Jesus that Your will is revealed to us so we do what we can of it immediately and pray for the rest of it to come about.

O Lord, may we not only thank You for the trees and bees and seas, but may we thank You for the storms and trials of life. And may we rejoice in repeatedly seeing Your will happen right before our eyes.

Just as Jesus is our intermediary in Heaven, may we be Your intermediary here on earth.

Amen

∞

Prayed at a Monday Night Prayer Meeting. This prayer is the result of reading Matt 4, Luke 4:16-30, Matt 12:38 and Matt 26:53.

Lord Jesus,

When You were at Your weakest point, You rejected the temptation to make bread out of stones to satisfy Your hunger and prove You were God's son.

When tempted, You refused to dazzle folk by jumping off the pinnacle of the temple.

On a mountaintop, You refused to bow down to Satan, refused to take a shortcut to establish Your Kingdom here on earth.

Later You refused to do miracles in Your hometown because of their unbelief.

You said no to the Pharisees when they demanded a sign to prove You were the Messiah.

At Your arrest You said You could have summoned twelve legions of angels.

O Lord and Master, help us know when to say no and demonstrate self control. And give us the desire, the strength, and the drive to do it for every temptation.

Lord, when we're at our weakest point and, for that matter, at every other point, too, give us the strength to reject the temptation to satisfy our own desires or take a dare to prove who we are.

Lord, may we not try to dazzle folk with our brilliance or impress them with our words or our deeds, but may we merely give them Jesus or merely give them Your Word.

Lord, help us refuse to bow down to Satan—may we refuse to take a shortcut to personal growth, or church growth, or growing Your Kingdom here on earth. Help us to not rely on self, others, the work of others, but help us to totally rely on You.

Lord, may we also refuse to do wonderful works in our hometown until Your Holy Spirit tells us precisely when and what to do.

Lord, may we say no to the Pharisees in our church and of this world who demand that we live up to their expectations.

Lord, help us to be submissive to Your will even when we want to take the easy way out.

Help us to know that we have more than twelve legions of angels at our call, we have You. Help us to be bold enough to be Your witness and do Your will no matter what.

O Lord, may we constantly seek to know Your will for us; and give us the patience to wait for it, the discernment to recognize it, the desire to do it, and the wherewithal to carry it out.

And may Satan cringe.

Amen

∞

Prayed at a Monday Night Prayer Meeting.

Precious Savior, we thank you because

- now that You've paid the price, we can be forgiven,
- now that Your body has been broken, we can be whole again,
- now that Your work on earth is done, we can find rest in You,
- now that You've fulfilled the Law, we can live by grace,
- now that You've experienced death, we can experience abundant life,
- now that You've won the victory, we can win every battle with sin,
- now that the curtain has been torn, we can pray directly to the Father,
- now that You've emptied yourself on the cross, we can be filled with the Holy Spirit,
- now that You've died for us, we can live for You.

O Lord, now that we <u>have</u> been forgiven, help us to so focus on how deadly our sins were and what You did for us on the cross that we will be properly thankful.

O Lord, now that we <u>can</u> be whole again, help us to bury our old life and live as new creatures in You.

O Lord, now that we <u>can</u> find rest in You, help us to remember that Your Word says that You gave us eternal life and we shall never perish and that no one can snatch us out of the Father's hand.

O Lord, now that we <u>can</u> live by grace, help us to not only quit striving to live up to a set of rules but also to do only that which is expedient and beneficial.

O Lord, now that we <u>can</u> experience the abundant life, help us so love You and our fellow man that our life overflows onto others so that they feel Your love through us.

O Lord, now that we <u>can</u> win every battle with sin, help us to be preemptive. Help us to take every thought captive to Your obedience. Help us to purposely take measures to avoid those temptations that we need to avoid and can. And for those situations in which we can't avoid the temptation, give us the patience and strength to find and exercise the way out that You promise us.

O Lord, now that we <u>can</u> pray directly to You, help us to so involve ourselves in prayer, spend so much time in prayer to You that we become so desirous of and submissive to Your will that we find our prayers being changed from what we initially want to what You want and that we find You are speaking directly to us.

O Lord, now that we <u>can</u> be filled with the Holy Spirit, help us not to quench the Spirit by not responding to His promptings, but rather help us to encourage the Spirit by obeying His every urging.

O Lord, now that we <u>can</u> live for You, help us to die to self, take up our cross, and follow You.

Amen

Used as an offertory prayer at an 8:30 Sunday Morning Worship Service.

Lord God Almighty,

Up in Heaven there is worship going on that makes what we're doing down here look kind of shabby.

There is unbelievable splendor in Heaven's throne room where seraphim worship You day and night crying:

Holy, holy, holy
Lord God Almighty,
Who was and is and is to come. (Rev 4:8 Amp)

There's lightning and thunder, living creatures full of eyes, and four-and-twenty elders who fall on their faces and cast their crowns before Your throne. They worship Him who Lives Forever and Ever saying

You are worthy, our Lord and God,
To receive glory and honor and power. (See Rev. 4:9-11)

And the celestial choir will be comprised of many angels, the living creatures, the elders of the Heavenly Sanhedrin, and those who the Lamb has redeemed out of every tribe and tongue and people and nation. They will number 10,000 times 10,000 and thousands and thousands. And they will be joined by every created thing in heaven and on earth and under the earth and on the sea and all that is in it lifting their voices, all eternity will echo with the sound of their praise as they sing

Blessing and honor and glory and power
Be to Him who sits on the throne and to the Lamb
Forever and ever. (See Rev. 5:11-13)

Lord, we can't top that. We can't even come close. But what is important about this worship service isn't that You receive more praise and glory, but that we give it.

I read recently that worship without commitment is worthless worship.[45] Lord, I pray that all of us here will truly be worshipping you at the end of this service because we have made a commitment to you—either a commitment of our lives to You for the very first time or a further commitment to You greater than we have ever made before. Lord, may this worship service focus on causing us to recognize the need to just turn our lives over to You completely and allow you to change us according to Your plan. May Your Holy Spirit overwhelm us with our sin and our helplessness to change ourselves. O Lord, we come to offer ourselves to You, not just during these moments of worship, but for the rest of our lives. Help us to love you with all our heart, with all our soul, and with all our might and our neighbors as ourselves. Help us to depend completely on You. Help us learn to serve, forgive, share, and love.

O Lord, you have no need to be glorified any more than You are, but we can't help but do it anyway—considering what Jesus did for us on the cross.

Amen

∞

Prayed during a Monday Night Prayer Meeting.

O Lord Who Gives Us Faith,

I ain't quite got it all figured out, but I think I've got a leg up on it. In man's way of thinking, *for the most part*, you get what you deserve—you get what you earn. You suffer the consequences of your actions. What goes around comes around. Why even for the evil people who seem

---

[45] Drace, Jerry. "Observations of an Evangelist." *Purpose4u.com*. CrossPurpose International, n.d. Web. 6 July 2013. <http://www.purpose4u.com/ JerryDraceObservationsofanEvangelist.html>.

to be prospering we think: "'Vengeance is mine,' saith the Lord.' and think that they're going to get theirs in the end.

But in Your economy, *to some extent,* you get what you believe. You can be a convicted mass murdering, pedophilic, child molesting, adulterous, serial bank robber. Yet, if you find Jesus and believe He died on the cross for your sins and you're going to Heaven, guess what—you're going to Heaven. I guess one could sum it up with Matthew 21:22: "Whatsoever you ask in prayer, believing, you shall receive." So when he asked Jesus to come into his heart, believing, He did. Now that's not to say that the blab-it-grab-it folk, those of the Faith Movement, are all going to be rich because they ask and believe—because the believing has to be for the right reason—and definitely selfishness isn't the right reason. It seems to have more to do with believing because it is in Your Word or because we're sure it's Your will.

Lord, because You told us to ask and because we believe
- Would you honor the prayers of all who want to invite Jesus into their lives?
- Would you convict us of our sins—especially those little sins that we've gotten comfortable with and those sins like self-pride and arrogance and aloofness that aren't even on our radar but everybody else seems to see in our lives and those sins of omission that make it obvious that You're not living through us? And would You convict all the lost people that we pray for, too?
- Would You show us how much You love us by continually chiding us and disciplining us and pruning us so that we end up confessing our sins and repenting regularly—even immediately after committing them, so that we end up having an ongoing, close relationship with You?
- Would You send trials and tribulations our way so our character will have a chance to grow? (See Rom. 5:3-4)

- For every temptation that comes our way, would You help us find the way out that You provide and give us the desire and strength to exercise it?
- Would You grow our faith?
- Would You engage us as we study Your Word, as we pray, as we fast, and as we give ourselves to Your endeavors?
- Would You help us to work out our salvation through fear and trembling? (See Phil. 2:12)
- Would You draw us close and excite us to Your work?
- Would You awaken us spiritually and fill us with Your Holy Spirit?
- Would You give us discernment so we can recognize Your will and can tell the difference between better and best?
- Would You give us the gift of evangelism?
- Would You bless us with Your presence?
- And would You meet all our needs according to Your riches in glory? (See Phil. 4:19)

Amen

∞

Prayed during an 8:30 Sunday Morning Worship service.

Jehovah Jireh, God Who Provides,

You were a living presence to the Israelites,
    The god who guided them in a pillar of cloud by day and a pillar of fire by night,
    The god who gave them manna every morning,
    The god who provided water from the solid rock,
    The god who protected them from Pharaoh's army,
    The god who met Moses at the burning bush and on Mount Sinai and spoke with him one on one,

The god who brought them out of the wilderness and into the Promised Land.

We praise You, Lord, because You are a living presence in our lives,
   The god who guides us with Your Word and Your Holy Spirit both day and night,
   The god who gives us our daily bread every morning,
   The god who provides living water and is our Solid Rock,
   The god who protects us from Satan's army,
   The god who meets with us as we study Your Word and in our quiet times and communicates with us one on one.

O Lord, we praise you for the great provision which brought us out of our wilderness and is going to take us to Your Promised Land, a provision named Jesus.

O Lord, we pray that Your presence will manifest itself here this morning in a powerful way.

Just as the first thing You required of Moses when he found himself in Your Presence was to take off his dirty shoes, the first thing You require of us when we find ourselves in Your presence is to get rid of the dirt. In fact, You never speak to us about anything else until our sin is taken care of. After all, You don't use dirty vessels, only broken ones. For that reason, Lord, would you convict us of those sins for which we haven't repented—whether it be sins of omission like not studying our Sunday School lesson this week or not having our quiet time, or sins of commission like stealing from our employer by not giving a full day's work or repeating information about someone when we're not absolutely sure the information is true or lusting in our heart?

O Lord, if need be, allow Your Holy Spirit to work on us this whole service. Wear on us our until we become broken vessels. Then, Lord, use Your Holy Spirit to speak Your message for us through Your preached Word and Your Holy Word—may we understand what it is that You're wanting us to know and do. Lord, it is said that worship without commitment is worthless worship.[46] May Your presence here be so strong that none of us experience worthless worship here this morning.

Amen

∞

Prayed during a Monday Night Prayer Meeting.

O Lord Who Desires To Be in Constant Communion with Us,

We praise You because not only do You seek us but You also put a desire in us to seek You.

Lord, Your son walked this earth and we say that He was wholly man and wholly god. And in one way of thinking we'd say he couldn't sin and he would have perfect knowledge of Your will. Yet the periods of time He spent in prayer are measured in terms of hours and days and nights. O Lord, we confess that there are times when we claim to know Your will without having followed Your will to spend large amounts of time in prayer seeking Your will. And there are times when we try to lead a holy life without seeking Your help.

O Lord, remind us again and again that without You we can do nothing (See John 15:5) and that when we lean on our own understanding we are violating and disobeying Your Word. In other words, we're sinning.

O Lord, help us to follow Jesus' example in prayer—to pray often for large amounts of time with the result that Your will is done.

---

[46]   Drace, Jerry. "Observations of an Evangelist." *Purpose4u.com*. CrossPurpose International, n.d. Web. 6 July 2013. <http://www.purpose4u.com/ JerryDraceObservationsofanEvangelist.html>.

Lord, a month ago or so we cast a net over this town with door hangers. Having done that and having seen the short-term results—that, basically, we didn't catch any fish, we now beg You to show us how to cast the net so that the net is overflowing. Show us which side of the boat to cast the net on. Show us which net to use.

Lord, I lift to You those whom we pray for who fall into the category of hard hearted. I lift to You Jay. I lift to You a sister named Betty. I lift to you church members' husbands: Charles, Steve, Jeff, John, Roy and Larry. I lift to You each person who came to the minds of those here when I said 'hard hearted.' Lord, from experience I know that the way to get a bone away from a dog is by throwing him a steak. O Lord, would you use us or whoever needs to do it to present Your Good News in such a way to these that it appears like a steak compared to that old bone they're gnawing on?

Lord, we recognize that this praying business isn't as much about getting answers as it is about You fashioning our hearts to be like Yours. When we begin praying, our focus is on what we're praying for, but if we pray long enough our focus moves to You. We pray You will fashion our hearts to be like Yours and that we will experience that intimate contact with You. We pray that the ultimate result of our prayers be the same as the result of Jesus' prayer—that we be brought into total submission to You.

We pray for Your will, nothing more, nothing less, no matter what the cost.[47]

Amen

∾

---

[47]   The Amplified Bible. p. 131, footnote f.

Prayed as an offertory prayer on Mother's Day.

Father in Heaven,

We thank You for our mother on earth.

We thank You that You endowed her with a healthy dose of unconditional love for us, the kind that loves us and cares for us no matter how ugly, dirty, smelly, and ornery we are, the same kind of love You have for us.

Lord, the Fifth Commandment says we are to honor our mothers. Your Holy Spirit leads me to believe that wasn't telling us just to pay tribute to her once a year on Mother's Day by giving her a potted plant and taking her out to eat—seeing as how Mother's Day is only a recent invention. And seeing as how there were other Old Testament laws that said that if we hit our mother or curse her we are to be put to death, it seems that Your intent in the fifth Commandment was not that we pay tribute to her from time to time but that we should live our whole life in a manner that will bring honor to her.

Lord, use Your Holy Spirit to convict us of our sins so that we might bring honor to our mother by confessing and repenting of our sins.

Lord, use Your Holy Spirit to work on us all day long, so we might bring honor to our mother by keeping short accounts and staying in right relationship with You.

Lord, use Your Holy Spirit to draw us to become more intimate with You so that we can honor our mothers by knowing and doing Your will.

Lord, help us to be so thankful for what You and our mother have done for us that it causes us to help others in Your name.

Lord, help us to honor our mothers by honoring You with our lives.

Amen

Prayed during a Monday Night Prayer Meeting. VBS is Vacation Bible School, one of the main evangelistic efforts performed by FBC and many, many Christian churches every summer.

Heavenly Vinedresser,

Your Word says that Jesus is the vine and we are the branches, apart from Him we can do nothing, and that if we abide in Him and He in us we'll bear much fruit. (See John 15:5)

O Lord, we recognize that we're no better than a vacuum cleaner attachment—totally useless unless attached and the power turned on. O Lord, may we be a branch that is attached at the hip to You and may the power of the Holy Spirit be turned on in us and through us so that we'll bear much fruit for You.

O Lord, may we no longer be attached to worldly things. May our prize possession be You. May all our treasures be in Heaven. May no earthly possession possess us. May Your name reside on our lips, Your thoughts in our minds, and Your cause in our hearts.

O Lord, may no earthly appointments keep us from our appointments with You. May we honor the times we've set aside for quiet time. May we not miss any of those divine opportunities You've set up with those we come into contact with that are in physical need or who are in need of You.

May we not become so attached to our families that they take priority over You. But may we turn their care and protection over to You and yield them to You for use—either here or in Heaven.

May we not be so attached to any habit, process, hang up, or methodology that we can't allow You to show us a better way.

Lord, we confess that our attachment to You is not as strong as it needs to be. Please prune us and chide us and make us aware of our sins so that our attachment may be made stronger.

O Lord, help us to empty ourselves of everything but You, so You can fill the void in our life with Your Spirit. O Lord may we be attached to nothing but You.

O Lord, attach us to You by involving us in Your work, by sending us on Your trips, by concerning us with Your concerns. Use us for Your purpose.

O Lord, attach us to You through trials and tribulations, and by helping us to know You better. May Your written Word enlighten us, may your preached word excite us.

O Lord, we pray for those of our church whose attachment is very weak—so weak they don't even come to church any more. Please use Your Holy Spirit and us to draw them back to You and Your church.

And, Lord, for those who are completely unattached to You, we lift them to You. We pray for those spouses of our church members who claim You not. We pray for all the children who will be here for VBS who know You not. We pray for all those of our community who choose You not. Use our hands and feet and voices to provide opportunities for Your Holy Spirit to do its work in their lives as need be.

O Lord, help us to abide in You by abiding in us.

Amen

∞

Used as an offertory prayer at the end of an 8:30 Sunday Morning Worship service.

O Lord Who Invited Us to Pray,

We come before You praying because, not only did You invite us to pray, but you encourage us to pray. Why, Your Word tells us to pray without ceasing and to pray at all times. (See 1 Thes. 5:17 and Eph. 6:18)

Lord, the very prospect of actually being in your presence in Your throne room scares the devil out of us, literally, and we come before You praying in humility because, in effect, we are bringing our requests into Your very presence in Your throne room, causes us to be so in awe of You that our meager concerns are completely forgotten and we can think only of honoring and worshiping You and doing Your every request. So out of humility we come asking not for our selfish concerns, but only for exactly what we think You want.

We come before You praying in Jesus' name—not because invoking His name renders any magic, but because we have His permission to use His name because we are His representatives here on earth and, as such, we're going to be asking exactly what we think He would ask if He were standing here. (See John 14:13-14)

We come before You praying in the Spirit. (See Jude 20) We come asking because we think Your Holy Spirit is the one who is responsible for us being here in this place and praying at this moment; and He is the one who is impressing upon us what to pray.

We come before You praying in Jesus. We believe that when He abides in us and we in Him we have the mind of Christ or at least one that thinks just like His, and therefore what we're about to ask is what Jesus would ask.

We come before You praying out of the desires of our own mind. Lord, it isn't that we're just repeating what Jesus or the Holy Spirit has told us to say, but we sincerely want what we are about to ask.

We come before You praying in faith—faith in Your ability to grant our request, faith that You care enough about us to grant our request, faith enough in what we're asking to know You're going to grant our request because what we are asking is in Your best interest.

O Lord, take our money here this morning before we become too attached to it. Use it for Your purposes. Take our minds. Change them, mold them, remake them, use them for Your purposes before the world gains control of them and us. Take our time; use it for Your purposes before we waste it frivolously. Take our children and grandchildren and the children of this church. We turn them over to Your care and protection before we worry about them again. And use them for Your purposes.

O Lord, keep us from the Evil One.
Help us to get caught up in the spirit.
Cause us to be focused on Jesus.
Bless us with Your presence.
Fill our minds with your Word.
Use us for Your Kingdom.

And as we go from here in just a minute, may each of us be in search mode, diligent to find who it is that is in need or in need of You that we're supposed to share Your love with this week.

Amen

∞

Used as an offertory prayer at the end of an 8:30 Sunday Morning Worship service. This prayer was built from 1 Chronicles 29:10 and the verses that follow.

Father in Heaven, Lord God Almighty,

Truly You alone are worthy of worship, worthy of praise, worthy of our spending an hour or two every week honoring with our presence, words, and attention.

Be praised, adored, and thanked, O Lord God of Israel, God of all Christians who have gone before us, and our God for ever and ever.

Yours, o Lord, is the greatness and the power and the glory and the victory and the majesty. For all that is in the Heavens and the earth is Yours. Yours is the Kingdom, o Lord, and You are to be exalted as head over all. (See 1 Chron. 29:11)

Both riches and honor come from You; and You reign over all. In Your hand are the power and the might. In Your hand it is to make great and to give strength to all. (1 Chron. 29:12)

Now, therefore, our God, we thank You and praise Your glorious name and all those attributes that Your name denotes.

But who am I, and who are we as a people, that we should retain strength and offer these tithes and offerings so willingly?

For all things come from You, and of Your own hand we have to give to You.

For our days on earth are like a shadow; and there is no hope or expectation of remaining.

I know that You try the heart and delight in uprightness. In the uprightness of our hearts, we freely offer these gifts to You. O Lord God of Abraham, Isaac, and Israel, keep forever such purposes and thoughts in the minds of Your people, and direct and establish our hearts toward You. (See 1 Chron. 29:17-18)

O Lord, accept our humble attempt to worship You here this morning and accept our meager offerings because both are sincere.

And now, Lord, help us to live our lives the rest of this week so that our every action is an act of worship and our every deed glorifies Your name.

Amen

Used as an offertory prayer at the end of an 8:30 Sunday Morning Worship service.

Eternal Father,

We praise You because You are from everlasting to everlasting. You are the Alpha and Omega, the Beginning and the End. Whom have we in Heaven but You? We desire You more than anything on earth. Our health may fail, our spirits may grow weak, but You remain the strength of our heart. O Lord, be our portion forever. (See Ps. 73:25-26) May You be ours and may we be Yours 'til the cows come home.

O Lord, we confess that we wasted much of our time during the past week, either goofing off or doing things that have no positive lasting value.

O Lord, help us focus on eternal things and not waste our time on things that have no long-term value. May we spend much time in prayer and thinking about Your attributes and praising You. And when our minds wander and we find ourselves engaged in earthly thoughts or activities of no eternal value, use Your Holy Spirit to discipline us and to help us to refocus on You.

O Lord, Your Word endures forever. Heaven and earth will pass away, but Your words will remain forever. (See Matt. 24:35) Your Word is for all time and for all people. May we relish Your Word and fill our minds with it and store it in the memory banks of our brain. Help us to loosen our grasp on the world and to hold on tight to what You have said and written so we can find out what is on Your mind and heart. O Lord, may we focus on magnifying Your Word here on earth, both by making it more important and more plain, but also by spreading it.

O Lord, Your Word indicates that people are eternal—that they'll either spend eternity in a sinner's hell or with You. Help us to spend much of our limited time here on earth focusing on people in a manner such that many of them choose to spend eternity with You.

O Lord, take these tithes and offerings and focus them on efforts that will make an eternal difference.

Amen

⚮

Used as an offertory prayer at the end of an 8:30 Sunday Morning Worship service.

O Lord Who Slept in a Manger and Had Fishermen for Best Friends,

You created us and gave us our freedom. Then, after we abused that freedom and found ourselves enslaved to this world and to sin and, with the aid of your Holy Spirit, came to our senses, You bought our freedom back with your blood and made us Your children.

O Lord, we come before you as poor excuses for loving children. Instead of spending significant amounts of time in Your Word we have played the harlot and spent most of our spare time worshiping our idol, the television. We have pushed the power button and allowed the ways of the world to flash upon the screen and invade our minds and influence our children. We have sat in front of it as it has moved our culture from denouncing homosexuality and promiscuity to celebrating them and we didn't say a blessed word. But even worse, Lord, instead of spending quality time with You in prayer, we've allowed it to mesmerize us, make its values our values, and make us slaves once again. It has made us a part of the world and worldly. We watch the NFL or the NCAA or Big Brother or American Idol while most of the folk we call neighbors are dying and going to Hell and we've never even prayed for them by name much less invited them to come to church.

O Lord, during this service may our attention be so focused on Your great love for us and how You rescued us from slavery to sin and on Your great sacrifice that out of thankfulness, out of the urging of Your Holy Spirit, we decide to go all out for You. O Lord, use Your Holy spirit to help us put our hand in Your hand and let You guide our every step.

O Lord, may we become overwhelmed by the idea that is much harder and much more costly not to do Your will than to do it. O Lord, when this service ends may we find ourselves standing smack dab in the center of Your perfect will with a firm resolution to stay there no matter what you ask us to do or what the world tempts us to do.

O Lord, may we stand at the ready, ready to obey. When You ask us to shout down the walls of Jericho, may we obey. When You tell us to go up against 135,000 Midianites with an army of 300, may we obey. When You ask us to go up against a 9'9" giant clad in armor, us armed with nothing but a sling and a couple of smooth, round, river rocks, may we obey. O Lord, when You ask us to pray without ceasing, may we obey. O Lord, when You ask us to be holy as You are holy, may we obey. O Lord, when You ask us to take up our cross and follow You, may we obey.

O Lord, our ways are self-absorbed—they call attention to ourselves, they are designed to eliminate discomfort; they are focused on the immediate. Your Word says that Your thoughts are completely different from ours, and Your ways are far beyond anything we can imagine. For just as the Heavens are higher than the earth, so are Your ways higher than our ways and Your thoughts higher than our thoughts. (See Isa. 55:8-9) O Lord, help us to follow Your ways rather than our ways so we may bring glory to You.

O Lord, use Your ways to draw us to the throne of grace, to purify us, to wean us from the world, and to make us long for Heaven. O Lord, keep us dependent on You. Draw us closer to You. Let us know Your ways so we may know You.

And may our surrender surely bring us closer to Your heart. O Lord, teach us to rely totally on You.

Amen

∞

Prayed during a Monday Night Prayer Meeting.

Precious Lord Jesus—our crucified, resurrected, ascended, and enthroned Savior,

We worship and adore You. What magnificent love You have shown to this for-the-most-part thankless human race.

We come acknowledging that Your Holy Spirit awakened us to the fact that we were sinners and made us want to solve the problem. However, all our attempts at righteousness were like filthy rags. Lord, we thank You that Your Holy Spirit made us so poor in spirit that we mourned over our sins and bought into Your plan. Lord, we thank You because You still cause us to hunger and thirst after righteousness. And we thank You because Your awesomeness and discipline cause us to be meek and submissive to Your will. And, Lord, we're thankful for the mercy and forgiveness shown to us by You so that we now feel merciful and forgiving to others.

O Lord, how can we be co-intercessors with You? How can we be prayer partners with You?

Give us the eyes to see others as Your eyes see them. Give us a heart like Yours that bleeds because of the tragedy of sin, the lostness of mankind, and the bondage with which Satan enslaves the world. Give us a heart like Yours that loves the church and Your own.

O Lord, fill our eyes with your tears and Your vision, fill our souls with Your hatred of sin and love for the lost, fill our wills with strength to resist every sin, and fill our spirits with determination to do Your will.

Then, Lord, may we be so in tune with You that we pray the very same prayers You pray in Heaven.

O Lord, we give ourselves to You anew. Take us. Take all of each one of us. Take us and so fill us with Your spirit that it is not we but You living in our bodies, not our love but Yours pouring through us, not our power but Yours propelling our actions.

Help us to pray persistently, vicariously, and victoriously. Help us to back Satan off and force him to retreat from stronghold after stronghold.

May Your Kingdom expand within us and within or to those we pray for.

Amen

Written after reading *Might Prevailing Prayer* by Wesley Duewel.

Prayed during an 8:30 Sunday Morning Worship service.

God of Grace,

You are the Lord; there is no other.
You formed the light and created darkness.
You bring prosperity and create disaster.
You, the Lord, do these things. (See Isa. 45:6-7)

We didn't come here for the status quo. We didn't come for three hymns with a side order of special music followed by a feel-good sermon and an offering where we give you money and an invitation where we look around to see if anybody else made a decision.

We're not here to play games; we're not here to play church. We came here to invest an hour or so to allow You to try to get through to us. You see, we know things aren't perfect in our lives by any stretch of the imagination and that we need some mid-course corrections. We came in hopes that You're going to tell us exactly what we need to hear. So use the music and the sermon to get Your message across. Cause this preacher to cut to the chase and say exactly what enables Your Holy Spirit to put the thoughts in our mind that cause us to be convinced of and convicted by your Message for us. May each of us hear what You want us to hear.

Lord, we want to be upfront with You. Remind us of our shortcomings so we can confess and make things right with You again. And, Lord, just so You know You aren't wasting Your time here this morning, we want You to know beforehand that we plan to obey. So if you'll get Your message across to us and convince us that it's from You, we plan to say "Yes, Lord, yes." So send Your message, make it clear, make it powerful, get our attention, then expect results. We're not going to let what other people think get in the way.

Lord, we don't want you to be just lord of our lives; we want You to be lord of our every moment. Lord, we don't want You to be just lord of our minds; we want You to be lord of our every thought. Lord, we don't want You to be just lord of our bodies; we want You to be lord of our every action.

Lord, we pray for those we know who know You not; may they find out what they are missing.

Guard us from ourselves and keep us in Your Word.

Amen

Prayed at a Monday Night Prayer Meeting.

O God Who Desires to Be Known,

We praise You because You are knowable.
We praise You because You are accessible.
Thank You for sending Jesus so we might come to know You through Him.
Thank You for the gift of prayer that we might have access to You.

O Lord, we confess to praying so seldom that when we do pray we often have forgotten the blessings You have blessed us with since last we prayed and more importantly we have forgotten some of the sins we committed since last we confessed. O Lord, we need Your help.

O Lord, we confess that there have been times when You wanted to talk with us and we were busy watching TV.
There have been times when You wanted to tell us Your will for our lives when we weren't at Burger King, but we were so involved with getting it done our way, that we didn't give You the opportunity to tell us what was really best for our lives.
We confess that when You wanted to be sovereign in our lives that our appetites or the pleasures of this life had our attention full time.
We confess that when You wanted to provide for us, we were busy being self-sufficient.
And when You wanted to direct our paths, we'd already installed our Garmin.

O Lord, we "have been lured into living for the fleeting pleasures of the body and mind rather than the spiritual delights of knowing and serving you."[48]

O Lord, against You only have we sinned because we don't know You as we should and haven't experienced You as we should. Give us a

___
[48] John Piper, *A Hunger for God*, p 47.

hunger for You and Your Word like we've never had before. And when we experience You and involve ourselves in Your Word, may Your Kingdom reign in our lives.

May we no longer pray for the selfish things that we want, but may we find ourselves praying for Your burdens.

First off, Lord, we lift to You closed doors. Would You use Your powers to open the doors of North Korea, Iran, Saudi Arabia, Maldives, and other countries that have a closed door policy to Your missionaries and Your Message? And would You work behind the scenes to keep the doors open in countries that are trying to close them—like Russia?

Then, Lord, would You use Your Holy Spirit and us, Your humble servants, to open the doors to Your love in the lives right here that we come into contact with who worship a god who is convenient, a god who allows them to pursue their own agendas, a god who can justify their prejudices, a god who allows each of them to follow the leading of their inner self?

And also, Lord, we're attempting to throw open the doors in our own lives that have been closed to You. O Lord, help us to open them wide—wide enough for You to come in. And help each of us to not withhold any part of our life from You.

O Lord, wrap Your arms of love around us, pull us close, give us Your peace, and let us feel the love.

May we see with the eyes of God, think with the mind of Christ, and operate with the power of the Holy Spirit.

Amen

∞

Prayed at an evening session of a Winter Bible Study. January Bible Study has been a fixture in many Southern Baptist Churches. It is usually an intense Bible study of one book of the Bible over a short period of time in January. At FBC, Tullahoma, it morphed into Winter Bible Study as it slipped out of January into February or March.

Precious Jesus,

Some folk, as they study Your Word this evening, will do so with the intent to discredit it, some with the intent to relegate what they read to fit into the niche of their preconceived ideas, some with the intent to explain away what it obviously says by saying it isn't relevant or that Paul was merely reflecting the mindset of the times, some with the intent of gaining scholarly knowledge, some with the intent of finding their personal understanding of what it says.

O Lord, we confess that our understanding of Your Word is shallow. All too often we have read or heard the words of others and have followed along—or we have leaned upon our own understanding.

O Lord, some of us meditate on Your Word by relying on human logic to consider the various options and to ask the logical questions, and to draw conclusions that natural thinking would provide. O Lord, help us instead to meditate in a manner that allows Your Holy Spirit to inject truth into our minds. O Lord, help us to discern the meaning of Scripture rather than decide it.

Only after we discern what it means instead of what it means to us may we ask, "How does it apply to me or my situation?" Then, Lord, help us apply it appropriately.

May Your Word be alive and powerful and sharper than any two-edged sword. May it penetrate to the depths of our soul and expose our every desire and purpose and bring about Your will in our lives. (See Heb. 4:12)

Amen

Prayed at an 8:30 Sunday Morning Worship Service.

O Lord,

So many of our acquaintances have major misconceptions about You. Somehow they've grown to the age they are, become responsible, productive human beings, but don't really understand who You are.

Some of them say that they're not perfect but they are not all that bad. In fact, they say that they're a lot better than a lot of the so-called Christians they know that go to church. They think that when judgment time comes, You'll look favorably on them.

O Lord, Adam took just one bite out of the apple, and You kicked him out of the Garden. Moses merely struck the rock, and he couldn't go into the Promised Land. For one sin, Elijah's servant got leprosy. And Ananias and Sapphira were struck dead for one act of deceitfulness.

O Lord, may those who are deceived gain an understanding of Your holiness—how You are so holy that You cannot even abide one sin and how only the blood of Jesus can pay for a sin no matter how small. O Lord, use us to get the message across as Your Holy Spirit leads. May these become so aware of who You are, how great You are, and how holy You are that they invest their life in You.

Forgive us for whatever part we played in their ignorance of you. Chide us properly and use Your Holy Spirit so it doesn't happen again.

We praise You because even though the high priest of the Old Testament was able to enter the Holy of Holies only once a year, that because of the spilt blood of Jesus we can enter Your presence any time we want to. Even as we speak to You on a personal basis through the prayer at this moment, we ask that in the moments ahead, as we go through an effort to try to worship You, that You would speak to each one of us here this morning through Your Holy Spirit using Your preached word, Your written Word, and Your living Word to convey Your message to us here this morning just as clear and straightforward as if Moses himself were reading it from stone tablets.

Lord, I read that if one doesn't have at least one head-on collision with the devil per day that it probably means you and he are headed in the same direction. Lord, I lift to You those of our congregation who are not struggling with sin. Lord, wake them up to see those signs along the road that say "To Heaven" are lies. O Lord, may Your Holy Spirit work continually pointing out our sins to us and making us feel guilty about them. And may our relationship with You grow as we confess and repent of those sins.

And may Your glory know no bounds,

Amen

∞

Prayed at a Monday Night Prayer Meeting.

O Lord,

We could be a church that majors on social ministry but just makes the world a better place to go to Hell from. Or we could be a church that majors in evangelism but walks by those in need. Or we could be a church with a beautiful sanctuary and a professional-quality worship service every Sunday but which doesn't read or heed Your Word. Or we could be the richest church in town but have its tithes and offerings rejected because it doesn't defend the cause of the weak and the fatherless. Or we could be a church that majors on Your Word—spends hours studying it, memorizing it, and holding each other accountable to it, but comes across as legalistic instead of loving. Or maybe we could be one of those megachurches which justifies its ways by its numbers and by saying, "We give the people what they want." (Instead of what You want them to have.)

And, Lord, we confess that to some extent we're guilty of being every one of those churches.

O Lord, instead of the church we are, move us to be a church that isn't run by the pastor or the church staff or the members or by the denomination or denominational leaders. Rather may we be a church that gets its guidance and marching orders from You and You only. May each member be so involved in studying Your Word and in prayer that You are able to communicate Your desires not only for the individual but for the whole church through whatever individuals You choose. And may Your Holy Spirit enable the congregation to recognize Your will when it's brought before it.

O Lord, will You require of us to do whatever we must do to become that one congregation in all history—past, present, and future, that comes closest to being all that You want it to be? And not for our pride, but only for Your glory.

O Lord, we lift to You the lost, the hungry, the outcast, the poor, the oppressed, the down-and-out, the widow, the orphan. May this church meet the needs of these as Your Spirit leads.

Lord, may we be so overwhelmed by Christ's love that it compels us to live, not for ourselves, but for Jesus. And may we keep growing in knowledge of You.

Amen

∞

Prayed at a Monday Night Prayer Meeting.

For all that is in Heaven and in earth is Yours,
Yours is the Kingdom, O God, and You are exalted as head over all.
Both riches and honor come from You and You reign over all. In Your hands are power and might.

In Your hand it is to make great and to give strength to all. (See 1 Chronicles 29:11-12)

O God, we praise You because neither death, nor life, nor angels, nor principalities, nor powers, nor things present, nor things to come, nor height, nor depth, nor any created thing shall be able to separate us from Your love which is in Christ Jesus our Lord. (See Romans 8:38-39)

But we come confessing that while nothing or no one can snatch us out of Your hand, we have broken fellowship with You, we are not living in communion with You because we have repeatedly sinned and failed to confess it to You and repent of it. O God, we have been selfish or we have thought less of others than we should or we passed up the opportunity to witness that you put in front of us or we were lazy or we said something we shouldn't have said or we were late to a meeting or we failed to pray for someone You put on our mind—and then we didn't confess and repent; and now we're out of fellowship with You. Therefore we're not experiencing the power and strength You want us to have.

O God, we confess that we know there are a multitude of sins we have not confessed. Please wipe the slate clean and let us begin anew. We are sorry and don't want to go down that road again.

O God, deliver us from ourselves. Use Your Holy Spirit to cause us to acknowledge our sins when they occur; and may we feel about them as You do. Help us to keep our account with You very short. O Lord, cleanse us of every evil desire and selfishness. Breathe Your breath into us again. Rekindle our slowly dying fire. Revive us.

Saturate us with the oil of Your Spirit then set us on fire for You. Consume us with Your work and Your fire. Use us for Your purpose. So fill us with Your Spirit that we become obsessed with You. So fill us with Your Spirit that we have a burning compulsion to do Your will and to see the lost come to You. May the world take note that here are men and women who have been with Jesus.

O God, then empower us with Your strength to resist temptation and to do Your will. Then God, may we be part of Your efforts here on earth to draw men and women to Christ and make them instruments of blessing to others. Move us to a point where we regularly see sinners begging to receive Jesus.

O God, may we experience that peace and joy that only comes from knowing You, knowing Your will, and doing it. And may you receive the glory and the praise that only You deserve.

O God, help us to never be out of fellowship with You again for more than a few seconds.

May we be filled with the knowledge of Your will in all spiritual wisdom and understanding so we may walk in a manner worthy of You to please You in all respects, bearing fruit in every good work and increasing in the knowledge of You. (See 1 Col. 1:9-10)

Amen

∞

Prayed at a Monday Night Prayer Meeting.

Lord Most High,

We praise You because Your seat of honor is far higher than that of any of our officials.
We praise You because Your love is higher than the heavens and Your faithfulness reaches the skies. (See Ps. 108:4)
We praise You because when it comes to forgiveness, Your ways are higher than our ways and Your thoughts are higher than our thoughts just as the heavens are higher than the earth. (See Isa. 55:9)
We praise You because You have ascended higher than the heavens in order to fill the whole universe. (See Eph. 4:10)

O Lord, You are higher than the mountain tops and Your reach is beyond the farthest star.

We praise You because You are higher than anything and truly worthy to be worshipped.

Lord, we come confessing. We are a bunch of liars. Our actions prove we are liars. We say we believe You are omnipresent and watching us at all times. Yet if my momma was watching me at all times, I wouldn't eat that second and third piece of cake. Yet I blatantly do it in front of You so I must not really believe You are watching me at all times. Lord. I confess to saying I'm concerned about the earthquake victims in Haiti and the flood victims in Pakistan. But my actions, basically doing nothing—not even sending a dime to help, proves I'm lying.

O Lord, basically most of us are just a bunch of liars. We even justify it—we do it to avoid pain and to avoid conflict and to avoid having to pay higher taxes. Or we justify it by saying that it advances Your Kingdom or more properly stated: "our agenda."

O Lord, we're liars because our actions don't match our words. O Lord, take us and shake us and help us recognize the problem, confess it to you, and repent.

Thank you for inviting us to draw near to You. Thank You for giving us faith. Lord, I remember going on a hospital visit to one who had been told he had only a short time to live. He was a dedicated church member, but he was scared to die—not sure what was going to happen when he died. Lord, my regular doctor, after seeing all the scans that were sent her way told my wife I'd be dead within a year. The online information that we looked up said the average life expectancy for someone with my condition was nine months. So after I went through the denial phase, I sat down and checked out whether I was ready to die. I remembered the story of the Boy Scout, the smartest man in the world, and the old pilot who were in the plane that was about to crash and they only had two parachutes. The smartest man in the world grabbed one of the parachutes, said "Sorry, but the world needs my abilities." Then he jumped out of the plane. The old pilot said, "Son, you go ahead and take that other parachute. I've had a long, fulfilling life and you're young and just getting started." Whereupon the Boy Scout said, "Don't worry about a thing. We still have two parachutes. The smartest man in the world took my backpack."[49] I evaluated all the major religions and decided I'm involved in the only one that really has parachutes.

Then I had to ask if I had that parachute on my back and had the rip cord in place. And, Lord, when I starting asking the questions about whether I'm really saved and going to Heaven I thought I'd have so much doubt, but instead You gave me so much faith that I had perfect peace about dying. Thank You for giving me faith way beyond what I thought I had.

O Lord, help us to match our actions with our words so our actions don't make liars of us.

Lord, I'd like to lift to You every person in this church that is scared to die or isn't 100% sure of their salvation. Would You use Your Holy Spirit to grow their faith?

O Lord, as we draw near to You would you draw near to us?

O Lord, move us to quit treating You as our hobby and become our all-consuming passion.

O Lord, instead of ignoring our worship, would You ignite our worship?

And, Lord, as we study Your Word, would You make sure it doesn't return void to You?

---

[49] I first encountered this story in *Faith and Doubt* by John Ortberg on pages 24 and 25.

Pursue us with a desire to be like You that we can't outrun.

We invite You, Lord, to be high and lifted up, reigning upon each of our hearts.

Amen

∞

Prayed during a Monday Night Prayer Meeting. A US-2er is a two-year NAMB (North American Mission Board) missionary. A Journeyman is a two-year IMB (International Mission Board) missionary. These are usually college graduates who spend two years on the field to decide if they want to be full time missionaries, then usually attend seminary or gain further training before becoming full-time missionaries.

O Lord Who Desires that All Men Be Saved,

We praise You because Your Word was not only the agent of creation, but also died on the cross so all men could be saved.
We praise You because You are a god who carved the words that became known as the Ten Commandments, which become the school teacher in the New Testament that teaches each of us that we are sinners.
We praise You because You are a god who spoke the words that pronounced judgment over the House of Eli and carried it out so we might understand that the consequences of sin is death.
We praise You because You are the God Who Gave Us the Final Word in Your son Jesus.
We praise You because You are the God Who Left Us Your Written Word that We Might Understand Your Living Word.

Lord, help us to take Your Word to those who haven't gotten the word.

Lord, we confess, we have sinned against the harvest of souls by not praying for more workers. O Lord, give us a burden for the lost not only here but worldwide.

Lord, we confess, we haven't done the job of taking Your Word far and wide. Last time I was involved in visitation, we only visited folk who had first visited us. And while, when I first came to this church, it was a church that talked and walked and breathed missions, by comparison missions has become secondary.

Lord, there was a time here when every Southern Baptist missionary got prayed for by name regularly. But now we don't even know their names.

Lord, I would like to thank You for the work of the Holy Spirit in calling each Southern Baptist missionary currently on the field. Be with every full-time missionary, every Journeyman, and every US-2er. I lift them to You as a group. Bless them with Your presence, with discernment of Your will, and with the peace that comes from knowing Your will and doing it.

I especially lift to You Sharon's son, Doug, Southern Baptist Missionary to India, who is gravely ill in a hospital in Thailand. Lay Your healing hand on him.

I pray for our mission team doing construction in Mississippi this week. Use them wisely, give them a sense of accomplishment, and bring them home safe and sound.

I pray for E. Lord, protect his life. Keep him from harm. Give him inroads to the people he is trying to reach. Lord, I understand he currently has only a temporary visa and unless he gets a permanent one he'll have to leave. And I understand this is the sticking point that is keeping N. and family from joining him there in Southeast Asia because without the permanent visa E. won't be able to get N. into the schools. Lord, get E. that permanent visa. Then may N. join him there and do a great work in the schools there such that there are so many saved that a church may sprout. And out of that church raise leaders who will evangelize the whole people group.

I'd like to lift to You Brian, a young man who is planning to go to college this fall to become a youth minister. Help us as a church to undergird him with prayer and funds as necessary. Lord, I pray that he will get enough scholarships so that money is not a concern for him and that he will get a position at a church there in Arkansas as a youth minister or associate youth minister so he can get OJT and start fulfilling Your dream for his career.

I'd also like to lift to You Kevin and Leslie. May their work in enabling other missionaries in Russia continue to be successful.

Lord, I lift to You Charles and Jason for salvation.

O Lord, may we know You like the back of our hand.

Amen

∞

Prayed during a Monday Night Prayer Meeting.

Sovereign Lord,

We praise You because You are not a god to be messed with.
We praise You because You depose kings and unseat emperors,
and You elect presidents and establish rulers.
and You bring about pestilence and disease
and cause death and hurricanes.
You give life and provide love.
We praise You because You answer to no one.
We praise You because what You plan You do.
We praise You because no obstacle or adversary can hinder Your plan
from happening.
We praise You because You are afraid of nothing, ignorant of nothing,
and need nothing.
We praise You because what You want You get.
We praise You because You can accomplish whatever You want.

We praise You because You see history from beginning to end.

We praise You because You are in control of everything.

We praise You because You're over the stuff we see and the stuff we don't see.

We praise You because we can study chapters in the Bible as history that were originally written as prophecy.

We praise You because there is no such thing as luck or coincidence.

Lord, we're not here to mess with You. We praise You not to butter You up, but to follow Jesus' example in the Model Prayer and to put ourselves in the right mindset to pray: namely, You are the Lord God Almighty and we are but bits of dust in the passing wind by comparison.

O Lord, we confess. We are far from the creatures You want us to be. Take us and shake us and wake us up to what it is that is keeping us from delighting in Your abundance in our lives. Help us to feel Your abundant pardon every day.

Help us to put ourselves in a position where Your Word can flow through our lives moment by moment—and may it not return void.

May we become so in love with You that we delight in You and in Your work—and it shows.

May we be overwhelmed by Your greatness.

Keep us from thinking that anything apart from You can ever satisfy us—whether it is baseball, football, TV, someone else, or something on the internet.

Pursue us by putting in us a desire to be like Jesus that we can't deny or outrun. We invite You, Lord, to be high and lifted up, reigning upon the throne of each of our hearts.

Your way, in Your time, every time.

Amen

Written after reading *Gripped by the Greatness of God* by James MacDonald (See p. 69+).

Prayed during a Monday Night Prayer Meeting.

O Lord Who Walked and Talked with Adam in the Garden of Eden,

We praise You because You are a god who created us for fellowship with You,
We praise You because You are a god who invented prayer.
We praise You because You are a prayer-hearing god.
We praise You because You are a prayer-answering god.

O Lord, we confess that one of the essential elements of prayer, confession, we're not very good at or we forget it altogether.

O Lord, we confess that we are a people who do not confess our sins in our prayers.

Some of us were nurtured into joining the church, giving our lives to Jesus to be our Savior because we loved Him. And we missed out on that experience of grieving over our sins, confessing them to You, repenting of them, and then inviting Christ to come into our lives and be Savior and Lord. Therefore, we haven't had that tremendous experience of feeling the guilt removed from our lives and so maybe don't feel the necessity to confess our every sin to You for the rest of our lives as others do.

Too many of us arrive at bedtime and say, "Lord, forgive me of my sins." And we can't think of a single one! We either have so grieved the Holy Spirit by ignoring Him so often that He has given up on us or we're not keeping a short account with You.

Some of us are so self-righteous that we wouldn't confess our sins to You much less to one another—as Your Word suggests. And maybe that is partially the sin of the church—because there seems to be nowhere where confessing sins one to another is part of the program of the church. No one else is doing it. Why should I?

The leadership of the church never confess their personal sins or the sins of the church at church. The people of the church seem so perfect—all dressed up, putting on their best attitudes, smiling and friendly, and apparently not having problems with sin in their lives. So why should I?

We look at the non-Christians that we know; and some of them are more Christian than the Christians! And why? Because we Christians are stagnated; we're not growing to be more like Jesus every day because we're not confessing and repenting of our sins ASAP and getting the Holy Spirit's help to not repeat the sin. Some of us say to ourselves, "Well, I rarely sin." Heaven forbid! The closer we are to Jesus the more sins we see in our lives—especially sins of omission.

And then, Lord, when we have a major problem at the church— like an extended period of time without any baptisms or a decline in membership, our leadership addresses the problem by coming up with new programming when what needs to happen is we need to be on our knees in tears at the altar either pleading for some lost soul or asking You what sin we've committed so we can confess, repent, and get right with You. We're too scared to give up the false security of our self-righteousness to admit that maybe we're the cause of the failure of the church. We're afraid that if we let our guard down and admit even a little sin, that our whole kingdom will fall.

O Lord, disturb the waters of our life once again. Bring us to our knees as individuals and as a church. Give us the strength to overcome our self-righteousness. O Lord, jolt us out of our complacency. Help us to recognize the lies we tell ourselves.

Lord, You didn't come for the righteous, but You came for the sinners. We confess that even though all our sins were forgiven when we invited You into our life, we still sin. We sin regularly and need to confess and repent regularly. We desire that fellowship, that closeness with You that comes from our confession and following Your will.

Help us to recognize our every sin.
Help us to feel remorse for our every sin.
Help us to confess our every sin.
Help us to repent of our every sin.
O Lord, bring us to the point where we can confess "Jesus is Lord" and it be 100% true for our life.

O Lord, take us and shake us and wake us up.

Amen

∞

Prayed during a Monday Night Prayer Meeting.

O Lord Whom Paul Identified as the Unknown God in Athens,

We praise You because You are a god who is not unknown to us.

We praise You because You are a god who provides evidence of Your invisible traits, Your eternal power, and Your divine nature to all men.

We praise You because it wasn't by any of our efforts that we came to know You, but rather it was You who chose us, gave us evidence of who You are, drew us to You, enabled us to believe in You, and sealed us for salvation.

We praise You because we can take no credit for either our knowledge of You or our salvation.

Lord, help us to find the people who are as ignorant and as lost as the Stoics and Epicureans of Athens. Help us to encounter the atheists, the agnostics, the deists, the secular humanists, the deceived, the Muslims, the New Agers, the Buddhists, and the Hindus.

Lord, give us the insight that You gave Paul so we might see an inroad on how to reach these, give us the boldness that You gave Paul to proclaim You to them regardless of the perceived futility of such efforts and the danger, give us the tact that You gave Paul so we might not scare them away. O Lord, help us to be confrontational with these as Your Holy Spirit leads so that some of them might be saved.

O Lord, I'd like to lift up E. and all foreign missionaries witnessing in Muslim countries. Keep them alive and healthy. Would You provide inroads for them to proclaim Your Word boldly and tactfully? And may Your Word not return void.

O Lord, grow Your church. And grow it through us.

We praise You because You made the world and everything in it. We praise You because You are the Lord of heaven and earth, do not dwell in temples made with hands. Neither are You served by human hands as if You needed anything since You Yourself give to all life and breath and all things. (See Act 17:24,25)

Lord, You are a god in whom we may greatly glory, and greatly glory in You we do.

Amen

∞

Prayed during a Monday Night Prayer Meeting.

The Lord is my shepherd...Jehovah Rohi (The Lord our Shepherd).

I shall not want...Jehovah Jireh (The Lord who provides).

He makes me to lie down in green pastures. He leads me beside the still waters...Jehovah Shalom (The Lord our peace).

He restores my soul...Jehovah Rophi (The Lord who heals).

He leads me in the path of righteousness for His name's sake...Jehovah Tsidkenu (The Lord our righteousness).

Yea, though I walk through the valley of the shadow of death, I will fear no evil, for You are with me. Your rod and Your staff, they comfort me...Jehovah Shammah (The Lord is there).

You prepare a table before me in the presence of mine enemies... Jehovah Nissi (The Lord our banner).

You anoint my head with oil; my cup runs over...Jehovah Mekoddishkem (The Lord who sanctifies).

Surely goodness and mercy shall follow me all the days of my life; and I will dwell in the house of the Lord forever.

Amen

The Twenty-third Psalm is taken from the ESV. The inserted names of God are taken from a table on page 33 of *Experiencing the Spirit: The Power of Pentecost Every Day* by Henry and Melvin Blackaby.

∞

Prayed at Monday Night Prayer Meeting.

O Lord Who Created the Stars,
The One who brings them out at night and knows exactly how many there are and calls them by name,
> Because of the greatness of Your might and because You are strong in power not one is lost or lacks anything. (My poor rendering of Isaiah 40:26)

O Lord Who Created Human Beings,
The One who knows how many hairs are on each of our heads and calls us by name to follow Him,

Because of the greatness of Your might and because You are strong in power not one who follows You is lost or lacks anything.

O Lord, we praise You because (Repeat this with indented phrases below or not.)
> You weren't off doing Your own thing when it came time to knit us together in our mother's womb,
> You weren't watching TV when it was time to draw salvation's plan,
> You weren't taking a nap when it was time to send Jesus,
> You didn't conveniently forget to raise Him from the dead.
> You omitted nothing that we needed.

O Lord, we confess that we are proud of the fact that we see very little sin in our lives, but because of that fact we are sorry excuses for Your children because we are constantly committing the sin of omission and not even recognizing it.

O Lord, (Repeat this with indented phrases below or not.)
- the people who would have been saved if we had but prayed for them,
- the people who would still be coming to church if we'd but gone to visit them when they quit coming,
- the people who would have been so much better off if we'd but ministered to them when we felt Your tug at our heart to help,
- the spiritual growth we'd have experienced if we'd but spent the time poring over Your Word as often as Your Holy Spirit prompted us,
- the Scripture we'd have stored in our memories if we'd just memorized all those memory verses You put in front of us,

- the promises in Your Word we could have claimed if we'd but accepted Your challenges,
- how close we could have been to You if we'd just confessed our sins as soon as Your Holy Spirit first convicted us,
- the glory You would have received except we didn't follow Your leading,
- the people who should have gotten a personal witness from us whom we ignored,
- the fruit that would have been produced in our lives except that we ignored what the Holy Spirit was telling us to do,
- the light this world might have received except we were too concerned with ourselves,
- the doors You opened that we could have gone through except we didn't want to leave our comfort zone.

O Lord, we're like the priest and the Levite (from the story of The Good Samaritan). We don't help those who are in our path and are in obvious need—rather we roll up our car window, try not to look at them, make excuses, and think their signs are inappropriate.

O Lord, we're like the Laodiceans who say they are rich and have need of nothing but, according to Jesus, are wretched, pitiable, poor, blind, and naked (list stolen from *Amplified Bible*, Rev. 3:17).

O Lord Your Word says that whoever knows to do right and fails to do it, for him it is sin (James 4:17 the way I memorized it long ago). O Lord, we have sinned. Show us all we have left undone so we might rightly confess it and repent.

Then Lord, give us the strength of commitment to do everything Your Holy Spirit is telling us to do.

Amen

Prayed during an 8:30 Sunday Morning Worship Service. This prayer was influenced by one of John MacArthur's New Testament Commentaries. Anytime one uses a commentary one needs to be aware of the author's theology. For example, MacArthur is known to be a fundamentalist, a Calvinist and a dispensationalist and advocates young-earth creationism.

O Lord of Peace,

We praise You because (Repeat this with indented phrases below or not.)
    You are a god who does not worry,
    You are a god who is not anxious about anything,
    You are a god who fears nothing,
    You are a god who is as calm as a cucumber.

Did You see what I just saw? Once again Your invitation was given here at FBC, and there was no visible response.

You know why; and I think I know why. It is because, instead of growing toward Your perfect peace every day, we've settled for the devil's peace.

Yes, the devil is rocking men in the cradle of false security, singing a lullaby, "I've got peace like a river" when actually they are standing at a precipice that leads to Hell.
One thinks he is worthy before God because he is good.
Another thinks he is going to Heaven because of his good deeds.
A third boasts he has peace but wallows in sin.
A fourth says he is going to Heaven because he is living according to a set of rules.
O Lord, rock their world and wake them up.

But, more importantly for us, the devil also sings a peace lullaby to us Christians singing, "If you're happy and you know it, clap your hands; if you're happy with the status quo, clap your hands." And we're all clapping our hands because we already know how and it's non-threatening. But this explains why we haven't responded to Your invitation and publicly rededicated our lives in umpteen years. Lord, may we work out our salvation with fear and trembling daily. (See Phil. 2:12) And may You who began a good work in us develop and perfect it one day at a time until Jesus returns. (See Phil. 1:6)

Lord, Your word says that "...righteousness and peace have kissed each other." (Ps. 85:10 Amp). May we obtain peace by waging war on the sin in our lives.

O Lord, the devil has so mesmerized us that the lost visitors in our midst are for the most part lost—they are not here. Yet Your Word tells us to compel the poor, the lame, the crippled, and the blind to come to the feast and to go out in the highways and hedges and invite the multitudes. (See Luke 14:13,23) O Lord, we have become so comfortable in the devil's peace, that we only give lip service to having a concern for the lost.

Help us to respond to Your chastening.

Then, Lord, help us to become peacemakers by being confrontational with Your Good News when and where Your Spirit leads.

And may we experience peace, not the kind that lulls us to sleep, but the kind that gives us a deep confidence that all is well between us and You and that we need to keep on keeping on. O Lord, may You become our peace.

May these tithes and offerings be used to bring more of Your peace to this world.

And may Your Word spread quickly, run its course, be glorified, and triumphant. (See 2 Thes. 3:1)

Amen

This prayer was written after reading *The MacArthur New Testament Commentary: 1 & 2 Thessalonians*, pp. 312-316.

∞

Prayed during an 8:30 Sunday Morning Worship Service. I began with the following introductory remarks:

Before I pray, I'd like you to take a moment to think of a friend, a family member, an acquaintance, or a co-worker that is lost that you would like to see saved. When I get to the point where I am specifically praying for an individual to be saved, I'm going to lift that name silently and allow you to say your person's name silently.

O Lord, they don't call You the Hound of Heaven for nothing.
We thank you that when it came to pursuing us You didn't leave the big dog on the porch.
We love You with all our heart, with all our soul, and with all our might.
We love Your Word.
We love Your Son.
We love Your Spirit.
We love Your chastening.

Lord, we would like to lift to You all those who have not been caught in Your web of love, but most specifically we'd like to lift to You _____ for salvation. We know You're at work in his life. Help us to join You.

We praise You because You loved us so much that You sent Jesus to die for all our sins: past, present, and future.

We praise You because You loved us so much that when we accepted Your invitation to accept Jesus as our Lord and savior, all of our sins—past, present, and future were forgiven, such that no matter what sin we might now commit, not that we want to, whether suicide, murder, adultery, or blasphemy, it is already forgiven and it won't keep us out of Heaven.

We praise You because You loved us so much that both You and Jesus hold us in Your hand and nothing we or anyone else can do can cause us to be released.

We praise You because You love us so much You want us to ask for forgiveness a second time for those sins we commit after we're saved, not because those sins can cause us to lose our salvation, but because those sins cause us to separate ourselves from fellowship with You, cause us to move away from that love relationship with You. O Lord, help us to get that relationship restored ASAP.

O Lord, the blanket prayer we often pray for forgiveness, the one similar to what we find in the Model Prayer, just doesn't give us the closeness that asking forgiveness for a specific sin does. Would You please use Your Holy Spirit to call attention to our every sin immediately after it happens, even our sins of omission?

O Lord, we are so blind to our own sins. We need Your help. For example, if our spouse compliments the meat loaf, and we bask in the praise—we just sinned. If a football player can give God the glory on TV for the touchdown he scored, why can't we give You the glory for a good meat loaf? And yet we come to the end of the day and can't remember any sins we committed that day! O Lord, help us see our every sin so we can restore fellowship with You ASAP.

And may we become Your hands, feet, and voice on earth so that in combination with Your Holy Spirit many others may be caught in Your web of love.

Use these tithes and offerings to spread Your love.

May Your word spread quickly, run its course, and be glorified, and triumphant. (See 2 Thes. 3:1)

Amen

Prayed during an 8:30 Resurrection Sunday Morning Worship Service.

Omnipotent, Omniscient, Omnipresent Lord,

There is a type of prayer called an 'invocation' in which Christians often try to 'call in' or invoke Your presence. But Your Word says,

"If I ascend up into heaven, You are there;
if I make my bed in Sheol, behold, You are there.
If I take wings of the morning or dwell in the uttermost parts of the sea,
Even there shall Your hand lead me, and Your right hand shall hold me."
(Ps. 139:8-10 Amplified)
It seems foolish to ask You to join us here this morning since You are already here, as well as everywhere else we could go.

Additionally, Your Word indicates that the body of each Christian is a temple of the Holy Spirit which has indwelt him. (See 1 Cor. 6:19) So it would seem even more foolish for a Christian or a group of Christians to ask for Your Holy Spirit to join us here this morning since He already lives within each of us. So for our invocation here this morning instead of asking for Your presence which we think we already have, we ask You to make us more aware of that presence.

Just as on the road to Emmaus, the disciples didn't recognize Jesus, we oftentimes don't recognize Your Spirit within us. As the threesome approached the village of the two disciples, Jesus acted as if He would go on further. But the two urged and insisted that He stay a while with them. And when He broke bread with them, they recognized Him. After he then vanished, they said their hearts burned within them while He talked on the way and He opened and explained the Scriptures. (See Luke 24:28-32)

O Lord, in the same way we urge You and insist that You abide with us this morning in a way that we recognize You and that our hearts burn within us as the Scriptures are opened and explained.

And just in case You missed it, Lord, and because we know You are courteous and won't do Your thing where You are not invited, we again extend to You a personal invitation to cause us to recognize You working in our lives this morning by causing our hearts to burn within with a desire to love You and to do Your will.

And when this service is over, may each of us be able to say that the Lord was in this place, my heart burned within me, and I personally experienced Him.

Amen

∞

Prayed during a Monday Night Prayer Meeting. Dewey was one of the faithful at Monday Night Prayer Meeting until his cancer got so bad he couldn't make it any more.

Lord of Abraham and Isaac and Jacob whose name You changed to Israel,

We praise You because You are the god who provided a Way whereby no matter how sinful we are we can be completely forgiven.
We praise You because You are the god who provided a Way whereby no matter how desperate our situation we can find hope.

O Lord, the Israelites had the Red Sea in front of them, mountains on both sides of them, and the Egyptian army fast approaching behind them. And You made a way.

O Lord, Dewey's oncologist has suggested he consider hospice; his surgeon has said he couldn't put the stents in that Dewey needed; Dewey is currently receiving nothing to treat his cancer; his cancer is growing as we speak; his family can't provide as much support as he needs; and his church family more often than not can't get in to see him. O Lord, would You make a way for Dewey?

O Lord, I picture a chair in Dewey's room in which no one is sitting. Seemingly, Dewey is having to go through all this alone for the most part. O Lord, would You sit next to Dewey and hold his hand? Would You be there for him to remind him of Your love and Your Word?

Would You change his worries to prayers and his fears to faith?

And would You do this all in a way in which You receive all the glory?

We give thanks to You because You are so good.

We praise You, Lord, because Your mercies and loving-kindness endure forever.

Amen

∾

Prayed during a Monday Night Prayer Meeting. Age of accountability is that age (different for every child and situation) at which a child becomes accountable for his own sins.

O Lord Who Is a Consuming Fire,

We praise You because You are the god who provided the fire that consumed the offering, the altar, the stones, and the water on Mount Carmel at Elijah's behest.
We praise You because You are the god who provided the fire that did not consume the bush that Moses encountered.
We praise You because You are our everything.

Lord, Elijah apparently knew of Your promise in Deuteronomy that said that if the Israelites turned aside and served other gods that Your anger would be kindled and You would shut up the heavens so there would be no rain (See Deut. 11:16-17) but it didn't happen until he claimed Your promise. And then it didn't rain for three and one-half years. It's almost as if on earth Your will, even when it is recorded in Your Word, doesn't happen unless and until we pray for it.

For that reason, Lord, let me remind You that I know of Your will as stated in 1 Timothy that all men be saved. Therefore, I humbly request that Your will be done here on earth just like is in Heaven and that Charles be saved and that every child at or above the age of accountability that attends our Vacation Bible School next week be saved.

O Lord, I would like to confess to doing a poor job of obeying You. I find myself weighing Your commands to see if I am going to do them. Help me to obey instantly—without thinking twice. May I obey even when it's not prudent or comfortable or logical.

Secondly, Lord, I would like to confess the sin of self-examination. O Lord, it is fraught with faults—the temptation to sweep stuff under the rug, the temptation to make excuses for my sins, the ability of pride to blind me to my sins, the inability to even have a clue about most of my sins of omission. O Lord, may I instead be like David and say: Search me, O God, and know my heart, try me, and know my thoughts. And see if there be any wicked way in me, and lead me in the way everlasting. (See Ps. 139:23-24) May Your Holy Spirit be on a seek-and-destroy mission in my life bringing to my attention my every sin and causing me to hate each one.

Lord, Your Word says that if we abide in You and Your Word abides in us we may ask what we may and it will be done for us. (See John 15:7) We would like to further claim this promise to reinforce our claims in the prayer.

We pray for Your will, nothing more, nothing less no matter what the cost.[50]

Amen.

∞

---

[50]   The Amplified Bible. p. 131, footnote f.

This was prayed in a Pre-service Deacon-Pastor Prayer Time (before an 8:30 Sunday Morning Worship Service) with fellow Deacons, the pastor, and visiting evangelist.

Lord of Salvation,

We praise You because You are a God who in every sense and in every tense, past present, and future—You are our savior.

We thank you Lord because in the past You did all the work to bring about our justification experience, that moment in time when we became in Your sight just as if we'd never sinned. O Lord, help us to be reminded how thankful we should really be.

And now, Lord, now that we're in the present trying to work out our salvation with fear and trembling, (See Phil. 2:12) thank you for providing the encouragement and blessing us at every step.

And thank you that the hope that we have for our future glorification is not hope like the world experiences it, but hope like only Your children can experience it—as surety.

Lord, we ask that You would not let Todd get in the way of Your Word and Your Spirit here this morning. But rather may he so boldly preach sin, repentance, and the gospel this morning that he so exposes Your Word and enables Your Holy Spirit that Your children here will be inspired by Your Word and Your Spirit to do Your will and take Your Word with them everywhere they go and spread it around to Your glory. May Your Word spread quickly, run its course, be glorified and triumphant. (See 2 Thes. 3:1)

May Your Word accomplish everything You intend for it to here this morning.

O Lord, may our hearts be so melted that we become single-minded, wanting only to know You and love You more so that we are continually praying and searching Your Word.

May we be Your Jesus here on earth to those we've mentioned who have problems, may we visit, call, touch, heal, encourage, pray for and with these as Your Holy Spirit directs.

Amen

∞

Prayed at a Monday Night Prayer Meeting.

O Lord Who Asked Us to Pray Without Ceasing, (See 1 Thes. 5:17)

We praise You because You are a god who wants to be intimate with us.

We come confessing that when it comes to the confessing part of prayer we have ceased to pray. We might pray for the sick; and we lift to You at this time those whose names we've called this evening. But we never get serious about our sins, Lord.

Some of us have a particular sin that we don't really want to confess to You because we really don't want to get rid of it. Others of us only pray generically when it comes to our sin. We say, "Forgive us of our sins." or "Forgive us of our sins as we forgive those who sin against us." But we don't pray concerning each sin separately. So You can't really help us deal with them. So the next day, next week, or ten years later we're still asking for forgiveness for the same sins because we're still committing the same sins.

Some of us actually try not to sin just so we won't have to confess our sins so we don't have to deal with You—we're doing just fine without You! But to even think that we don't have sin in our lives or to think we can handle it is pure arrogance. (See 1 John 1:8)

Then there are the many who have been duped into identifying sin as committing a homosexual act, obtaining an abortion, murder, having sex with someone we are not currently with, or committing armed robbery or some such list and nothing else. Therefore they never sin. However, they lie and exaggerate, exhibit pride and arrogance, show greed and selfishness, live lives of materialism, and lose their temper on a regular basis.

Lord we need Your Holy Spirit and Your Holy Word and Your preached word to work on us this evening to break our heart. But we don't need to be broken hearted for the starving in Somalia, we don't need to be broken hearted for the poor in Haiti; we don't need to be broken hearted for the lost in India. We just need to be broken hearted for the sin in our own life.

Lord, we really don't even need a preacher here at church. What we really need is an ER doctor with those paddles. You see, You asked us to do something some time back. And we said, "No." And we said it repeatedly. We drew the line as to what we'd do and not do for You. And now You've about quit asking us. Lord, we're flat lined. We're so dead we can't see our sin. Lord, shock us back to life here this morning. Make us broken hearted for our sin.

Amen

∞

Prayed during an 8:30 Sunday Morning Worship Service.

Lord of Hosts,

We praise You because You are a mighty military commander who can with a single word summon legion upon legion upon legion of angels to protect us.

Lord, Elisha's servant awoke to see that he and Elisha were surrounded by a great army. He was scared. Elisha prayed that the servant's eyes would be opened. Then the servant saw that the army was greatly outnumbered by horses and chariots of fire and warrior angels.

Lord, I pray that You would open our eyes this morning that we can see what we don't ordinarily see. May we be able to see behind the scenes and see You and Your Holy Spirit and Your angels at work bringing about Your will through Your children here on earth.

O Lord, after the altar was prepared on Mount Carmel, Elijah didn't do anything but pray. And the result was that the people saw a miracle and made a recommitment to the one true god. They didn't go home saying what a great prayer that was or what a great prophet Elijah was. They went home saying, "The Lord, He is God. The Lord, He is God. The Lord, He is God."

I pray that everyone here will see at least one miracle here this morning, experience Your Holy Spirit moving in their life to make a new commitment, and go home saying, "The Lord, He is God."

Amen

∞

Prayed during an 8:30 Sunday Morning Worship service in which the Lord's Supper (Communion) was served.

Precious Jesus,

It's a right humbling thing to be died for. And it's downright embarrassing to consider how long it's been since we just sat quietly and meditated, like we did this morning, on the fact that Your lifeblood was poured out atoning for our sin and Your body was sacrificed for us and how thankful we need to be!

O Lord, it is beyond human capability to be properly thankful for Your sacrifice on the cross for us; and that was just the beginning of a long list of things You've done for us that we need to be thankful for.

We are thankful that because of what we've seen in our own lives and in the world around us, we have the confidence that You, who began a good work in us, will continue until You return, developing that good work and perfecting it and bringing it to full completion. (See Phil. 1:6) And, o Lord, help us to do our part with fear and trembling.

We are thankful for the fellowship we've had together here at FBC advancing the Good News from when we joined until now.

Lord, we are thankful that we don't have to face the challenges ahead alone—that You are always there for us and that our fellow church members are there to pray for us and support us.

O Lord, we thank You because we have every confidence that as we apply ourselves to Your Word, we will grow
- In love
- In knowledge
- In the ability to discern between good and bad and between better and best
- In character
- Living fruitful lives.

May we fasten our eyes upon You and live closer to You each day.

We pray especially for some folk here who are maybe not as thankful as they could be. For those who have health problems, would You grow their faith?

For mates whose spouses are lost, help them to be good witnesses.

For parents whose grown children don't go to church, hear their prayers.

For those looking for work, help them find Your plan for their lives.

For those with financial problems, may they honor You with their lives.

May our offerings this morning reflect our love and thankfulness.

Amen

The following prayer was used as an offertory prayer after a sermon entitled "The Compassionate Heart" based on Leviticus 19:9-10:

Sovereign Lord,

We praise You because You reign over the entire universe.
We praise You because, despite the fact that You have allowed Satan to have certain powers here on earth, You ultimately will reign over the entire earth.
We praise You because almost every person here can say that You are the Lord his god and that You reign in his life—at least part of the time.

Unfortunately we must confess that we have been polluted by the world. For example, we find ourselves wasting time watching and being influenced by TV shows which are attempting to spread a world view vastly different from ours. And we find ourselves watching and being influenced by movies produced by Hollywood directors who are out to move the standards of decency and acceptability beyond the current standards.

Lord, we are a church which has a reputation for praying for and ministering to the sick. Perhaps no church in Tennessee does a better job in this area. I probably wouldn't be alive today except for the prayers of people in the church offered in my behalf.

However, when it comes to having compassion for the foreigner, namely the lost, we are lacking.

Lord, we know that we become most like the person we spend the most time with. Lord, help us to spend less time watching TV and movies and more time in prayer and in Your Word so that Your compassion for the lost rubs off on us. May we find ourselves shedding tears for the lost as You do; may we find ourselves agonizing over the lost just as You do.

Lord, may these tithes and offerings be used to show compassion to the foreigners—the lost.

And as we leave this place in just a bit, may we take Your Word boldly with us, may we take Your Good News boldly to the lost.

In the name of the one who reigns on high with God forever and ever.

Amen

∞

Prayed at a Monday Night Prayer Meeting, this prayer is based on Acts 4:23-32 (NIV)

Sovereign Lord,

How great You are.

You made the heavens and the earth and the sea, and everything in them.

We praise You because of Your greatness and Your great provision.

Peter and John had been arrested for preaching Jesus. The authorities warned them not to preach in that name any more, then released them. They went back to church, where with one accord they all lifted up their voices. In their prayer they first identified Your greatness, just as I did in this prayer. Then they quoted Your Word back to You. Lord, I quote those same words back to You: "Why do the nations rage and the peoples plot in vain? The kings of the earth take their stand and the rulers gather together against the Lord and against His Anointed One." Then they spoke to You of the threats out there: "[And] now, Lord, consider the threats and enable Your servants to speak Your Word with great boldness."

O Lord, may the fear of persecution and the thoughts of what others might think not hinder our witness. May we, like Peter and John, choose to obey You rather than man.

Then the place began to shake and they were filled with the Holy Spirit and began to speak the Word of God with boldness. May we, too, be filled with the Holy Spirit and begin to witness with boldness such that the lives of many who need You are shaken.

May we take Your Word as You will, when You will, and where You will.

Amen

∞

Prayed during an 8:30 Sunday Morning Worship service.

God of grace and God of glory,

We praise You because You, and You alone, are worthy of worship.

It is our intent to worship You as a corporate body—as Your church here this morning. The music has been selected, a sermon prepared, and we come prepared to give.

Unfortunately we know from past experience that sometimes we sing the hymns, listen to Your Word preached, and give our offerings; but when it comes time to go home we are each the same person we were when we entered the sanctuary. On those occasions we were just like the Israelites who were careful to bring their prescribed animal sacrifices, but they didn't obey other commandments. May none of us go home unchanged this morning.

O Lord, we're not here to worship You in our way this morning, but to bow down to You and worship You on Your terms. May any unconfessed sins we have come to mind. May we offer You a contrite heart. And may sin and Satan himself be crushed by our submissiveness to you.

May Your Holy Spirit grow our faith; may we commit to a closer walk with You. May we become more like Jesus through our worship here this morning. May our attention be drawn to what Your will for our life is at this time.

We pray for Your will, nothing more, nothing less, no matter what the cost.[51]

Amen

∞

Prayed during an 8:30 Sunday Morning Worship service. The preacher preached on compromise.

Sovereign Lord,

We praise You because You are the god who deposes emperors, establishes kings, and elects presidents. We praise You not only because You reign over us, but because You also rain on us. We thank You for the rain we had this week.

Lord, we come confessing—confessing that we think there is a political solution to our nation's problems and we spend our time and effort in that direction instead of recognizing that our nation's problem is spiritual and we need to spend our time and effort praying for revival and seeking the lost.

O Lord, help us to trust in Your Word. May we not only honor it by obeying it, but may we honor it by spending large amounts of time reading it, studying it, and meditating on it. May we not just get into Your Word, but may Your Word get into us. May it guide our every action.

---

[51]   The Amplified Bible. p. 131, footnote f.

Great is Your faithfulness to Your Word. May we be as faithful to it.

Lord, use these tithes and offerings to spread Your Word throughout the world. May Your Word spread quickly, run its course, be glorified, and triumphant. (See 2 Thes. 3:1)

Amen

∾

Prayed at a Monday Night Prayer Meeting.

Our Lord and our God,

You are not only the Alpha and Omega of our lives, but You are the Beta, the Gamma, the Delta, the Epsilon, and everything else in between. O Lord, You are our everything.

And You have been in complete control from the beginning of time and will be in complete control until the end of time. We thank you because in Your eyes we weren't an accident. Our parents may not have planned us, but You did. We were Your intention from the beginning. You even made us in Your image; and You have a purpose for our life. Help us to find it, do it, and praise You for it.

And You not only have plans for us now but for later, too. May we be steadfast, always abounding in Your work, knowing that our labor is not futile but will be rewarded on Judgment Day. (See 1 Cor. 15:58)

Lord, in that moment in Your life here on earth when it seemed like You were not in control—when You were crucified, You actually accomplished the very purpose for which You were here on earth. Likewise, may we have the faith during those times when things seem to be going badly, when we're tempted to say, "How can God be in charge and let this happen to me?" that You are working out Your ultimate will for us.

May You be our alpha and omega. May we begin and end our day with You—and spend every waking moment influenced by Your presence.

Save us from ourselves.

Amen

∞

Prayed during a Monday Night Prayer Meeting.

O Lord Jesus Christ Who is the Way, the Truth, and the Life,

Help us to lose our way and find Your Way. Teach us Your Way, o Lord. (See Ps. 27:11) For there is a way which seems right to man, but its end is the way of death. (See Prov. 14:12) In other words, help us to find You.

And once we find Your Way, help us not to stray. In other words, once we find You, help us to not let go.

Lord, Your Word says that we shall know the truth and the truth shall set us free. (See John 8:32) Harvard University uses that verse as its motto, but unfortunately they're talking about academic truth.

May we not rely on the truth that is just a determined fact, but rather may we seek and find the truth that Jesus is the one and only Way that imparts divine vitality into us which results in eternal life and aspiring toward the abundant life.

May we find the Way, know the Truth, and experience the Life.

Amen

∞

Prayed during an 8:30 Sunday Morning Worship service. The preacher's sermon title was "Living Available"

Lord Who Provides the Living Water and the Bread of Life,

We praise You because You are always available.

We confess that when we look at the number of folk who have joined Your Kingdom as a result of our efforts that it appears we must not have always been available when You needed us. Lord, it appears that we have been passively leading the Christian life instead of living it actively pursuing Your goals. May we live more deliberately for You. May we set goals consistent with Your goals that cause us to commit to participating in certain visitation activities, to sharing Jesus with at least one person a week, to being responsive to Your Holy Spirit when He urges us to witness.

And as we must need go through Tullahoma or Normandy or Shelbyville or Estill Springs on our way home, may we pray that You'll provide a divine appointment for us; and may we meet our every obligation. May we do the will of Him who sent us.

May we make available to You a portion of the money You have made available to us so that Jesus becomes more available to those who need him desperately.

We pray for more workers for the harvest is ripe. And may we become one of those who is considered a worker rather than a shirker for Your Kingdom.

And may it all be for Your glory.

Amen

Prayed during a Monday Night Prayer Meeting.

Glorious Father,

We praise You because, just as Horton in *Horton Hatches an Egg* by Dr. Seuss said, "I meant what I said, and I said what I meant. An elephant's faithful one hundred percent." You meant what You said and You said what You meant. To Your Word You're faithful one hundred percent.

For that reason, Lord, we come praying for Your church what you asked us to pray for in Your Word.

We pray that our love in this Your church will keep on growing in knowledge and discernment so that we can determine what really matters and can be pure and blameless in the day of Christ. May we be filled with the fruit of righteousness that comes through Jesus Christ, to Your glory and praise. (See Phil. 1:9-11)

We pray we'll do nothing wrong, not that we appear to pass some test, but that we may do what is right, even though we appear to fail. May we not attempt to do anything against the truth but only for the truth. May we rejoice when we are weak and You are strong. We pray for our sanctification and maturity. (See 2 Cor. 13:7-9)

We pray that You will consider us worthy of Your calling and will by Your power fulfill every desire for goodness and work of faith You have for us so that the name of our Lord Jesus will be glorified by You through us and hence You be glorified by Him through us. (See 2 Thes. 1:11-12)

Pour Your Spirit out on this church. Give us a burden for the lost. Raise up more laborers for the harvest. Break our hearts over the sin in our lives. Fill our hearts with love for each other. May our attitude be that of Jesus Christ. (See Phil. 2:5)

Help us as a local church members to
- Love one another (See John 13:34)
- Be devoted to one another (See Romans 12:5)
- Honor one another (See Romans 12:15)
- Serve one another (See Galatians 5:13)
- Forgive one another (See Ephesians 4:32)
- Encourage one another (See 1 Thessalonians 5:11)
- Offer hospitality to one another (See 1 Peter 4:7)
- Confess our sins to one another (See James 5:16)
- Pray for one another (See James 5:16)[52]

Guard us with Your love.
Guide us with Your Word.
Gird us with Your power.

Amen

∞

Prayed during a Monday Night Prayer Meeting.

"Father of Compassion and God of All Comfort," (2 Cor. 1:3 NIV),

"How majestic is Your name in all the earth." (Ps. 8:1 NIV)

We don't say You *were* the God of Abraham, Isaac, and Jacob, but rather we say You *are* the God of Abraham, Isaac, and Jacob because while Abraham, Isaac, and Jacob died a physical death, they are alive with You in Heaven. And You are not the God of the dead but of the living. (See Luke 20:38)

And we are proud to say our God is the God of the living because we have been raised from being dead in sin to eternal life (See Romans 6:13) which began when we gave ourselves to You.

---

[52] List found in Harris, Joshua, *Why Church Matters*, p. 66.

We praise You because we walk in newness of life.

We praise You because rivers of living water flow through us.

Lord, we come confessing that we have too much self in these lives that You have given us; We've been using them for our purposes rather than Your purposes. Help us to shake off complacency. (See Rev. 3:19) Help us to so involve ourselves in loving You and doing Your work that our lives become empty of self love, self ambition, and self will. Fill us with Your Holy Spirit so we might resist doing the things we know we shouldn't and instead witness so that Jesus might be glorified.

And may those we witness to seek You while You still may be found, call upon You while You are near, forsake their wicked ways and unrighteous thoughts and return to You. (See Isa. 55:6-7)

May we not just profess Jesus but may we possess Him and He us.

And may we feel compassion for and provide comfort to our fellow man.

Amen

Prayed during an 8:30 Sunday Morning Worship service.

Jehovah,

We come before You in the name of Your precious son, Jesus Christ, to thank You that You aren't just Jehovah, but You are also Jehovah Jireh, the God Who Provides.

We thank You for the provisions that sustain us in this world, oxygen, sunlight, water, food, and shelter, but ever so much more we thank You for the sustenance for which You are really called Jehovah Jireh: You provided Jesus so we might be saved.

We praise You because Your Word says that You knew the thoughts and plans that You had for us, thoughts of welfare and peace and not for evil, to give us hope in our final outcome. (See Jer. 29:11) And then You worked behind the scenes to bring us to the point where we should call on You and pray to You and need You and repent and ask Jesus to come into our hearts. And we did. And in our human way of thinking we say that we found You, but, in reality, You found us.

O Lord, we count everything as loss compared to the priceless privilege of knowing Jesus Christ our Lord and of progressively becoming more deeply and intimately acquainted with Him. (See Phil. 3:8)

Lord, we confess that anytime we try to do things on our own we encounter failure. And we confess that whatever lasting success we've had in our lives is due to Jesus dying for our sins, us following the instigation of the Holy Spirit, and You loving us.

May our thanks, in some very small way, be expressed this morning in the gifts we bring to support this church and Your Kingdom worldwide.

And may we be dismissed in just a few minutes and as we go may we have so much love for our fellow man and for You that when people look at us they see Jesus.

Amen

∞

Prayed during an 8:30 Sunday Morning Worship service.

O Holy One,

We praise You because You alone are holy. There is none like You.
We praise You because You are always holy and Your Truth is holy and
Your righteousness is
holy and
Your justice is holy.

Indeed, Lord, all of Your attributes are holy because You are altogether holy.

O Lord, we praise You because You are Holy with a capital 'H'.

And we, Your followers, are also called holy with a little 'h' because we have been set apart to do Your work here on earth. But, Lord, we confess that, for the most part, we are failures.

What one of us can say we have really loved our neighbor as ourself? Even when we do good deeds they are tainted with wrong motives. What one of us can say we have loved You with all our heart, with all our soul, and with all our might?

We regularly display conduct unbecoming to a saint. We fail not so much because we fall short, but more because we are enticed by our own desire to do something completely different from what You want us to try to do. We fail to witness to the lost and can't overcome the influence of the world in our lives.

We show more enthusiasm for our favorite football team than we do for You. We gossip, speak critically of others, harbor resentment, become impatient, act selfishly, succumb to materialism. We are anxious about things, we worry, and we get frustrated over things like our computer or our printer not working.

And we are ungodly—we go for hours on end and sometimes days with little or no thought of You!

The Psalmist said he pants for and thirsts for You and Your Living Water just as the deer pants for and thirsts for fresh running water. (See Ps. 42:1) O Lord, use Your Holy Spirit to cause us to pant for and thirst for You. May we go hard after You so much that we establish that time to pray and be in Your Word every day

Then, Lord, may each of us here be filled with the knowledge of Your will and please You by doing it and bear much fruit.

May we eat for Your glory, may we drive for Your glory, may we work for Your glory. May we put our monetary offerings in these plates this morning in a way that will bring You glory. Indeed, Lord, may everything we do be for Your glory

In the name of all that is Holy,

Amen

This prayer was written after reading Jerry Bridges' *Respectable Sins*

∞

Prayed during a Pre-Service Deacon-Pastor Prayer Time for an 8:30 Sunday Morning Worship Service.

Omnipotent, Omniscient, Omnipresent Father,

We praise You because of your ability to omni-focus—to see and listen and attend to the needs of seven billion people at the same time with such ability that for each of us down here on earth it's as if You are our God and Father and our God and Father alone.

O Heavenly Father, we confess that we, especially we men, aren't any good at multi-tasking. For that reason we have a hard time focusing on You while other things are going on. But, Lord, may we so focus on You this morning that what happens at 8:30 is not just another worship service where out attention wanders to other things and we go home unchanged, but may we find our eyes so focused on Jesus, our hearts so focused on You, and our minds so attentive to Your message that we, in effect, prostrate ourselves before You such that we are silent, such that we are still, such that we are completely submissive to Your will without even knowing what it is. Then, Lord, reveal Your will to us so we may do it. And may we do it as unto You. (See Col. 3:23)

This morning may our sanctuary be turned into the Holy of Holies in which we all show up and have a divine appointment with You.

Attend to each of these we've mentioned here this morning who has special need of a healing touch from You in such a way that they feel You've shown up personally to take care of their needs. After the service today focus our attention on the one of these You want us to pay special attention to.

Amen

∞

Prayed during an 8:30 Palm Sunday Morning Worship Service.

Hosanna to the Son of David. Blessed is He Who Came in the Name of the Lord. Hosanna in the highest, (See Matt. 21:9)

On Palm Sunday the people couldn't resist praising Jesus any longer. They had to praise Him for the miracles he had done and for who He was.

O Lord, considering how great You are and how much You have done for us, we look absolutely ridiculous sitting idly by when we could be praising You. O Lord, we insult You with our dearth of praise. The first element in the Model Prayer is adoration or praise and yet I often hear prayers offered in this church on behalf of the whole congregation that don't contain any praise.

O Lord, on this Palm Sunday, we would be remiss if we didn't make a special effort to praise You. As we partake of communion, may we praise you as we are reminded of the miracle of You living a perfect life so you could spill Your blood for our sins instead of Yours so we might have life and have it more abundantly and have life eternal. And Lord, I personally want to thank you for the many times I've done stupid stuff with cherries on top that should have gotten me killed, but you intervened and I'm here to give you glory for it. And there's probably not a one of us here that can't give a similar testimony.

Lord, may we find ourselves, like the original Palm Sunday participants, in a situation where we so recognize the miracles You've done and come to the realization of exactly who You have to be so that we just have to praise You.

Then, Lord, inhabit our praises and change the spiritual climate around here. May our praises usher in Your presence and may we be ushered into Your presence. May we have the perfect atmosphere for hearing Your Word. And may the preacher so sense Your presence that he feels a special anointing in his preaching this morning.

We understand that You can't resist praise—that when You are properly praised You have a tendency to release Your power. When the Israelites were obedient to Your instructions and finally in unison raised their voices on that seventh day in praise, the walls of Jericho came tumbling down. May our praise this morning cause You to release Your power such that some of the walls in our lives come tumbling down.

Over in 2 Chronicles when the Israelites praised You with all their might, You defeated their enemies without them even having to raise a hand. O Lord, we pray for what You want to happen here when we praise You with all our might.

O Lord, praise looks so good on us. May we wear it all the time.

Crucify our pride, help us to feel humble, and cause us to become godly as we praise You.

Amen

∞

Prayed as an offertory prayer during an 8:30 Sunday Morning Worship Service

Holy Fruit Inspector,

You'd think a Sunday morning worship service should be non-threatening—just a few hymns, some special musical, and a sermon. But, Lord, we must praise You because Your Holy Spirit doesn't want us to be comfortable; in fact, He doesn't want us to go home unchanged. He knows us well; and He knows what needs to be pruned and what needs to be cultivated.

O Lord, we confess that all too often we judge ourselves based on how good we are, how we compare to others, how busy we are down at the church house, or how we don't commit the big sins. But Your Word says that You are the Vine. We are the branches. He who abides in You and You in us bears much fruit. Apart from You we can do nothing. (See John 15:5) Lord, can the others we encounter see the fruit in our lives? Do they accuse us of having the patience of Job? Do they see the peace in our lives or do they see us fretting about first one thing then another? Do they see us demonstrating self-control or do they see us losing it ever once in a while? Do they see us demonstrating love or do they see us ignoring the person who is holding a sign at the intersection asking for help? Do they see us demonstrating faith or hear us repeatedly praying for the same thing over and over? Can they see the joy, meekness, peace, faith, self control, patience, goodness, gentleness, and love in our lives? Can we name the people who have given their lives to Jesus based on our witness? Do others hunger and thirst for Your Word because they've recognized our love of studying and teaching Your Word?

Your Word indicates that if You abide in us and we abide in You that we are going to bear <u>much</u> fruit. Lord, based on the response to the invitation not just each of us as individuals but the church as a whole isn't bearing much fruit. O Lord, prune us. Cut out the dead and throw it away so we may bear more fruit. Give us more fruit in our lives. Give us more opportunities to witness. Help us to grow. Conform us more closely to Jesus. Use us to make others want to know You.

And, Lord, as we study Your Word, when we (Repeat this with indented phrases below or not.)

> See Your promise, may we claim it,
> See Your command, may we obey it.
> See Your warning, may we heed it, and
> See Your encouragement, may we accept it.

May we not leave here this morning unchanged. Help us, Lord, to abide in You.

May our giving be sincere and generous.

Amen

This prayer was written after reading *My Heart's Cry* by Anne Graham Lotz.

∞

Prayed during an 8:30 Sunday Morning Worship Service. Later I was told that that was the first time they'd ever heard a joke in a prayer, (Everybody laughed at the punch line.) but that's not a joke—that's designed to get your attention and to convey something deadly serious. The sermon title was "Life Is Short, but Eternity Isn't." One of our Deacons preached the sermon. The major employer in the area had issued about one hundred layoff notices on Friday.

Eternal Father,

We praise You because You were the same yesterday as You are today and will be tomorrow and forevermore.

We lift to you those of our number who recently received their layoff notices. May they find Your will for the rest of their lives.

Lord, we thank you for life—even if it is short. We thank you for those we know who blessed our lives and whose life was cut short. Lord I ask you to be with those who had a miscarriage, lost a toddler, or a young child like the 8-year-old in the Boston Marathon bombing or the first graders killed in New Town, or lost a teenager, or a grown child. Lord, those hurts never go away; and we ask that You comfort these parents and grandparents even today.

Lord, being reminded that life is short brings to mind a story I tell my Sunday School boys every year. It's about the Boy Scout, the old pilot, and the smartest man in the world. They were in a single engine plane over the jungles of South America, The engine was on fire and they were about to crash into a mountain. The other problem was they only had two parachutes. The smartest man in the world hollered, "Sorry, but the world can't do without me." He grabbed one of the parachutes and jumped out. The old pilot then said, "Son, I've lived a long life and you've still got a lot of living to do. You take that other parachute and jump out." Whereupon the Boy Scout said, "Don't worry about a thing, the smartest man in the world just took my backpack and jumped out."[53] Lord, I'd like to lift to you all those here and those we know who don't have a parachute. Use Your Holy Spirit to convict them of their sin and convince them of their need for Jesus and do it quickly.

Lord, I'd also like to lift to you all those of our number here who think they have a parachute but are carrying a backpack. Your word says that if we abide in You and You in us we'll bear much fruit. Apart from You we can do nothing. Lord, some of us who have thought we had a parachute for umpteen years don't have any fruit. (See John 15:5) There's no joy, meekness, peace, faith, self-control,

---

[53]   I first encountered this story in *Faith and Doubt* by John Ortberg on pages 24 and 25.

patience, gentleness, love, and goodness. O, we might have a little bit of some of those, but the Word seems to indicate we get them all together. We experience impatience; nobody accuses us of having the patience of Job. We worry about things instead of demonstrating faith; we eat too much or lose out temper instead of showing self-control. And we can't name any folk who have given their lives to Jesus because of our witness. Lord, I'd like to lift to you all of us who are deceiving ourselves by carrying around backpacks. May we come to know the Truth.

Lord, use the money put in these plates and the commitments made this morning to provide more parachutes for those that don't have them.

In Jesus' name,

Amen

∞

Prayed during the 8:30 Sunday Morning Worship Service of September 8, 2013. The sermon title was "I Need You." Our preacher was out of town. Our Minister of Administration and Education preached. The way I memorize these prayers is by praying them out loud over and over until I can say the whole prayer comfortably. The memorization process is also an editing process, because once I start hearing how these prayers sound aloud I hear things that need to be changed. For example, this prayer had two additional paragraphs to it when I started and numerous minor changes were made to make it sound more natural to end up with what is written below.

Heavenly Father,

We sometimes use the expressions 'Good God' and 'Good Lord' as interjections and probably are not giving You the proper respect when we do. But, o Lord, You are a good god and a good lord.

O Lord, we praise You because You are good.

We thank You because all that You made was good.

We especially thank You because when You made man it was very good.

We praise You because You only do good things for us.

We praise You because when we have sinned and have committed iniquity and have done wickedly, (See Ps. 106:6) You respond with good. Only under those conditions it is called mercy.

O Lord, You are a god who is merciful and gracious, slow to anger, and abundant in loving kindness, mercy and abundant in goodness, extending mercy to thousands, forgiving iniquity and transgression and sin. (See Ex. 34:6-7)

And Your goodness goes even further. It is evidenced at times as great love, as when Jesus died on the cross for our sins. O Lord, we thank You for Your great love.

Because You have been good to us, may we be good to others.

Because You have been merciful to us, may we be merciful to others.

Because You have shown us great love, may we demonstrate our great love to others.

Because You have shown us great love, may we help others acknowledge and accept that great love. Then, surely, Your goodness and mercy shall follow them all the days of their lives. And they, too, will dwell in the House of the Lord forever. (See Ps. 23:6)

And may these tithes and offerings reflect our goodness and our mercy to others and our great love for You.

Amen

To be prayed during an 8:30 Sunday Morning Worship Service

My Lord and my God, (Thomas' confession in John 20:28 that Jesus is God.)
Our God and Savior Jesus Christ, (Peter's term for Jesus in 2 Peter 1:1)

We praise You because You are "the perfect imprint and very image of [God's] nature, upholding and maintaining and guiding and propelling the universe by… [Your] mighty word of power." (Hebrews 1:3 Amp)

We praise You because You are (Repeat this with indented phrases below or not.)

- The bread of life. No one who comes to You will ever be hungry again. (See John 6:35)
- The light of the world. Those who follow You will never walk in darkness. (See John 8:12)
- The door. Whoever enters by You will find pasture. (See John 10:9)
- The good shepherd who lays down his life for the sheep. (See John 10:11)
- The resurrection and the life. The one who believes in You, even if he dies, will live. (See John 11:25)
- The way, the truth, and the life. No one comes to the Father except through You. (See John 14:6)
- The vine. Apart from You one can do nothing. (See John 15:5)

(These parallel the seven I Am statements in John)

We lift to You those that consider You only as a great teacher or a great prophet. C. S. Lewis said those who deny Your deity are, in effect, calling You a liar or a lunatic. Your Word says You say You and the Father are one. (See John 10:30)

Jesus, we pray that all will say You are who You say You are. We recognize You not as just a great teacher and/or great prophet or just as <u>a</u> god, but as <u>the</u> God.

May You not just sit next to the Father and reign over the universe, but may You reign in and over our lives forever.

Amen

∞

To be prayed during a Monday Night Prayer Meeting.

Precious Jesus,

Would that we could, we would latch onto the fringe of Your garment and hang on for dear life until You healed our issue of blood (See Luke 8:42-48) whether it be an affliction or a handicap or a loved one who has died we want raised from the dead or a relationship we want healed or a wayward child we want returned. But alas, Lord, we know You're not around so we can grab onto the fringe of Your garment. Plus Paul prayed three times for his thorn in the flesh to be removed. And You said, "My grace is sufficient for you: for my strength is made perfect in your weakness." (See 2 Cor. 12:9-10) Plus You aren't really into satisfying our selfish desires.

But instead, Lord, may we see so clearly who You are that we recognize how trivial we are and how unimportant our needs are when compared to what You need. Lord, lay upon us one of Your burdens. Lord, instead of being so concerned about our needs, may we so dedicate ourselves to You that we're so transformed that we find exactly what Your good and acceptable and perfect will is for our lives. (See Rom. 12:1-2) May our sacrifice to You be a broken spirit and a contrite heart, broken by the sin in our life. (See Ps. 51:17) And may Your burden burden us such that we are totally dedicated to what becomes the desire of our heart—meeting the need You've laid on our heart. Then, Lord, as Your eyes search to and fro throughout the whole earth, may they fall on us such that You show Yourself strong on behalf of Your work we're working on. (See 2 Chronicles 16:9)

And may we just think of You, dear Jesus, who endured such grievous opposition and bitter hostility that our difficulties pale in comparison so we don't grow weary or lose heart. (See Heb. 12:3 Amp)

And may Your kingdom grow and grow. And may You get all the glory.

Amen

Written after reading Chip Ingram's *Holy Ambition*.

Prayed during a Sunday Evening Worship Service. Early in the service there was a skit whose catch phrase was 'You're as dumb as a stick.' The reference was added to the prayer extemporaneously. Barna does research on churches in America.

Jehovah, Lord of Heaven and earth, High and Lofty One who inhabits eternity,
Whose very name is holy, (See Isa. 57:15) Who is the "Creator… and Governor of all worlds,"[54]
"Who bears up the pillars of the Universe,"[55]

---

[54] Article II, Sunday School tract, written by Thomas Sawyer presenting the doctrines of the Christian Universalism.

[55] "The Loaded Wagon," A sermon delivered on Sunday Morning, August 24, 1862, by Rev. C. H. Spurgeon at The Metropolitan Tabernacle, Newington, England.

And to whom all the powers in Heaven and earth and Hell are subject,[56]

You are the glorious one to whom we address our prayer because Jesus Christ paid for our sins with His blood and tells us we may ask in His name. Lord, we know not exactly how or what we should pray, but are confident that Your Holy Spirit will translate our words and yearnings into requests that You desire to hear.

Lord, first off, I ask You to give us understanding or redirect our steps. In the words of Jonathan and Chad's skit, I must be 'as dumb as a stick.' I just don't understand how anyone who hears the Good News of Jesus Christ can possibly turn You down. Seriously, Lord, is there anyone in their right mind on the face of the earth that doesn't want forgiveness, eternal life, and abundant life? Lord, is the message not getting communicated properly so that they can't really understand? Have we so distorted Your Word that people can't straighten it out? Have we so clothed it in the mystery of religious verbiage that people don't have a clue? Are we living our lives so that people don't listen to what we have to say? Are we trying to witness in our own power? Lord, do we just think we're spreading Your Good News?

Or are we actually failing to try to spread the Good News? Did You actually save some of us and not give us a testimony? Are we so thankless that we're not bubbling over to share Your Good News far and wide with everyone we meet? Lord, are we so selfish we want to keep You all to ourselves? Have we spent so little time with You that the world can't sense Your love for them through us? Are some of us so isolated that we don't actually run into people we can witness to? Have we hidden Your message in our hearts and in our homes and in our church houses lest someone steal it from us? Do some of us actually read Your Word regularly but never get Your drift? Are

---

56 Bunyan, John, *Visions of Heaven and Hell*, p. 23, spiritlessons.com/Documents/
John_Bunyan_Hell/Bunyan_Heaven_and_Hell.doc.

some of us so caught up in missions studies, missions committees, missions giving, and missions projects that we forget to carry out the Great Commission in the Jerusalem and Samaria's right here in Tullahoma? Are some of us so involved in friendship evangelism that we forget the evangelism part? Do some of us read Barna so we can cite statistics to justify not using certain evangelistic methods? Lord, are some of us actually led by the Holy Spirit to stay home and do nothing?

Lord, are we still willing to call a visitation program that only visits folk that first visit us outreach? Are we actually satisfied with the few lost sheep that stumble in our door when You were willing to leave the ninety-nine to go look for the one who was lost? Lord, are we so busy playing church that we can't be a praying church? Is the only person we listen to when we pray ourselves? Are we spending so much time trying to protect what we have that we can't seek and save that which is lost? Lord, are we wasting our time praying for the revival when we should be praying for new life? Lord, are we wasting our time praying for You to bless us when we should be praying for You to break us? O, Lord, we humble ourselves before You, affirming once again our conviction, our commitment, to learn Your heart, to know You, to love You, to trust in the certainty of Your Word, to wait patiently for Your chosen time, to listen quietly for Your voice, to persevere in prayer so that we may gain understanding or have our steps redirected such that Your Word spreads quickly, runs its course, is glorified and triumphant. (See 1 Thes. 3:2) Convict us of our shortcomings, convince us of Your desires, and incite us to Your work.

O Lord, may You get our act together so that more people tune into Your Good News and then turn onto You than tune into the 6 O'clock News so that Your glory knows no end.

Amen

343

In 2013, the North American Mission Board (NAMB) encouraged each Southern Baptist church to hold a TenTwo Prayer Service on October 2, 2013—ten-two because it was October 2 and because of Luke 10:2 (NIV)—'He told them, "The harvest is plentiful, but the workers are few. Ask the Lord of the harvest, therefore, to send out workers into his harvest field."' This special service on Wednesday night was set up to pray for more workers and for the efforts of our North American Mission Board (NAMB) missionaries and missions here in the United States. We as a church also undergirded our church-wide Appalachian mission trip to Tellico Plains (TN) October 6-12 with prayer. The format of the service was a corporate worship song, then praying as directed (for example, the first prayer time was for praise) in small groups, then another corporate worship song, then praying in your small group according to the leader's direction. I had to pray the prayer below piecemeal.

Lord of the Harvest,

We praise You because You are a god who is concerned for the lost. We praise You because You are a god who leaves the ninety-nine to search for the one who is lost.

We come confessing that many of us consider we have done our part by holding the rope and by praying and writing a check to support others who go. Others of us seem to participate in a mission trip, consider that as having done our part, and sit back and do nothing to evangelize Tullahoma. Luke 10:2 was the beginning of Jesus' instructions as He sent the seventy out two by two to visit in homes in the cities He was going to pass through.

Lord, I lift to you all those who are currently following in the footsteps of those seventy who went out two by two to spread the Good News and the twelve who were sent out earlier who went through the towns and preached the Gospel. I lift to You all those who are full-time or part time missionaries employed by the North American Mission Board, our state convention, and our local association who are planting churches or inviting people to church and to come to Jesus. Bless their work with visible results, with lost souls coming to Jesus. I lift to You those that are going on the Appalachia Mission Trip. May Your will be accomplished and may Your work be done and may the angels in Heaven be rejoicing.

Lord, indeed the harvest is plentiful. Bring more workers. Use Your Holy Spirit to change some of us shirkers to workers. Then, Lord, would You also give some of us the gift of evangelism so Your message might spread more quickly. Then cause us to be so concerned for the lost we stand in the gap and pray for them until they come to You. Cause us to be so concerned that we go and engage them and invite them to come to church and to come to You.

O, Lord, show us what net to use and what side of the boat to cast it on. Provide us with leadership to organize and incite the work. May we find Your combine, oil it, grease it, fill it with fuel, and drive it up and down the streets of Tullahoma and the surrounding towns and reap Your harvest.

And may You get all the glory and Your Kingdom grow by leaps and bounds.

May Your Word spread quickly, run its course, and be glorified and triumphant. (See 2 Thes. 3:1)

Amen

∞

To be prayed at an 8:30 Sunday Morning Worship Service. This one is waiting in the wings.

Precious Cornerstone, (See 1 Peter 2:6)

Peter says that, like living stones, we are being built into a spiritual house to be a holy priesthood, offering spiritual sacrifices acceptable to God through Jesus Christ. (See 1 Peter 2:5) In OT times, the priests offered up animal sacrifices, but You have offered up the sacrifice to end all animal sacrifices. Now we are to offer up spiritual sacrifices on the altar of our heart. But just as in OT times, sacrifices were to be blameless, spotless, without defect to meet God's requirements, our spiritual sacrifices should meet God's requirements, too.

Lord, we offer up to You our mind and every part of our living body to become Your instruments of righteousness. (See Rom. 12:1-2)

Lord, we offer You the sacrifice of praise and worship here this morning. (See Heb. 13:15)

Lord, we offer to You the good deeds we have done—things that have honored You and have helped others and are consistent with Your person and Your work. (See Heb. 13:16)

Lord, we offer You our possessions—everything we own and hope to own for Your use. (See Phil. 4:18)

Lord, we offer up to You the names of those converts that we are in some way responsible for. (See Rom. 15:15-16) You know who they are.

Lord, we offer our sacrificial love for one another, the same kind of love You showed when You died on the cross for us. (See Eph. 5:1-2)

And, Lord, we offer up to You not only this prayer but all the prayers that we have prayed in accord with Your will. (See Rev. 8:3-4)

Lord, we now put in these offering plates sacrificially from our resources to meet the needs of others. (See Heb. 13:16)

We praise You because we'll never be disappointed in You. (1 Peter 2:6)

We praise You because You called us out of darkness into Your marvelous light. (1 Peter 2:9)

May all our spiritual sacrifices be pleasing and acceptable in Your sight.

Amen

This prayer was written after reading *The MacArthur New Testament Commentary: 1 Peter,* pp. 113-117. The seven spiritual sacrifices noted correspond to the ones MacArthur identified.

PRAYER

BIG PICTURE: God created the whole universe and put us in it so He could have fellowship with us. In Heaven, His perfect will is accomplished. On earth His perfect will is accomplished via prayers. (As a result of our praying, He sometimes does His will on earth or convinces us to do it!) The reason He accomplishes His will on earth primarily through our prayers is that He gets the fellowship He wants in the process.

Matthew 21:22 (KJV) "And all things, whatsoever ye shall ask in prayer, believing, ye shall receive." We don't get what we ask for because we don't believe it will happen. We get what we ask for because what we ask for is identical to what God wants to happen: therefore, we believe it will happen.

James 5:16 (KJV) "The effectual fervent prayer of a righteous man availeth much." It's not because the righteous man is so good or so spiritual that something good happens as a result of his prayer. Rather it is either because

- He is so in tune with God that what he prays is identical with what God wants to happen or
- He is so submissive to God's communication to him that God is able to accomplish His will through him.

Note that "availeth much" doesn't necessarily mean that he is going to get what he asks for. It may just mean that something good completely unrelated from what he asked for is going to happen.

John 14:13 (NIV) "And I will do whatever you may ask in my name so that the Father may be glorified in the Son." The phrase "in Jesus' name" tacked onto the end of a prayer is not magic. In fact, there is no magic formula of prayer that guarantees that you get what you ask for. Rather, "in Jesus' name" means in Jesus' nature or Jesus' character. In other words, if our prayers are to be effective we must grow into a person who is so like Jesus that our prayers are an expression of his concerns and love. In other words, when Jesus was saying to pray in His name, He was saying to submit to His transforming power in our lives and "let His mind be in us." (See Phil. 2:5) Then we pray exactly what Jesus would pray if He were in the same situation. Such prayers are answered.

Jesus said that if "two of us on earth agree about anything, that we may ask and it shall be done for us by His Father who is in Heaven." (See Matt. 18:19) The reason it shall be done is because the two of us are agreeing not just with each other but also with the Father who is in Heaven.

Phil 4:6 (Amp) "Do not fret about … anything, but in every circumstance and in everything, by prayer and petition [definite requests] with thanksgiving continue to make your wants known to God." Why should we pray asking for selfish things? Not because you're going to get everything you pray for, but because

- We have to (our desperate situation forces us to pray)
- The more we ask and beg for something from God, and the more God fails to give it to us, the more assurance we have that God understands us and will carry us through difficult times.
- It keeps the lines of communication open. Then He can communicate to us. (Note: God doesn't normally speak to us with an audible voice. Normally he communicates to us by putting thoughts into our mind that coincide with His will.)
- The Holy Spirit intercedes for us. When we attempt to pray to God, the Holy Spirit prays to God on our behalf, overcoming our limitations and short sightedness in prayer. In our immaturity, we pray for what we think we need. The Holy Spirit corrects this by praying for the things we really need.

Matthew 6:8 says that God "knows what we need before we even ask." So why ask? Because it is so important to have that line of communication open. Because prayer calms us down in times of trouble, because God will comfort us when we hurt. Because He'll encourage us when we're down. Because prayer is a crutch. Praise God we don't have to be self-sufficient all the time.

Perseverance: Luke 11:9 (Amp) "So I say to you, ask and keep on asking, and it shall be given to you..." Sometimes God does allow us to have what we ask for even though it is not the best thing for us, but we also suffer the consequences. More often what happens is that God gradually changes what we are asking for to what He wants done. Perseverance is important because it allows God time to work in our life. Prayer is not an attempt to get God to give us what we want. Rather it is a process wherein people spiritually surrender so that they might become instruments through which God can do His work. If we were supposed to ask God for something only one time and sit back and in faith wait for it to happen, God wouldn't be able to have that communication line open so He could try to communicate to us and change what we're praying into what He wants us to pray or to convince us to do His will in some area.

Besides our requests, prayer often includes adoration, confession, and thanksgiving—all of which move us toward subjugation to God and His will so that as a result we will be saying "Not my will, but Thine be done." Luke 22:42.(KJV)

Prayer changes people. It changes us from wanting our desires to wanting God's desires.

Will God miraculously heal people who are sick? For example, James 5:14-15. First, all healing comes from God. All healing is miraculous. We are to pray for the sick. If it is to God's glory and in His will, He will perform a miracle to heal. Sometimes the result of our praying is that we are convicted that we are to minister to these who are sick. Sometimes it is to God's glory that the person dies. Many times praying for our own healing results in our accepting the situation in which we find ourselves!

Ever since I was thirteen I've been ending my prayers with 'In Jesus' name, Amen.' Even though I didn't think there was any thing magic about the phrase, I thought I was being true to Scripture. Now I understand that the phrase 'in Jesus' name' really means in his character or according to his nature so that we shouldn't be praying anything that Jesus wouldn't have prayed. I no longer end with that phrase but feel that I should only pray the words, the thoughts and the will of Jesus.

When you do that it limits what you pray. I've gone through several phases with this. At one point I refused to pray anything but phrases right out of the Bible. That'll put you to the test—send you to your Bible, also. Then I refused to pray for anything I wasn't 100% absolutely sure was God's will. The week before a revival I decided I would pray for only two things and that I do my best to try to pray constantly. One of the things I prayed for concerned one of these prayers God had birthed. Many months before our interim pastor even announced we were going to have a revival, God had birthed a revival prayer and had fine tuned it and prepared it for use. As the week began I prayed that if it be to God's glory He would use that prayer in the revival. As the week progressed I prayed that if it be to His glory it be used in the 11 O'clock Worship Service on Sunday. As it got closer I prayed that if it be to His glory it be used during both Sunday morning services. Before I left for church Sunday morning I was praying that God use that prayer for His glory in both worship services. I got to the early services about two minutes early and about a minute later Bob came all the way up to where I was sitting in the front and got me to help usher. And that prayer got used in that early service. And events transpired that it got used in the second service also. Exactly what I prayed for occurred.

However, the main thing I had been praying for was for a boy in my Sunday School class to be saved. He had moved to my number one prayer request back in February. That week I prayed fervently and as close to constantly as I could for that young man. That young man came to Sunday school that morning. I dismissed my other boys five minutes early so I could have a word with him. I just asked him, "Well, have you accepted Jesus Christ as your Lord and Savior?" And he said, "Yes." Again exactly what I had prayed for occurred.

Now, you may be saying to yourself

he persevered long enough so God answered his prayer
he prayed hard enough so God gave him what he asked for
he believed so God gave him what he asked for
he changed God's mind to get what he wanted or
he changed God's timing

Now let's look at some Scripture where it's obvious that we can draw some of the same conclusions. But again all the conclusions are wrong. In Exodus 32, Moses is on Mount Sinai with God, the Israelites are at the base of the mountain having fashioned a golden calf to worship. Verses 11-14 (NIV): But Moses sought the favor of the Lord his God. "O Lord," he said, "why should your anger burn against your people, whom you brought out of Egypt with great power and a mighty hand? Why should the Egyptians say, 'It was with evil intent that he brought them out, to kill them in the mountains and to wipe them off the face of the earth'? Turn from your fierce anger; relent and do not bring disaster on your people. Remember your servants Abraham, Isaac and Israel, to whom you swore by your own self: 'I will make your descendants as numerous as the stars in the sky and I will give your descendants all this land I promised them, and it will be their inheritance forever.'" Then the Lord relented and did not bring on his people the disaster he had threatened. We literalists don't have any problem saying that Moses changed God's mind. But we have a problem. 1 Samuel 15:29 says, "He who is the glory of Israel does not lie or change his mind for He is not a man that he should change his mind." We have a contradiction. How do we resolve it?

Clue number 1. "If God changed His mind in response to Moses' prayers to spare the Israelites, does it mean that Moses was more merciful than God? Does it mean that Moses taught God a lesson in forgiveness? Does it mean that Moses helped God cool His anger so He wouldn't do something He would ultimately regret? Was Moses' wisdom greater than God's? Does God make rash decisions in the heat of anger, then later repent?"[1] "Was it Moses' character that influenced God where others could not?"[2] If so, Moses would have been able to convince God to allow him to go into the Promised Land. "Surely Moses was more deserving of mercy than the Israelites…[were]."[3]

"Or is this the way it happened? God, in His sovereignty and infinite wisdom, decides it is best to destroy Israel because of their idolatry. Moses makes a passionate plea on their behalf. God listens and decides, 'Moses has a point there. I hadn't thought of it like that. I'll change my mind and do it Moses' way.'"[4] At this point we can say that we know enough about God and Moses to say that it couldn't have happened any of those ways. So maybe our interpretation is a little off.

Clue number 2. Moses is a Levite, not from the tribe of Judah. God had already declared that Jesus would be born of the tribe of Judah. If he is really serious about destroying all these and making a nation of Moses, then he would be going against his own prophecy. Therefore we realize that God wasn't going to destroy the Israelites, He was only using this as a threat to get Moses to think about the Israelites the same way He did.

Clue number 3. There is an identical situation in Ezekiel 22. God lists the sins of the Israelites just before the Babylonian captivity. "In both cases the people have brought upon themselves God's righteous judgment. In both cases God's desire is to circumvent the natural course of events."[5] Ezekiel 22:30 (NIV) says, "I looked for a man among them." And we can add the phrase "to intercede." Actually it says, "to stand before me in the gap…" None was found. The people are conquered and taken captive. Analogously in Exodus 32:7-10, God reminds Moses that these are Moses' people and Moses is their leader—a job which includes a call to be intercessor for them. God kept talking to Moses telling him this and that until Moses' heart and

---

1   Dean, Jennifer Kennedy, *The Praying Life*, (Birmingham, Alabama, New Hope, 1993), p. 6.

2   Ibid.

3   Ibid.

4   Ibid. pp 6-7.

5   Ibid. p. 9.

mind were so aligned with God's purposes that Moses interceded for them. And the people were saved.

So God never wanted those Israelites destroyed. His mind was never changed one iota. Rather he talked to Moses until Moses heart was aligned with His.

What does this teach us? God pours out His wrath on folk not because they sin, but because no intercessor is found. In other words, your next door neighbor is lost and going to Hell not because he is a sinner; he is lost and going to Hell because we aren't interceding for him. God works through intercessors to overrule judgment. "Moses did not change God's mind. He shared God's mind. Moses did not alter God's plan, he implemented it."[6] Prayer does not change God's plan, it implements it.

"Thy will be done on earth as it is in Heaven." (Matt. 6:10 KJV) God's perfect will is done in Heaven, and two places in the Bible it talks about how intercessors stand in the gap between heaven and earth and pray God's will down—basically you can think of it as a flood of mercies in Heaven just waiting for intercessors to pray them down.

The result of prayer is not an answer (although we can talk in those terms); it is submission to God and His plan. God weans us from what we want to what He wants and then uses us to accomplish it. Prayer is the primary way in which God's will is implemented on earth. (if we're not praying for it, it's not happening!)

Why does God ordain prayer as the appointed way of accomplishing His will? Because He created us, the world, and the whole universe for one reason—because He wants a relationship. We were created for friendship and fellowship with Him. Through prayer He wants to reproduce His heart in us.

Now let's go back to my experience. God changed my prayer concerning that prayer time and time again until it was what he wanted. Then He used me to get it accomplished. You see, in the first service after Bob came and got me I, volunteered to lead in prayer. For the second service, the leader of our deacon prayer time didn't show up,

---

6   Ibid.

so I took over and appointed myself to say the prayer. God changed my heart until it agreed with his about that prayer then He used me to implement His plan. I was praying exactly what I should have been about that young man all along. But as the week went on his salvation became the most important thing in the world to me. I would have died for that young man to be saved. I never wanted anything else ever as much as I wanted that young man to be saved. I actually prayed that if the rapture came that God would leave me down here to witness to him. What I didn't tell you was that I couldn't stand it any more. On Monday I had to write that young man a letter begging him to give his life to Christ. So when I asked him the question in Sunday School he was answering my letter. Once again, God changed my heart until it agreed with his about that young man and then he used me to implement his plan.

The ultimate resolution to a prayer isn't a yes or no, but an aligning of our hearts with God's and His using us to implement His plan.

The purpose of prayer is not answers. The purpose of prayer is relationship and God's will being done.

Note: The entire development about God changing Moses' mind follows very closely Jennifer Dean Kennedy's development in *The Praying Life*.

WHY I BELIEVE IN PRAYER

Let me tell you why I believe in prayer. One reason is because I can't explain some things that happen any other way than that God answers prayer. Let me give you a case in point. About two years ago on a Monday evening in October, I came to prayer meeting. Lyle was there, too. We usually went visiting together after prayer meeting. After spending an hour in a spirit of prayer, we checked out the visitation cards to see where the Holy Spirit might be leading us. We both went out of the church empty handed.

We got in my car, and I led in prayer saying something like, "Lord, Your Holy Spirit didn't direct us to choose any of those visitation cards to go visit tonight, but we know You have a divine appointment for us tonight. We know there is someone in this town that You want to give their life to Jesus tonight. Lord, I'm going to start this car and drive; but, Lord, I don't know where to go. Will you direct us? Will You point us to exactly where You need us to be tonight?" So I started driving. I was driving out toward Continental Apartments when Lyle said, "You know, we once said we ought to do some visiting in Brandywine sometime." So I turned in. I then asked Lyle, "Where do you suppose the Lord wants us to start—down at the far end or up here at the front?" Lyle said he didn't know, so I parked in the middle. Then I led us in prayer telling the Lord that we sensed that maybe He wanted us here but we didn't know where to begin. I told Him that if he'd open the door, we'd walk through it. When we got out of the car I told Lyle I thought maybe the Lord would want us to begin down at the far end. So we walked to the far end. Brandywine is set up like a lot of apartment complexes around here—with an entryway from which you have access to four apartments—two upstairs, two on ground level. We went upstairs first and knocked on a door. It was a black man and his wife. He had his Bible open on the kitchen table. He was a Church of Christ preacher over in Cowan and was preparing a sermon when we interrupted him. His wife recognized my last name. She was a nurse and had worked in Dr. Harvey's office when my kids were growing up. I explained what we were doing there that evening and then said to him, "You know, I'll bet we're wasting our time here because I'll bet you've been all over these apartments checking on folk seeing if they need the Lord." He said that was exactly the case, except there were two families that had moved in over the weekend in the unit across the street. So we had prayer with him and his wife and left. We knocked on the other door upstairs and didn't get an answer. As we got downstairs, a man was just leaving one of the apartments, we exchanged pleasantries with him; and he went on.

So we knocked on the other door downstairs. A black man answered. We exchanged pleasantries and found out his name was Michael He invited us in. His wife and little girl were inside. As I was fixing to sit down, remembering a pointer from a soul-winning course I'd had many years ago that one of the partners should turn off the TV, I said, "Oh, let me turn down the TV." Then I proceeded to turn the volume down on the TV—and much to my surprise the TV shut off. I'll still tell you that I didn't do anything to that TV to turn it off. But anyway, we discovered the man was a Black Muslim and that his wife had an AME background. After a tad more conversation, Lyle began trying to win him to the Lord. I began praying for God's will to be done in this man's life and at the same time paying close attention to see if Lyle needed any support. Lyle brought the man to a point of decision and the answer was "No, I just can't do that." Lyle kept pushing—If you've ever been out soul winning with Lyle you know he doesn't give up easily. About twenty minutes later, after this man had repeatedly said no, he invited Jesus into his life. I went out to the car and brought in some tracts to give him. As we finally were leaving, his wife followed us out the door because she wanted to tell us something. These are her exact words: "Thank you, the prayer of my life has been answered tonight." The next morning at work the first person I encountered was Gary. Gary lives in Tullahoma, pastors a black Baptist church in Fayetteville, and pastors all the people in the building where I work. I told him what happened. He immediately called Bro. C. of Mt Zion to go by and see him and invite him to church. We went back a month later and Michael and his wife had joined an AME church over in Shelbyville. We checked back about six months later and they were still going to church but were in the process of moving to Nebraska—and hoped to find a good church there.

When I put two and two together to try to get four out of these events, I don't get one big coincidence. I find that here was a wife who had been desperately praying for her husband for many years. And here were two guys who were only interested in being completely submissive to the Lord's direction; and He used them to answer this lady's prayer.

COGNITIVE DISSONANCE

"Cognitive dissonance is the term used in modern psychology to describe the state of holding two or more conflicting cognitions (e.g., ideas, beliefs, values) simultaneously. The theory of cognitive dissonance in social psychology proposes that people have a motivational drive to reduce dissonance by altering existing cognitions, adding new ones to create a consistent belief system, or alternatively by reducing the importance of any one of the dissonant elements.

"An example of this would be the conflict between wanting to smoke and knowing that smoking is unhealthy; a person may try to change their feelings about the odds that they will actually suffer the consequences, or they might add the consonant element that the short term benefits of smoking outweigh the long term harm. The need to avoid cognitive dissonance may bias one towards a certain decision even though other factors favour an alternative."[1]

My introduction to cognitive dissonance came about because of one of my fellow workers. Bill was a very intelligent man. He was well organized, well dressed, and well liked. However, Bill was very frugal and quite proud of what a good shopper he was—and liked to brag about the bargains he purchased. In the 1970's there was a time when we experiences shortages—in things like gasoline and mayonnaise. Well, news was out one summer that there was a shortage of potatoes—and, indeed, prices suggested that there was a shortage. So Bill came into work bragging about how he had gone over to Manchester (known

---

[1]   Theory of Cognitive Dissonance - Home, http://cognitivedissonancetheory. weebly.com/ (accessed July 7, 2013).

as a potato-growing area around here) and purchased 200 pounds of potatoes at twenty cents a pound. He put the potatoes under his house for storage. Come Christmas time one could find door-buster prices on potatoes at five cents a pound. However, when we pointed this out to him, Bill would never admit he made a mistake even though he still had 180 pounds of potatoes he'd purchased at twenty cents a pound.

The second incident is downright funny. Bill bought a new car and justified his purchase by telling everyone what good gas mileage he was going to get. Well, once a week for several weeks while Bill went down to the cafeteria for a coffee break, two of my coworkers went out to the parking lot and poured a gallon of gas into Bill's gas tank. And for several weeks we never heard the end of Bill bragging about his great gas mileage. Then for the next several weeks my two coworkers proceeded to retrieve their gasoline from Bill's gas tank one gallon per week. Bill ceased bragging about his gas mileage. However, if we asked him how his gas mileage was, he maintained that it was still great.

Cognitive dissonance is not confined to the secular world and non-Christians. And, unfortunately, most people don't recognize that they are guilty of sinning by not being truthful to themselves unless someone else points it out to them. And I see it in the church and in my own life fairly often.

BIBLIOGRAPHY

An Unknown Christian. "The Victorious Life." *Bibleteacher.org.* Christian Digital Library Foundation, n.d. Web. 5 July 2013. <http://www.bibleteacher.org/VictoriousLife.htm>.

The Baptist Faith and Message, A Statement Adopted by the Southern Baptist Convention, (Nashville: The Sunday School Board of the Southern Baptist Convention, 1963.

Baptist Hymnal. Nashville: Convention Press, 1991.

Blackaby, Henry T. & Blackaby, Melvin. *Experiencing the Spirit: The Power of Pentecost Every Day.* Colorado Springs: Multnomah, 2009.

Blackaby, Henry T. & King, Claude V., *Experiencing God: Knowing and Doing the Will of God,* Nashville: Sunday School Board of The Southern Baptist Convention, 1990.

Bridges, Jerry. *Respectable Sins.* Colorado Springs: Nav Press, 2008.

Briggs, Edward C. *A Pilgrim's Guide to Prayer.* Nashville: Broadman Press, 1987.

Bunyan, John, *Visions of Heaven and Hell,* See http:/www.spiritlessons.com/Documents/John_Bunyan_Hell/Bunyan_Heaven_and_Hell.doc

Dean, Jennifer Kennedy. *The Praying Life*. Birmingham, Alabama, New Hope, 1993.

Doctrines of the Christian Universalism in a Sunday School tract written by Thomas Sawyer in the late 1880's. See http://www.auburn. edu/~allenkc/chr-univ.html

Drace, Jerry. "Observations of an Evangelist." *Purpose4u.com*. CrossPurpose International, n.d. Web. 6 July 2013. <http://www. purpose4u.com/JerryDraceObservationsofanEvangelist.html>.

Drace, Jerry. "The Work of the Evangelist." *Uu.edu*. R. G. Lee Society of Fellows, n.d. Web. 6 July 2013. <http://www.uu.edu/centers/rglee/ fellows/FALL97/Drace.htm>.

DeHaan, M. R. *Hebrews*. Grand Rapids: Zondervan, 1959.

Duewel, Wesley. *Might Prevailing Prayer*. Grand Rapids: Zondervan, 1990.

Gordon, S. D. *Quiet Talks on Prayer*. New York: Revell Company, 1904.

Hallesby, Ole, *Prayer*. Minneapolis: Ausburg, 1994.

Harris, Joshua. *Why Church Matters*, Colorado Springs: Multnomah, 2004.

Hybels, Bill. *Just Walk Across the Room*. Grand Rapids: Zondervan, 2006.

Ingram, Chip. *Holy Ambition*. Chicago: Moody Publishers, 2002.

Jeremiah, David. *Captured by Grace*. Nashville: Thomas Nelson, 2006.

Jeremiah, David. *Prayer, the Great Adventure*. Colorado Springs: Multnomah, 2004.

"The Loaded Wagon," No. 466 a sermon delivered on Sunday Morning, August 24, 1862, by Rev. C. H. Spurgeon at The Metropolitan Tabernacle, Newington, England

Longfellow, Henry Wadsworth. *The Poems of Henry Wadsworth Longfellow.* New York: Thomas Y Crowell Company, 1896.

Lotz, Anne Graham. *The Glorious Dawn of God's Story.* Dallas: Word Publishing,1997.

Lotz, Anne Graham. *My Heart's Cry.* Nashville: W Publishing Group, 2002.

Lucado, Max. *A Love Worth Giving.* Nashville: W Publishing Group, 2002.

McArthur, John. *The MacArthur New Testament Commentary: 1 Peter.* Chicago: Moody Publishers, 2004.

McArthur, John. *The MacArthur New Testament Commentary: 1 & 2 Thessalonians.* Chicago: Moody Publishers, 2002.

MacDonald, James. *Gripped by the Greatness of God.* Chicago: Moody Publishers, 2005.

Murray, Andrew. *With Christ in the School of Prayer.* Springdale: Whitaker House, 1981.

Ortberg, John. *God Is Closer than You Think.* Grand Rapids: Zondervan, 2005.

Ortberg, John. *Faith and Doubt.* Grand Rapids: Zondervan, 2008.

Piper, John. *A Hunger for God.* Wheaton: Crossway Books, 1997.

Ravenill, Leonard. *Sodom Had No Bible.* Minneapolis: Bethany House Publishers, 1979.

Rice, John R. *Prayer: Asking and Receiving.* Murfreesboro: Sword of the Lord Publishers, 1942.

Stowell, Joseph M. "Who Needs God," *Moody*, Jan/Feb 1997.

Taylor, Jack. *Prayer: Life's Limitless Reach.* Nashville: Broadman Press, 1977.

The Amplified Bible. Cedar Rapids: Zondervan Bible Publishers: 1965.

Theory of Cognitive Dissonance - Home, http:// cognitivedissonancetheory.weebly.com/ (accessed July 7, 2013).

Thompson, Francis, *The Hound of Heaven.* New York: Dodd, Mead and Company, 1926.

Torre, R. A. *How to Pray.* Springdale: Whitaker House, 1983.

Vaughan, Curtis (ed.). *The Bible from 26 Translations.* Grand Rapids: Baker Book House, 1988.

Warren, Rick. *The Purpose-Driven Church.* Grand Rapids: Zondervan, 1995.

Westminster Shorter Catechism, General Assembly of the Church of Scotland, 1648.

Williams, William. "Guide Me, O Thou Great Jehovah." 1745.

Yancy, Philip. *Prayer: Does It Make a Difference?* Zondervan, 2006

CPSIA information can be obtained at www.ICGtesting.com
Printed in the USA
LVOW11s0044111014

408271LV00001B/13/P

9 781490 819